CORRECTING JESUS

At EXTERMINATING ANGEL PRESS,
we're taking a new approach to our
world. A new way of looking at things.
New stories, new ways to live our lives.
We're dreaming how we want our lives
and our world to be…

Also from
EXTERMINATING ANGEL PRESS

The Supergirls: *Fashion, Feminism,*
Fantasy, and the History of
Comic Book Heroines
by Mike Madrid

Jam Today: *A Diary of*
Cooking With What You've Got
by Tod Davies

Correcting Jesus

2000 Years of Changing The Story

BRIAN GRIFFITH

EXTERMINATING ANGEL
PRESS

Portions of this book first appeared, some in different form, on the Exterminating
Angel Press online magazine at **www.exterminatingangel.com**

EXTERMINATING ANGEL PRESS

"Creative Solutions for Practical Idealists"

Visit **www.exterminatingangel.com** to join the conversation

info@exterminatingangel.com

Book design by Mike Madrid

Griffith, Brian.
    Correcting Jesus : 2000 years of changing the story /
Brian Griffith.
    p. cm.
    Includes bibliographical references and index.
    LCCN 2009924468
    ISBN-13: 978-1-935259-02-2
    ISBN-10: 1-935259-02-4
    ISBN-13: 978-1-935259-05-3
    ISBN-10: 1-935259-05-9

    1. Jesus Christ--History of doctrines. 2. Jesus
Christ--Theology. 3. Christianity--Social aspects.
I. Title.

BT198.G75 2009   232.9

Printed in The United States of America

Contents

This book is dedicated to the Muslims,
Buddhists, Christians, and Agnostics in my
family, who all believe in
critical compassion.

For making the book, I want to especially thank
Tod Davies for her creative leadership,
Mike Madrid for his artistry
on the cover and book design,
John E. Daniels for his great technical support,
and Riane Eisler for her lifetime of teaching.

1. Correcting Jesus in Sunday School

During the Victorian age, best-selling portraits of Jesus showed him as a man of delicate features and soulful eyes, with hair so long and silky he looked hyper-feminine.[1] This Victorian Jesus seemed gentle, meek, and mild. But his legions of largely female soldiers could be militant in crusades for restricting alcohol, winning the vote, or putting an end to war. The idealists of those days stressed their own selections of Bible verses, mostly on the virtues of bleeding heart compassion. But that was only one brand of Christianity in the age of colonial wars. My grandparents lived in British Ireland in the aftermath of WWI, as several different Christian ideologies tore the country apart. My grandfather was a Protestant and my grandmother a Catholic. They eloped and fled Europe, as if escaping from a burning madhouse.

Forty years later in Texas, as kids of the me-generation arrived in Methodist Sunday School, we found our classrooms still decorated with those classical-looking Victorian pictures of Jesus, tenderly holding lambs or babies. We sang "Jesus loves the little children, all the children of the world." But of course that was for kids. By the time we got to mature class, we didn't go overboard for sentimentality. We heard the kindly instructions to forgive all wrongs and "resist not one who does evil." But I assumed nobody in their right mind would seriously follow that.

My pastor, the Rev. Russell Moon, was a scholarly graduate of Yale. I was impressed he spoke both ancient Greek and Hebrew, plus he'd read all those volumes on history and religion in his office. Rev. Moon gave us sermons explaining the historical context of Bible stories. He described

1

the political and economic situation in which the prophet Micah said, "They covet fields, and seize them; houses and take them away; they oppress householder and house, people and their inheritance . . . Should you not know justice? — you who hate the good and love evil, who tear the skin off my people, and the flesh off their bones; who eat the flesh of my people, flay the skin off them, break their bones and chop them up like meat in a kettle, like flesh in a cauldron." (Micah 2:2, 3:1b–3)

The way Rev. Moon explained things, it was almost as interesting as T.V. He gave us the impression that standing up for justice in biblical times was both simpler and more suicidal. He told us that Jesus was not the sort of Messiah people were expecting. To many observers Jesus was a big disappointment. He didn't liberate Israel from its conquerors, take the throne as king, establish justice across the world, or punish humanity's abusers. Most people concluded he couldn't be the expected One. Likewise, Rev. Moon said, we modern people had our own expectations, which determined what we wanted to see in Jesus.

In general, Rev. Moon seemed more interested in raising questions than in telling us what to do. And for most of us that seemed abnormal. We were expecting a pastor to give us expert advice from the law books of scripture. A lot of us also felt that religion should be an emotional thing. It should be more about changing hearts than minds. Besides, our American culture already had the basically right ideas. We had that almost Victorian optimism about our civilization, like when Charles M. Sheldon said, "Every day I have more and more confidence in the wonderful results which I believe God is going to bring about in the social and political life of the world."[2] Near as we could see, we didn't need a change of direction — just better motivation for success.

As a teenager, I didn't come to Sunday School on my own steam. But once our family got there, the group conversations sucked me in. Mostly we discussed how the ancient Jews and early Christians lived, and I assumed the game was to make our modern ways conform to theirs. I liked the notion of judging modern society by a different cultural standard, and only later noticed how unusual it was. In our world of white, Protestant, middle class Texans, most people felt the United States was the most developed and civilized nation ever. By comparison, all foreign countries and past societies were more primitive. Yet on Sundays we arrived in church, hoping to learn a better way to live. And our chosen teachers in this vital subject were a pack of impoverished villagers from ancient West Asia. What did those Old World peasants have to teach modern Americans? Well, that was the question we were there to discuss.

Our members mostly believed that the Bible was more or less inerrant truth. We didn't get too literalist, but we felt if it was in the book, then God put it there for a reason. But this basically shared assumption didn't help us much in agreeing what the book said. At first I thought our differences were between true believers, and doubters like me. Later I decided we disagreed because we favored different verses in the book. But even when talking about the same verse, our degree of disagreement was still amazing. I remember one exchange which shook me from a daydream, as somebody said that real Christians trust the Bible more than human reason. "Then why," another replied, "did Jesus ask 'Why can't you decide for yourselves what is right?' " (Luke 12:57) The answer was, "We can't because we're sinners."

Another thing that impressed me was learning that early Christians were pacifists. Our Sunday School teacher seemed impressed that the early martyrs preferred to be killed rather than swear obedience to the emperor, and they felt it was a sin to enlist in the Roman army. An early Christian book called the *Recognitions of Clement* presented their attitude: "Under the hope of future good things, I will not suffer men to take up arms and fight against one another, plunder and subvert everything, and

3

attempt whatever lust may dictate. And what will be the condition of that life which you would introduce, that men will attack and be attacked, be enraged and disturbed, and live always in fear? For those who do evil to others must expect like evil to themselves."[3]

To me it sounded inspiring, but quite unbelievable. Later I noticed that, near as I knew, nobody in my church was a pacifist, not even the Sunday School teacher. Almost everybody there bore a deep respect for our country's armed forces, and considerable contempt for so-called conscientious objectors. If somebody refused to swear allegiance to the American flag we'd think he had a mental problem. I supposed the issue in Rome was that their pagan rulers were evil tyrants, and swearing loyalty to them would have been like swearing to obey Adolf Hitler.

Obviously we were selective in reading the Bible. The book of Acts said the first Christians "shared all things in common," but we believed it was Christian to defend the sanctity of private property. The Bible praised charitable giving, even to the ridiculous extent of "giving away all that you have." But a lot of us felt that charity was counterproductive since it rewarded dependence on others. In some places Jesus said we'll be judged by how we treat other people, as in the line "I was hungry and you gave me food." But as Protestants we stressed that salvation depended on "faith alone," and "works" were of no avail. Jesus apparently said that those who forgive will be forgiven in turn. But we felt it was stupid to simply forgive offenders. They'd think they could get away with anything. At one point Jesus said that his followers "will do greater things than me" (John 14:12), but we tended to forget that verse because none of us believed it. The great theologian Reinhold Niebuhr said it straight out: Jesus' teaching was so idealistic that it was humanly impossible to follow in the real world. Therefore his ideals couldn't really apply on earth, and Christianity had no workable code of morals till it adopted the ethics of Roman Stoicism.[4]

After university, for a long time I decided that Christianity was just a form of ancient prejudice, leading to racism, nationalism, and war. I followed in my grandparents footsteps to reject religion, because it didn't live up to its own principles. I agreed with Frederick Douglas, who back in the days of slavery said "Between the Christianity of this land and the Christianity of Christ, I recognize the widest possible difference."[5] Later I heard of "red letter Christians," who tried to distinguish what Jesus said from all the other voices of tradition that came before or after him. For example, Rev. Ralph Blair put out a seemingly controversial pamphlet entitled, "What Jesus said about Homosexuality," and inside the page was a complete blank.[6] I started to suspect, like Rev. Tony Campolo, that people have "interpreted the Gospel so much, we've started to believe the interpretations instead of what Jesus said."[7] I wondered how much we've presumed to correct what Jesus said.

Reading over the gospel accounts, I noticed how much the first disciples tried to correct Jesus. When he said that men and women are equals in marriage, they answered, "If that is the position between husband and wife, it is better not to marry." (Matthew 19:10) Were lines like that from stand-up comedy routines? When confronted by a crowd of 5,000 hungry people, Jesus asked the disciples to share all the little food they had. And like most modern pragmatists they replied, "Are we to go and spend twenty pounds on bread to give them a meal?" (Mark 6:37) When Jesus said it was difficult for a rich man to enter the kingdom, the disciples "were more amazed than ever, and asked, 'Then who can be saved?' " (Mark 10:26) The disciples repeatedly argued over who should be greatest among them. They wanted to form a new monopoly on religious power: "John said to him, 'Master, we saw a man driving out devils in your name, and as he was not one of us, we tried to stop him.' " (Mark 9:38) When Jesus said that speaking or eating with "impure" people pollutes no one, the disciples admitted they didn't understand. They also admitted he replied, "Are you as dull as the rest?" (Mark 7:14–18) But soon enough, church leaders would be regularly "excommunicating" the sorts of sinners and prostitutes Jesus ate with.

Have we been generally "dull as the rest"? Have our churches taken the disciples' responses as expressions of orthodox faith? I'd like to ask people who claim to be Christians, and also critics of religion as they know it. Of course some church leaders reject this whole line of questioning. For example, in December of 2000, Cardinal Ratzinger's office in Rome (the Sacred Congregation for the Doctrine of the Faith) responded to critics who claimed that the early church was far more open about leadership roles for laypeople. The Sacred Congregation said it's invalid to use evidence from early Christianity to critique current church authorities.[8] But in this book, that's the main thing I want to do.

If we look over Christianity as we know it, what cases of officially correcting Jesus can we find? What is the record of Christians presuming to correct Jesus on subjects like Judaism, forgiveness, women, freedom, war, or charity?

What have been the results of correcting Jesus on these things?

2. Correcting Jesus' Jewish Religion

ince later Christians commonly treated Jews as heretics or ethnic pollutants, it's useful to recall that Jesus started out with the opposite prejudice. The gospels can be brutally frank about this, as in Matthew's report concerning a Canaanite woman: [His disciples urged him:] "Send her away; see how she comes shouting after us." Jesus replied [to her], "I was sent to the lost sheep of Israel, and to them alone." But the woman came and fell at his feet and cried, "Help me, sir." To this Jesus replied, "It is not right to take the [Jewish] children's bread and throw it to the dogs." (Matthew 15: 21–27)

At this point in his life, Jesus seemed to assume, like many Israelis today, that "Palestinians are garbage." In another verse he told his disciples "Do not take the road to Gentile lands, and do not enter any Samaritan town . . ." (Matthew 10:5–6) Later of course, he changed his mind. He went to Samaritan villages, rebuked his disciples for scorning them, challenged Jews to be like "the good Samaritan," etc. He started speaking to non-Jews as well, as in his three-days of preaching to a crowd of about 5,000 in the mainly Gentile region of Tyre and Sidon. But whether he spoke to Jews or Gentiles his topic was the same, namely how to follow the spirit of Jewish scriptures. He was a Jewish preacher who hoped to be a rabbi to the world. Later, his followers won much wider support from non-Jews. But then within several decades, these Gentile followers corrected Jesus' devotion to Judaism. For much of the next 2,000 years they made rejecting Judaism a fundamental principle of Jesus' religion.

We Gentile Christians tend to believe that Judaism is a tribal religion by nature; we think it's inherited only by birth, whereas Christianity is open to whoever chooses it. But in Jesus' time, no laws existed against Jews winning converts to their religion. Josephus said the Jews in Antioch "made proselytes of a great many of the Greeks."[1] In Rome, Seneca complained, "The ways of these dreadful people [the Jews] have taken deeper and deeper root and are spreading throughout the whole world. They have imposed their customs on the conquerors."[2] At that time there was no death penalty for converting to Judaism. That only happened later, when non-Jewish Christians took over the Empire, ostracized Jesus' people as traitors against Rome, and labeled the Jewish religion a heresy.

In this chapter I want to look at how this reversal happened in several steps. First, I'll discuss how it could possibly happen that the early church changed from promoting, to rejecting Judaism. The second question will be how the church switched political loyalties, from Jewish-style protest against Roman imperialism, to Gentile-Christian patriotism for the Empire. The third issue will be how Gentile converts changed Jesus' identity from a Jewish prophet to a Gentile-style deity. Last, I'll skim over the results of all these corrections down to recent years.

Jesus, Peter, and Paul on the Torah

As a Jew, Jesus believed the Law of Moses was God's vision for the world, and in saying so he could sound as legalistic as a Muslim mullah: "If any man . . . sets aside even the least of the Law's demands, and teaches others to do the same, he will have the lowest place in the kingdom of Heaven." (Matthew 5:19) His disputes with other rabbis concerned which laws took priority, as in: "You pay tithes of mint and dill and cumin; but you have overlooked the weightier demands of the Law, justice, mercy and good faith. It is these you should have practiced, without neglecting the others. Blind guides!" (Matthew 23:23–24) Like many later rabbis, he would ridicule a *Chasid Shote*, meaning a righteous fool, such as the idiot

8

of Talmudic legend who let a drowning woman die to avoid the impurity of touching her.[3] Basically, Jesus criticized legalistic control-freaks, but no more aimed at rejecting Judaism than any previous Jewish prophet. This would be too obvious to mention if not for later changes in church doctrine.

Paul also started out as a Jewish preacher, in the local synagogues across Turkey and Greece. So in Acts we read, "They now . . . came to Thessalonica, where there was a Jewish synagogue. Following his usual practice Paul went to their meetings; and for the next three Sabbaths he argued with them . . ." (17:1–2) He argued that Jesus taught people to go beyond Judaism's ritualistic requirements to an inner change, or "a circumcision of the heart." (Romans 2:29)

In Paul's home region of Asia Minor, many synagogues were already quite multi-cultural. As Seneca complained, they encouraged non-Jews to attend their services. They attracted "God-fearers," who were ethnic Gentiles, interested in the teaching of Jewish prophets, but often unwilling to "become Jewish."[4] One example was Paul's supporter Timothy, who came from a mixed Greek and Jewish family. Timothy had "from childhood been acquainted with the [Jewish] sacred writings," but he wasn't circumcised.[5] In synagogues outside Palestine, it seems the rabbis were seldom dogmatic about demanding conformity to all 613 laws in the Torah. They probably hoped to have a positive influence on surrounding cultures, and win them to Israel's ways step by step. In the same way, Paul hoped that Jesus could inspire both Jews and others.

All this mixing with historic enemies was still controversial back in the Jewish homeland. But even in Jerusalem, Peter also came to conclusions like Paul's: "I now see how true it is that God has no favorites, but that in every nation the man who is God-fearing and does what is right is acceptable to him . . ." (Acts 10:34–35) Basically, sharing values and fellowship between Jews and non-Jews seemed a good direction to Jesus,

Peter, and Paul. But within 100 years, both their Jewish and non-Jewish followers would basically forbid it.

From Fulfilling to Dumping the Torah

When Paul started preaching in Greece, he began one of history's great experiments with trans-ethnic religion. We could compare it to when preachers of Islam entered Indonesia, and tried to hold a balance between maintaining Arabian customs, and adapting Islam's spirit to an utterly different culture. But Paul's experiment had a more dramatic mix of remarkable successes with devastating failures. On one hand, his movement among non-Jews eventually succeed beyond his dreams. But the non-Jewish converts and his fellow Jews soon rejected each other. Basically, Paul won the foreigners to his cause, but lost his own people. His Gentile converts increasingly took the Christian movement as an invalidation of Jesus' own religion.

As he moved West, Paul went beyond preaching in synagogues, and directly addressed people of other religions. He was far from an all-or-nothing ethnic purist. If Jews like himself could reinterpret their whole tradition in light of Jesus' teaching, he felt people of other nations could do likewise with their traditions. As he built up hybrid Greek-Jewish communities, he grew determined to honor the Jewish and Gentile members equally. For him, Jesus' message cancelled the old hatreds of Pagan-Jewish wars. With enthusiasm he wrote, "Gentiles and Jews, he has made the two one, and in his own body of flesh and blood has broken down the enmity which stood like a dividing wall between them . . ." (Ephesians 2:14)

Paul faced critics who said he was corrupting ethnic purity. Some of these were proud Greeks, some were traditionalist Jews — like the ones who argued with Jesus. The more conservative Jewish Christians such as Jesus' brother James claimed that Jesus was a Jew, and so following him required honoring all Jewish laws. When some of these Jewish-Christian legalists visited Paul's followers in Galatia, they insisted his Greek companion Titus must be circumcised. They even violated Jesus' practice by refusing to eat with Paul's non-Jewish friends. And against this intrusion on his flock, Paul reacted by calling the visitors "sham Christians, interlopers who had stolen in to spy upon the liberty we enjoy in the fellowship of Christ Jesus. These men wanted to bring us into bondage, but not for one moment did I yield to their dictation." (Galatians 2:4)

When Jesus opposed legalistic Jews, he did it by appealing for better priorities in observing the law. For him the law was not a maze of nit-picky rules to be enforced on others. It was a matter of core values to be applied in each situation, as in the reasoning: As I would not be killed, so I would not kill. As I would not be robbed, so I would not steal. As I would not be lied to, so I would not lie. But Paul was more polemical. He replied to fundamentalists for the law in terms that seemed to dismiss all Jewish traditions: "Why let people dictate to you: 'Do not handle this, do not taste that, do not touch the other,' — all of them things that must perish as soon as they are used?" (Colossians 2:21) He was defending his flock of Gentile converts against a majority of Jewish Christians. He wanted his Greco-Roman friends to know he was on their side. To those who insisted that Gentile converts fit the mould of Jewish culture, he grew defiant: "Mark my words, I, Paul, say to you that if you receive circumcision Christ will do you no good at all . . . the only thing that counts is faith active in love . . . As for these agitators [for circumcision], they had better go the whole way and make eunuchs of themselves!" (Galatians 5:2–3, 6, 12)

Where Jesus always spoke of fulfilling the Law of Moses, Paul's more emotional attacks on legalism now seemed to flatly deny that Jewish ethical standards were at all relevant to non-Jews. Sometimes he went even further, giving arguments that seemed to invalidate the Law of Moses completely, even for Jews. In Galatians he claimed that Abraham had faith in God, and that this faith saved him. So if Abraham was "saved" long before the Jewish law appeared, then the law was not needed. As Barrie Wilson points out, this argument seemed to prove that the whole history of Judaism since Abraham — including Moses, the Exodus, and all the prophets — was basically irrelevant.[6] Though Paul didn't claim Jesus ever said so, he now suggested that the Law of Moses was obsolete. It applied to a time when "we were close prisoners in the custody of the law . . . until Christ should come." (Galatians 3:23-24) Now, it seemed, the Jewish moral code was simply replaced — by faith in Jesus himself.

At first, it was hard for Paul's Greek hearers to find out if he was contradicting Jesus. They probably had no written record of what Jesus said, because the first gospel of Mark didn't appear till about 15 years later.[7] So they had only Paul's word on the subject. It was those who had actually witnessed Jesus' sermons who objected to Paul's arguments. Back in Jerusalem, James warned of "trials" within the "synagogue" brought by deceivers arguing that "faith alone" was Jesus' message. James argued that religion was about living well, which required acting with compassion and justice: "what use is it for a man to say he has faith if he does nothing to show it? . . . faith divorced from deeds is lifeless as a corpse." (James 2:14, 26) Even Paul, after seeming to invalidate the Torah, immediately started preaching that freedom from the law was no excuse for "self-indulgence."

When Paul wrote his letters, the majority of Christians were still Jews living in Judea and Galilee. He was sticking up for an ethnic minority within the Jesus movement. But soon a growing majority of Gentile Christians echoed Paul's criticisms of Jewish legalists. Many adopted his words as scriptural proof that Judaism was stupid and irrelevant to Jesus' teaching. By the second century, a Gentile Christian *Epistle to Diognetus* ridiculed the "follies of Judaism": "As for their scrupulousness about meats, and their superstitions about the Sabbath, and their much-vaunted circumcision, and their pretentious festivals and moon-observances — all of these are too nonsensical to be worth discussing."[8]

From Jewish Anti-Imperialism to Roman Patriotism

As under the previous empires of Babylon or Greece, most Jews under Roman rule were firmly anti-colonial. Their scriptures were filled with stories of liberation from oppressors, and many Jews believed that all reverence for rulers or states was idolatry. Palestine's population was perhaps more defiant against the Roman Empire than that of any other colony. With famous fanaticism, their Zealots for independence waged a guerrilla jihad, risking martyrdom like Israel's fiery heroes in 2 Maccabees: "With his last breath, he said: 'Fiend though you are, you are setting us free from this present life, and, since we die for his laws, the King of the universe will raise us up to a life everlastingly made new." (7:9)

Of course Jesus was no empire loyalist himself. For him, it seems the Roman Empire was a huge edifice of egomania. Concerning its builders and defenders, he basically said, "Forgive them, for they know not what they do." Though he rejected violent resistance, he was a proud, independent Jew, who suffered the maximum Roman penalty for insubordination. It was lackeys of the occupation who accused him of treason, reporting to the Roman governor, "We found this man perverting our nation, forbidding us to pay taxes to the emperor, and saying that he himself is the Messiah, or King." (Luke 23:2) John has these traitors arguing, "If you release this man, you are not loyal to Caesar. Anyone claiming kingship of his own opposes Caesar." (19:12)

Patriotic Jews commonly referred to Rome as "Babylon," and its emperor as "the beast."[9] Even Paul wrote with seditious hostility, "our warfare is not against flesh and blood, but against the rulers, against the authorities, against the world powers of this darkness . . ." (Ephesians 6:12) And within a few decades, the "stiff-necked" rebels of Israel launched an anti-colonial war so murderous that the Romans' response was basically an indiscriminate slaughter of the Jewish nation. Even outside Palestine, Jews throughout the Empire faced death or prison for their presumed association with the rebel Jewish terrorists.

Yet soon after this we hear of patriotism and obedience to the emperor as noble Christian virtues. Where early Jewish Christians sympathized with Israel against its occupiers, we soon find non-Jewish Christians teaching that Jesus' real enemies were "the Jews." And soon these empire loyalists who viewed Jews with contempt began claiming that they were the real followers of Jesus.

The Pressure to Prove Paul's Churches Patriotic

We first glimpse empire patriotism in the Jesus movement among Paul's mainly Gentile churches in Greece or Rome. Many members were Gentile Romans, and everyone knew the government spied on private organizations. When Paul wrote to the church in Rome, there was probably real danger his letter would be inspected by government officers. Quite naturally he was careful to sound loyal. As if patriotism for the empire was an important part of Jesus' message, he wrote: "Every person must submit to the supreme authorities. There is no authority but by act of God, and the existing authorities are instituted by him; consequently anyone who rebels against authority is resisting a divine institution, and those who resist have themselves to thank for the punishment they will receive." And Paul knew perfectly well that the Roman government killed Jesus, just on the suspicion that he might be considered a "king of the Jews." We know Paul's real feelings from his lines in Ephesians on "warfare" against the rulers, authorities, and "world powers of this darkness." But what could he say in Greece or Rome? The survival of his church depended on claiming heartfelt devotion to Rome's colonial empire.

Paul's claims of patriotism may sound sufficiently submissive to

14

us, but to the Romans they weren't convincing. The Jews were already notorious for treason, and simple claims of innocence from a Jewish sect hardly dealt with the degree of suspicion. Paul could explain that followers of Jesus were not rebellious like other Jews, but Jesus had been killed by the government for treason. The Romans suspected everyone who claimed a lord aside from the emperor, or a kingdom aside from Rome. To protect the Jesus movement in a Gentile empire, Paul needed a public relations offensive. He lobbied the Roman governors of Judea and Crete, promising them that Christians were loyal, and even model citizens — more law-abiding, virtuous, and helpful than pagan ones. Paul tried to argue there was no conflict between Christian and Roman loyalties. God was the source of every authority, and He worked through the pharaoh — I mean the emperor — not against him. It might seem Paul was actually saying that it was impossible for the commands of any earthly ruler to contradict God's will. Some Christians in Nazi Germany certainly took it that way. But again, this argument didn't convince Paul's rulers. Of course such promises of collective virtue and loyalty were more than Paul could deliver. And Emperor Nero remained convinced that Christians in Rome were a fifth-column of pro-Jewish rebels. He eliminated most of them later, including Paul.

The Pressure to Ditch Judaism

After the Jewish nation's revolt passed from low-grade insurgency to full-blown rebellion, it grew even harder for Christians to prove harmless loyalty. In the Jewish war of 66–70, the Romans made few distinctions between Jewish sects and took few prisoners. In Caesarea, on the Palestinian coast, Roman forces and the Gentile population acted in "self-defense" to slaughter a reported 20,000 dangerous Jews. Josephus reported, "It was then common to see cities filled with dead bodies . . . unburied, those of old men mixed with infants, and women lying among them without any cover."[10]

Outside of Palestine, the Romans generally assumed that Jews and Christians were rebel sympathizers unless proven otherwise. In Antioch, someone started a rumor that local Jewish terrorists were plotting to burn the Gentile side of town. The suspects were seized, and mobs of Gentiles demanded they be burned alive immediately, without trial. Next, fearful Gentiles demanded every Jew take an oath of unconditional loyalty, and they killed anyone who refused. After that a big fire did erupt, and many assumed it was the predicted Jewish terror attack. Mobs of vigilantes massacred every Jew they could catch. After the soot settled, the Romans sent officers to investigate, and concluded that all the accused Jews had been innocent.[11] In the middle of this madhouse, Antioch's minority of Christians tried to survive any way they could.

In Egypt and Libya, the large Jewish communities remained quiet at news of the Palestinian revolt. But the suspicious Romans demanded that every Jew, even the children, had to publicly swear unconditional obedience to Rome. The results were the same as when later Christian martyrs balked at such an oath. As Josephus rather enthusiastically reported:

> They were subjected to every conceivable form of torture and bodily suffering, all of them contrived for the sole purpose of getting them to affirm Caesar as lord. Not a one of them gave in or was even able to declare it, but everyone maintained their resolve, victorious over coercion. As they endured the tortures and flames, it was as if their bodies felt no pain and their souls actually rejoiced in it. What especially amazed those who saw it were the young children, none of whom could be persuaded to call Caesar lord.[12]

By this point Rome's rulers saw all Jews as terrorist suspects. Emperor Vespasian believed that Judaism was fanatical by nature, and it would always seek to undermine Roman civilization.[13] How could Gentile Christians feel about this? It was natural for self-protection that Paul's Gentile churches downplayed any association with their mother religion. Even St. Peter did the same when accused of association with a condemned rebel. So, while imperial armies crucified the Jewish nation, most Gentile Christians denied they even knew the offenders.

After that war, the world of the early church was changed almost beyond recognition. The original Christian communities in Galilee and Judea were mostly slaughtered or scattered to the wind. Suddenly the majority of surviving Christians were Gentiles living outside Palestine. Instead of hoping to renew Judaism as Jesus did, these people increasingly emphasized whatever set them apart from Jews. Many of them seized on Paul's words which suggested the Old Testament Law was null and void. Christianity, they said, was a totally different religion.

Luke's Revision of the Record

Luke wrote his gospel account and the book of Acts after the Jewish revolt, and many textual signs plus his proficiency in Greek suggest he was a non-Jewish Christian.[14] Rather than emphasizing the continuity of Jesus' teaching with the Old Testament as in Matthew, Luke edited the record of early Christianity for a more pro-Roman, anti-Jewish slant. For example, where Paul had written that he fled the city of Damascus due to hostility from the Nabataean ruler Aretas (II Corinthians 11:32–33), Luke changed the story to claim that Paul fled to escape murderous anti-Christian Jews. (Acts 9:23–25)

Back in the 50s, Paul had criticized Peter for clinging to ethnically exclusive Jewish traditions. But writing about 30 years later in Acts, Luke described Peter as denying any relevance to Jewish tradition. He wrote that Peter addressed the Jewish national Sanhedrin saying, "There is no salvation in anyone else at all [save Jesus — apparently not even

Abraham, Moses, Elijah, or John the Baptist]; for there is no other name under heaven that has been given among men, by whom we may be saved." (4:12) Luke also had Peter correct Jesus, to make him seem more like a Gentile deity. Matthew had Jesus advise, "Not everyone who calls me 'Lord, Lord' will enter the kingdom of heaven." (Matthew 7:21) But Luke had Peter give a more optimistic promise: "everyone who calls on the name of the Lord will be saved." (Acts 2:21)

In his letter to Ephesians Paul showed the attitude of a patriotic Jew, a former Pharisee, and an agent of the national Sanhedrin, in condemning the rulers and world powers over Israel. But in Acts, Luke describes Paul as modeling the highest respect for Rome's officials. In a stirring re-composed speech (Acts 25: 10–11) he depicts Paul as a proud Roman citizen, appealing to the colonial power for defense from his fellow Jews. If association with rebel Jews caused contempt for his faith and suffering for Gentile believers, Luke would show the world that Christians were patriots. Christians, he claimed, had been persecuted by Jews, not Romans, and they looked to Rome for deliverance from Jewish oppression.

Luke's hope of befriending the Romans shows in his excitement over the centurion Cornelius' conversion in Acts 10 and 11. In his account of the first church council in Jerusalem (Acts 15), Luke describes greater enthusiasm over one Roman officer's conversion, than over Paul's reports of large-scale conversions among common people in Asia Minor and Cyprus.[15] Luke takes more space discussing this one Roman's conversion than he does in repeating the story of Paul's conversion three times.

Basically, Luke avoided any criticism of Rome, and blamed all the trials of Jesus and his followers on other Jews. This was the pattern for Gentile Christians after the Jewish War. It was far safer for Christians to blame their trials on dead Palestinians than on the mighty Romans. By around the year 100, the Gentile Bishop Ignatius of Antioch contradicted Paul by claiming it was an abomination for Christians to attend synagogue services: "If we are still living in the practice of Judaism, it is an admission that we have failed to receive the gift of grace."[16] Christianity, he said, was clearly a separate religion. Judaism was nothing but a post-war wasteland of "tombstones and sepulchers of the dead."[17]

And still the Gentile Christian efforts to appear patriotic failed to convince the Romans. Around 110, they killed Bishop Ignatius for failing to affirm that the emperor was a higher authority than the Jewish rebel Jesus. The Romans also murdered the second bishop of the Jewish-Christian church, Simon bar Clopus, reportedly because he was a cousin of Jesus, and they wanted to exterminate the lineage of King David.[18] A bit later, Palestine exploded again in the Bar Kosba revolt of 132–135, and the Romans executed Telesphorus, the bishop of Rome, presuming he must be guilty by association.[19] By 135, the original Jewish Christian community was nearly extinct by sheer dint of slaughter. The chastised Gentile Christians grew convinced they must cut their ties to Judaism even more completely.

The Emergence of Imperialistic Christianity

After Rome scattered Israel to the winds, most Christians had little choice but to see the Empire as their only country. Of course many Gentile Christians still felt it was apostasy to pledge devotion to the emperor. Till after 300, most of them still believed it was a sin to serve in Rome's army. But they increasingly accepted that Rome's occupation must be God's will, and obedience to the emperor their Christian duty. The trend toward empire patriotism slowly advanced, bucking the Bible's praise for resisting tyrants. By some point in the second century, the author of 1 Peter felt it faithful to advise, "Submit yourselves for the Lord's sake to every human authority, or to governors, who are sent by him to punish those who do wrong . . . Show proper respect for everyone, fellow believers, fear God, honor the emperor." (2:13–17) By around 200, even a colonial Egyptian admirer of martyr-protesters like Origen could instruct his readers that Roman rule was necessary to God's plan: "A peace [the famous *Pax Romana*] was prevalent which began at the birth of Christ. For God prepared the nations for His teaching so that it might not, because of lack of unity between nations due to the existence of many kingdoms, be more difficult for the Apostles to carry out the task laid on them by their Master when he said 'Go and teach all nations.' "[20]

All these calls to patriotism came as the Romans continued investigating and killing Christians, mainly for the treason of claiming there were higher authorities than the state. But after a particularly nasty round of executions in Gaul (late 200s), Bishop Irenaeus of Lyons tried to turn the page by extolling the spiritual advantage of a strong empire: "Earthly rule, therefore, has been appointed by God, and not by the Devil, for the benefit of nations . . . so that, under fear of human rule, people may not devour one another like fishes."[21] Clearly this religion from a rebel colony was showing its flexibility to switch loyalties, from Israel to Rome, and from conquered people to their rulers.

The Gentile Christian Rejection of Israel's Jealous God

Soon after the Bar Kosba Jewish revolt of 132, the Gentile Christian teacher Marcion proclaimed his message of final rejection for Judaism. The Old Testament and the gospel of Jesus, he taught, were utterly different in spirit. While the Old Testament was a record of "religious" wars, ethnic hatreds, and petty rules, Jesus had come to reveal the true God's love for all. How, Marcion asked, could these two utterly different testaments possibly come from the same God? Didn't accepting Jesus involve casting Judaism aside? Didn't Paul say that Jesus brought freedom from the curse of Old Testament law?

For Marcion, the issue was clear as black and white. He saw nothing but violence and heartless legalism in Judaism, and only loving brotherhood in Christianity. He typified Judaism by the cruelest episodes recorded in the Bible, and labeled the Jewish people accordingly. Of course Jewish Christians were also critical of Judaism's past. Their *Kerygmata Petrou* said the Old Testament contained corruptions in which certain writers attributed jealousy, hate, or violence to God. Marcion knew about these debates between Jews over the wheat and chaff of their tradition. But he preferred to just discredit the whole religion.[22]

Marcion's new teaching swept through the Gentile churches in the 140s in a popular wave. Probably most Gentile Christians were gratified to hear that Christianity contradicted Judaism on every point, and was a completely different and superior religion. But then Marcion wemt further to insist that the scriptures be purged of Jewish influence. He drafted a Jew-free version of the Bible. Of course it eliminated the whole Old Testament, but in addition it trashed the Gospels of Mark, Matthew, and John, the letters of James, Peter, John, Jude, and Revelation. The only books non-Jewish enough for Marcion were slightly corrected versions of Luke, Acts, and the letters of Paul. Fortunately, the Gentile clergy rebelled against this degree of disfigurement of the scriptures. How, they objected, could a loud-mouthed layman command such wholesale invalidation of religious heritage? Assemblies of bishops declared Marcion a heretic. They defended the authority of Jewish scripture, while at the same time invalidating Jewish people and their traditions.

Changing Jesus from a Jewish Prophet to a Gentile-style Deity

Our four canon gospels appeared over the thirty or forty-year period following the destruction of Israel as Jesus knew it. And this was the period when the Jesus movement was transformed, from a mainly Jewish sect within Palestine, to a mainly Gentile sect outside the Jewish homeland. Mark appeared in the immediate wake of the war, around the year 70. It's likely the destruction of Jewish Christian communities across Palestine spurred the author to make a written record, since oral memory was in danger. Matthew probably came second around 80, then Luke about 90 or 100, and John a bit after 100. Each gospel in succession shows an increased influence of Gentile culture. The accounts progressively shift from describing Jesus as a Jewish prophet, toward presenting him as a Gentile-style deity.

We can trace the rising theme of Jesus' superhuman status through the New Testament, from earliest writing to latest. In the 50s, Paul said simply that Jesus was "born of a woman of Judea." (Galatians 4:4) This first known reference to Mary mentions nothing of her being a virgin.[23] About twenty years later, Mark's gospel gives Jesus' story with no mention of his birth at all. To these writers, it didn't seem to matter. Concerning these accounts, Joseph Campbell says, "It is reasonably certain that in the earliest strictly Jewish stage of the development of this legend, the completely un-Jewish idea of the begetting of a hero by a god can have played no role, and that the episode of the initiatory baptism in the Jordan must have marked the opening of the Messianic career."[24]

Only with Matthew and Luke in the 80s and 90s do we first find stories of a virgin birth. But even then, with Jesus so literally called "Son of God," Luke still gives him a human genealogy going back to Adam, and lists Adam's father as "God." (3:38) Bart Ehrman finds cases where this text was later altered. The oldest and now best accepted manuscripts end the genealogy with, "Jacob, who was the father of Joseph, the husband of Mary, from whom was born Jesus, who is called the Christ" (1:16). But some later versions corrected this to read "Jacob, who was the father of Joseph, to whom being betrothed to the Virgin Mary gave birth to Jesus . . ."[25] Later books claimed that the gospel references to Jesus' "brothers and sisters" really meant step-siblings, or cousins, and the Council of Chalcedon in 451 required belief that Mary was *Aeiparthenos*, or "Ever-

Virgin."

In the synoptic accounts before John, Jesus was usually addressed as "teacher" or "rabbi." Peter called him the Messiah, but all Jews believed the Messiah was a holy human being. The disciples said he was God's son, but the Hebrew Bible said the same thing of Adam, King David, and all people of Israel, as when Hosea claimed to quote God: "When Israel was a child I loved him, and out of Egypt I called my son." (11:1) In Exodus, Moses was instructed to tell the Pharaoh "Israel is my firstborn son." (4:22) And Psalm 82 seemed to expand divine parentage to all humanity: "I have said, Ye are gods; and all of you are children of the most high." (82:6) But after Mark, this Jewish context for Jesus' role progressively fades from view. It is replaced by claims that Jesus was infinitely superior to all others, and true divinity belonged to him alone. Where Jesus spoke of God as "our Father," most Gentile converts insisted that Jesus was God's only child. The claim was offensive and idolatrous to Jews and Jewish Christians, but it was much in demand among Gentile ones. If Romans already addressed Augustus Caesar as "Lord," "Redeemer," "Savior of the World," "Son of God" and "God from God," then for many Gentile Christians, it seemed impious to call Jesus anything less.[26]

In the first gospel of Mark, the disciples often appeared as common buffoons, who were almost comically slow in grasping what Jesus told them. Jesus himself showed human feelings of anger, grief, and fear. He displayed amazing powers, but then encouraged his followers to do the same things. After Mark, however, the later gospels grew less candid and more worshipful toward both Jesus and the disciples. For example, in Mark, Jesus walks on the water, and the disciples "were utterly astounded, for they didn't understand about the loaves, but their hearts were hardened." (6:51–52) About a decade later, Matthew altered this story to say, "Those in the boat worshipped him, saying 'Truly you are the Son of God' " (14:33) In Mark, Jesus never said he was the Messiah. Peter called him that once, but Jesus told him not to repeat it, and the disciples obeyed. (8:30) But by the book of John, Jesus himself was constantly announcing that he was the Son of God, as if this was his main message to the world.

Comparing the earliest gospel of Mark with the latest one of John, Louis Ruprecht finds a remarkable shift in meaning. In Mark, Jesus is a painfully human figure. When facing arrest on his last night, "Horror and dismay came over him, and he said to them, 'My heart is ready to break with grief.' " (14:34) He prays in anguish, "take this cup away from me." (14:36) His last words on the cross are a shriek of naked despair: "My God, my God, why have you forsaken me?" (15:34) But in John, there is no horror, no grief, no doubt or tragedy. Jesus faces his death boasting of total self-control: "Now my soul is in turmoil, and what am I to say? 'Father save me from this hour?' No, for this is the purpose I have come to this hour." (12:27) Rather than praying to be spared suffering, he asks, "The cup that the Father has given me — shall I not drink it?" (18:11) When he dies, he doesn't cry out in pain or despair; he boldly announces, "It is accomplished!" (19:30)[27] Augustine found the difference between John and the other gospels obvious: "For the other three evangelists were walking as it were along the ground with their human Lord, and they said little about his divinity. But this one [John], as scorning to walk along the ground, at the outset launched himself, with a lightning flash, not only above the ground but above the encompassing air and heaven . . ."[28]

In John, Jesus doesn't share in human weakness. He is the incarnation of superhuman perfection. When he is asked, "What should we do to satisfy God?" he doesn't say, "love God and neighbor" or "follow the Ten Commandments" as in earlier gospels. John has him reply, "This is the work that God requires: believe in the one whom God sent." (John 6:28–29)

By the time John's gospel appeared, a clear majority of Christians were non-Jews, and the new religion shifted to meet their demands or expectations. Already the heroic teacher had changed to a superhuman divine being. For Gentile converts, the tales of Jesus' amazing powers were proof he was a superhuman deity, able to grant them supernatural help. Jewish Christians pointed out that rabbi Jesus expected his students to do the same miracles he did. When he sent out 72 disciples in pairs, he expected them to heal sick people, not just bring them to be treated by the Master. Peter reportedly joined Jesus walking on water, and even matched him in raising people from the dead, because Acts says Peter raised a female disciple named Tabitha from the grave. (Acts 9:36–43) For Jewish Christians, these stories suggested that Jesus wanted colleagues who would join him in his work, not just fawning devotees.[29] Like any good teacher he said, "A disciple is not above his teacher, but every one when he is fully taught will be like his teacher." (Luke 6:40, Matthew 10:24–25) And at first, this optimism was typical of Christian preaching. As Paul put it:

> . . . *the Spirit of God joins with our spirit in testifying that we are God's children; and if children, then heirs. We are God's heirs and Christ's fellow heirs. . .* (Romans 8:16-17)
> . . . *So shall we all at last attain to the unity inherent in our faith and our knowledge of the Son of God — to mature manhood, measured by nothing less than the full stature of Christ.* (Ephesians 4:10, 13)

Only much later would ecclesiastical courts rule that claiming such a goal was a capital offense.

Around the year 100, Ignatius, the Gentile bishop of Antioch, corrected the old Jewish attitude toward Jesus, explaining that real Christians accepted Jesus "not as Son of Man, but as Son of God." Apparently, Ignatius assumed there was a universe of difference between the two.[30] Like most Greco-Romans, he believed there were two main orders of beings in the universe, namely a) human and mortal, or b) divine and immortal. Since Jesus reportedly rose from the dead, he had to be an immortal deity. If he wasn't an immortal deity, then reverence for him would bring no benefit.

Such arguments may sound obvious or simply orthodox to our ears. But many traditional Jews believed that all souls were eternal, and everyone would be resurrected in the body. As Paul said, "I believe all that is written in the Law and the prophets, and in reliance on God I hold the hope, which my accusers too accept, that there is to be a resurrection of good and wicked alike . . ." (Acts 24:15) Of course Paul's hearers were also familiar with the story from Ezekiel: "Come, O wind, come from every quarter and breathe into these slain, that they may come to life! I began to prophesy as he had bidden me: breath came into them; they came to life and rose to their feet, a mighty host. He said to me, 'Man, these bones are the whole people of Israel'. . ." (37:9–11)

So if Jesus died, rose, and ascended into heaven, how in the Jewish sense was that so different from the fate of other souls? The Jewish-Christian "Ebionites" believed that Jesus was a human prophet who rose from the dead, which they took as a confirmation of traditional Jewish beliefs. They thought all just and good people would be resurrected, and the greatest prophets would rise first.[31] When Jesus told Lazarus' sister "Your brother will rise again," she replied like many Jews, "I realize that he will rise again at the resurrection on the last day." (John: 23–24) But most Gentile Christians saw the resurrection of Jesus as a miracle unique in history. This miracle showed he was the hoped-for deity, who had the power to raise both himself and his devotees from the grave. And this was what most Romans, Greeks, or Egyptians wanted from a religion. Most people didn't want a challenging path of learning to live with compassion and justice. They wanted salvation as an escape from the pain of life, and from mortality itself. Obviously only an immortal deity could grant this wish. So if Jesus was just a human prophet as the Jewish Christians believed, then he couldn't be a true savior at all. If Jesus was just a human being, then eternal life would not be his to give. So the popular demand for immortality fit together with faith in Jesus' divinity, in a bond strong as the desire to live.

If this was what most Gentiles wanted in an avatar, then the Jewish Christian view of Jesus seemed to them totally uninspiring. These Jews had missed the whole point of who Jesus was and what hope he offered. For Epiphanius of Salamis, the position of Jewish Christians was utterly ridiculous: "How do they define the savior a mere man from the seed of a man?"[32] The Church historian Eusebius dismissed Jewish Christians in a chapter called "The Heresy of the Ebionites": "These were properly called Ebionites by the ancients as those who cherished low and mean opinions of Christ . . . They regard [Christ] as plain and ordinary, a man esteemed as righteous through growth of character and nothing more, the child of a normal union between a man and Mary."[33]

In the late 20th century, Rev. Jerry Falwell was still refuting such "disbelief," explaining to modern Americans, "It is important to recognize that Mary was a virgin. If Christ had had a human father and if His mother had been an illicit woman, then He by nature would have inherited the fallen nature of His earthly father and would have needed someone to save Him. He certainly could not have been the Savior of the world."[34]

With the rise of this doctrine, Jewish rabbis increasingly ruled that Jesus worshippers were apostates from Judaism. It was the first big split in the Jesus movement, and the most basic of all divisions to come.

The Great Nature-of-Christ Debates

Over the next 250 years, belief in the "deity of Christ" rose to become the centerpiece of Gentile Christian orthodoxy. Several other views of Jesus remained among Gentile believers, but these were rejected one by one in the courts of bishops' assemblies. Within the Roman church, a series of pro or con decisions eventually rejected all views of Jesus but one.

After rejecting the Jewish belief that Jesus was a human being, the next heresy to be attacked was "docetism." This was a belief that Jesus was God, and he only appeared to take human form in order to play a role on history's stage. This view of Jesus seemed to make him a supernatural entity without any real relation to humanity. And at this early stage of church history, the traditional Jewish horror of deifying any human being remained influential. A series of church councils from the 140s on expelled teachers of Docetism from their churches. Later, in the 300s, the state church criminalized possession of either Jewish-Christian or "docetic" books, and both views were basically purged from the written record, till some copies were rediscovered in recent times.

Next, in the 260s, Bishop Paul of Samasota raised a dispute by claiming that Mark's gospel was basically right — Jesus had started off as a mortal Jew, whose birth and youth were not worth mentioning, till the day God's spirit filled him at his baptism. This view had a plausible basis in scripture. But it seemed to imply that any mortal could be filled with God's spirit, or claim to speak for God. A council of bishops discussed this in 268, and the majority voted to denounce it as a heresy of "adoptionism." The council also voted to sack Paul from his job. For the first time in church history, a conclave of bishops voted to expel a fellow bishop. From now on, a cleric could be fired for suggesting that Jesus had ever been a human being.

Then came the great "Arian heresy" of the 300s, in which an Egyptian priest named Arius unfortunately reasoned that if Jesus was God's son, then God existed before him, and Jesus was basically part of God's creation. The dispute this generated resembled the Islamic debate as to whether the Quran was created, or existed before the universe began. Some church leaders felt it was meaningless speculation, but the argument soon threatened to split the newly state-backed church. Different regional councils of bishops voted to back one side or the other, and pronounced excommunications on those of the opposite opinion. Emperor Constantine decided that only a council of all major churchmen in the empire could settle it, and called the great Council of Nicea in 325.

In these early councils, most of the bishops were Middle Eastern or North African men, often of Greek descent. Their conceptual worlds were mixtures of Near Eastern traditionalism with Platonic philosophy. In their world an assumption prevailed that the heavenly and mundane realms were composed of different substances.[35] As Bishop John Spong put it, they "assumed a dualistic world divided between nature and super-nature, body and soul, humanity and divinity."[36] All this made the question of Jesus' nature start to resemble a chemistry problem. If Jesus was both divine and human, how did those two obviously incompatible natures co-exist in him? Were they mixed in equal portions? Bishop Athanasius of Alexandria insisted there could be no middle term between "God" and "not God".[37] And somewhere in this argument over what substance Jesus was, the issue of what he taught about life began to fade into the background.

The arguments in these church councils often resembled winner-take-all theological wrestling matches. The losers in each debate were often expelled from the church, fined, and exiled to foreign lands. Since careers were at stake as well as doctrines, no one seemed willing to back down or admit a mistake. As the debates at Nicea wore on, many bishops hoped to explain that Jesus was a special soul in a normal body. Therefore he suffered physically, but was too perfect to sin. But what formula to express this decision that could satisfy the whole contentious church? To break the logjam, Emperor Constantine himself spoke up with a suggestion. Why not use the term *homoousios*, or "of one substance"? Why not just say that Jesus and God were of one substance?

The majority of bishops felt suddenly moved to endorse the emperor's insight. After all, he was now the state church's paymaster. A correct creed was soon drafted, which read in part, "We believe in one God, Almighty, Maker of all things visible and invisible, and in one Lord, Jesus Christ, the Son of God, begotten of the Father, God from God, Light from Light, Very God from Very God, begotten not made, of one substance with the Father . . ."

Of this statement, historian Frances Young points out, there was nothing about Jesus' way of living or what he taught.[38] It was just an assertion of his superhuman status. According to this creed, Jesus was never created, and was perfect from before the beginning. When it said he was "begotten, not made," it meant he was not made like any other creature in the universe.[39] In that case he never had to grow up from childishness to wisdom, though Luke said, "As Jesus grew up he advanced in wisdom." (Luke 2:52) Where Jesus had said, "my Father is greater than I." (John 14:28), and "I can of my own self do nothing" (John 5:30), the Gentile bishops ruled him an omnipotent Lord of the universe. They implied he knew everything that ever was or would be, though Mark quoted him saying, "But of that day or that hour no one knows . . . only the Father." (13:32) Though Jesus predicted his followers "will do what I am doing; and . . . will do greater things still . . ." (John 14:12), the new creed implied this was utterly impossible. Yet for most churches of the future, this creed served as the litmus test of belief in Jesus. On this basis, conservative writer Rod Dreher rejected Barack Obama's claim to be a Christian, saying "As a statement of minimal Christian orthodoxy — that is, what it is necessary to believe to be a Christian, the Nicean Creed is as basic as it comes." By this standard, Obama's dedication to service and his claim to be inspired by Jesus were not enough. For Dreher the most important thing was use of the term "begotten not made."[40]

As in other religions, these claims of infallible perfection for the prophet served to buttress claims to ultimate authority for the prophet's representatives. So in later Shia Islam, some clerics taught that "the executor of God's will, the Imam is . . . infallible and sinless, for 'sin would destroy the validity of the call.' "[41] Some of the more self-righteous mullahs claimed that the rightly-guided Imams were not created from dust like other people, but from eternal light. It seemed very pious. But as Jewish scholar Barrie Wilson points out, "The price tag of seeing Jesus as divine [and ourselves as not] is that we cannot identify with him, nor he with us, for we do not share the same situation, the same lot in life."[42]

I always heard that the Founding Fathers of Christian orthodoxy followed a golden mean, between the extremes of calling Jesus a mere man or worshipping him like a Gentile deity. But if the middle way was to call him both human and God, while insisting he was absolutely unique to have such a dual nature, then this was the same as saying he was infinitely more divine than any mortal being, which was the same as saying he was a deity. The doctrine which prevailed as Christian orthodoxy was very close to the earlier rejected "heresy of docetism." Jesus was the greatest divinity ever to appear on earth. Those who called him Lord would be saved, and he would punish the rest.

Later, this Gentile demand to deify Jesus involved "correcting" previous church history, including many early manuscripts of the New Testament. Textual analysts like Bart Ehrman find a host of such "corruptions," which often passed as inerrant scripture until scholars discerned which manuscripts were most original. Most of these changes were made to make Jesus look more like a superhuman deity. Examining the Codex Alexandrinus, Johann J. Wettstein found the text of 1 Timothy 3:16 had been changed by a later hand. Where the original writing spoke of Jesus "who was made manifest in the flesh and justified in the Spirit," later marks in a different ink altered the word for "who" to the abbreviation for "God," so that Jesus was described as "God made manifest in the flesh."[43] Ehrman finds that in manuscript 2766, the words of Luke 8:28 were changed from "Jesus Son of the Highest God" to "Jesus, the Highest God." And a third-century text changed 2 Peter 1:2. While the original text read, "May grace and peace be multiplied to you in the knowledge of God and our Lord Jesus Christ," the modified text omitted the word "and," to make it read "in the knowledge of God, our Lord Jesus."[44]

Robert Capon explains that the former heresy of "docetism" now passes for true religion in modern America. American believers generally see Jesus as a kind of supernatural hero who single-handedly saved the world. "The true paradigm of the ordinary American view of Jesus, he says, "is Superman": "Faster than a speeding bullet, more powerful than a locomotive, able to leap tall buildings in a single bound. It's Superman! Strange visitor from another planet, who came to earth with powers and abilities far beyond those of mortal men, and who, disguised as Clark Kent, mild-mannered reporter for a great metropolitan newspaper, fights a never-ending battle for truth, justice, and the American way."[45]

As Billy Graham put it, "Jesus is God in human flesh."[46] Of course, according to Jews and Jewish Christians, that broke the First Commandment.

Severing All Ties to Jesus' People

Both as a Gentile Christian and a military man, the first Christian emperor Constantine viewed the Jews as his enemies. He moved to sever the church from its Jewish roots with a series of decrees. One was to change the Christian Sabbath to Sunday, by ruling all government business would cease on that day.[47] Then he separated the dates of Easter from those of the Jewish Passover. As he told his bishops, "It appeared an unworthy thing that in the celebration of this most holy feast we should follow the practice of the Jews, who have impiously defiled their hands with enormous sin and are therefore deservedly afflicted with blindness of soul . . . Let us then have nothing in common with the detestable Jewish crowd."[48]

In 337, Constantine moved to block human relations between Jews and Christians. Literally banning love between the two, he proclaimed the death penalty for any marriage between a Christian and a Jew. He made it a capital offense for any Jew to preach his religion to Christians, or for any Christian to convert to Judaism. By dint of this death penalty, which continued in future law codes, he forced Judaism to become a strictly hereditary religion. Then Constantine stole Jerusalem for Christianity, by banning Jews from living in their holy city.

The whole history of Christian anti-Semitism to follow is well known, but I want to mention some details of the unfolding nightmare. Of all corrections to Jesus' religion, this one is probably the starkest.

Jesus' People under a Christian Curse

After Emperor Theodosius banned all religions but Christianity in the 390s, the temples and communities of all other religions suffered. But the vilification of Jews and synagogues was especially severe. In place of Jesus' devotion to the Jewish people, Christian bishops like John Chrysostom attacked the Jews as "vile," "dogs," "godless," "sick," "mad," and "fit for slaughter."[49] Such lectures commonly led directly to riots against local Jews, as happened across Europe when the Crusades were preached from the 1090s. Where Jesus made a point of eating with Gentiles and said it polluted no one, Christian authorities demanded social segregation of Jews into ghettos so they wouldn't contaminate Christians. The Franciscan scholar Duns Scotus contradicted the book of Exodus by claiming all Jews were slaves by divine decree. Christian princes therefore had the right to treat any Jews in their domains as slaves, and to forcibly baptize Jewish children. Scotus hoped the forced baptism would end Judaism.[50] With all this righteous abuse of Jews, Pope Innocent III felt responsible to remind his flock, "Jews are the living witnesses of the true faith. The Christian is not permitted to exterminate the Jewish race."[51] Instead of exterminating them, the rulers of France and England repeatedly expelled all Jews in their realms, and profited by confiscating their property.

In the 1400s Spain also expelled all Jews, ruling they could remain only on converting. But then even the converts were banned from holding any church office or official honor unless they could prove a genealogy free of Jewish blood. A Spanish church organization announced. "all of their descendants . . . are as if born with polluted blood. Therefore they are denied all honors, offices and titles . . . the abomination of their ancestors will cling to them forever."[52]

Martin Luther was as at least as contemptuous of Jews as any medieval Catholic cleric. He rebuked these repeatedly punished people as "poisonous, bitter, vengeful, deceitful snakes, assassins, and the Devil's children, who . . . do harm secretly, because they dare not do it in the open." In his 1543 essay "On the Jews and Their Lies," he said the Jewish people were a "plague of disgusting vermin" seeking to destroy Christendom and achieve world domination. To defend Christian society, Luther urged churchmen to burn the Jews' books, synagogues, schools and houses.[53] Where some Christian leaders wanted to pressure Jews to convert, Luther advised it was useless: "Yes, it is useless to argue with them about how God is triune, how he became a man, and how Mary is the mother of God. No human reason nor any human heart will ever grant these things, much less the embittered, venomous, blind heart of the Jews . . . Moses was unable to reform the Pharaoh by means of plagues, miracles, pleas, or threats; he had to let him drown in the sea."[54]

In the 1700s, Empress Elizabeth Petrovna of Russia moved that "from our whole empire . . . all Jews shall . . . be immediately deported, and shall henceforth under no pretext be admitted into our Empire . . . unless they . . . accept the Christian religion of the Greek persuasion." But when a Russian-German pact partitioned Poland in 1772, Catherine the Great allowed Russia's Jews to stay there, provided they stayed inside their "Pale of settlement."[55]

When the French Revolution of the 1790's rejected state enforcement of church laws, it overturned these old restrictions on Jews. Wherever the revolutionary armies prevailed, Jews were allowed to leave their ghettos and have the same freedoms as other people. In Rome, Pope Pius IX complained bitterly. He wrote that before the time of Jesus, Jews had been "children in the house of God," but since then "owing to their failure to believe, they have become dogs . . . We have today in Rome unfortunately too many of these dogs, and we hear them barking in all streets, and going around molesting people everywhere."[56]

Defeating the Jewish World Conspiracy to Destroy Civilization

As a series of movements for secular government, freedom of religion, and social equality took root across the continent, clerical leaders commonly blamed emancipated Jews for organizing opposition to church powers. These clerics claimed an evil alliance of Jews and revolutionary Freemasons was systematically destroying Christendom, and seeking to impose a godless socialistic order. In 1825, Fr. Ferdinand Jabalot warned that if Jews were not controlled, they "will finally succeed in reducing the Christians to be their slaves. Woe to us if we close our eyes! The Jews' domination will be hard, inflexible, tyrannical . . ."[57] Even in America with its tiny Jewish population, Christian politicians blamed their problems on Jewish plots. As the Civil War blockade forced disastrous inflation in the Confederate South, a Southern Congressman accused the handful of local Jews, who "swarmed here as the locusts of Egypt. They ate up the substance of the country . . . they monopolized its trade . . . The end of the war [will] probably find nearly all the property of the Confederacy in the hands of Jewish Shylocks."[58]

35

During the 1800s some thinking Christians turned once again to the problem of separating the Jewish heritage from Judeo-Christian religion. Why, they asked, if Christ rejected the Jewish law and was killed by the Jews, hadn't European Christianity purged itself from corrupt Jewish traditions? Joseph Arthur De Gobineau grew enthusiastic over the possibilities of a truly European religion, cleansed of Hebrew cultural pollution. In the Bible, which Gobineau claimed to believe in, there was only one creation of humanity. But Gobineau claimed that different races were different species with different origins.[59] Surely it was an abomination against God for his own Christian Aryan race to mix either sexually or culturally with the Jews. Matthew Arnold also complained that since the Protestant Reformation, the British seemed more "Hebraic" than the Roman Catholics. He felt it should be corrected. As he mentioned in a letter: "Bunsen used to say that our great business was to get rid of all that was purely Semitic in Christianity and to make it Indo-Germanic, and Schleiermacher that in the Christianity of us Western nations there was really much more of Plato and Sokrates than of Joshua and David . . ."[60]

Hopefully, a lily-white Christianity could be made to appear from behind the tarnished veneer of church history. Only one fact seemed to seriously block the quest: Jesus was a Jew. But where there was will, there had to be a way. Paul Lagarde proposed that Jesus was really an "Aryan Jew," who was crucified by "Semitic Jews."[61] Other churchmen claimed that Jesus was not a Jew at all, but an Aryan — and the Jews killed him because he exposed their racial inferiority.

During the 1800s a movement gathered steam to defend the European powers from the Jewish threat. Christian publications and newspapers trumpeted alarming revelations of evil. With willful mistranslation, they posted headlines concerning the Jewish Talmud, which reportedly required,

Jews must curse the Christian three times each day, and ask God for their extermination and destruction.

God permits the Jews to seize the property of Christians any way they can, by ruse, trickery, or theft.

Jews must view Christians as wild beasts and animals, and treat them accordingly . . . and if one of us encounters a Christian at a precipice, he should push him off.[62]

Like some modern alarmist publications concerning the threat of Islamic world conquest, official church publications like the *Cività cattolica* warned (in 1890), ". . . brotherhood and peace were and are merely pretexts to enable them to prepare — with the destruction of Christianity, if possible, and with the undermining of the Christian nations — the messianic reign that they believe the Talmud promises to them."[63]

As such preaching led to growing anti-Semitic riots over much of Europe, the Catholic newspaper *L'Unità cattolica* warned in 1892,

Far be it from us . . . to have the least thought of wanting with our writing to reheat the boiling pot of anti-Semitism which, having already scalded Romania and Russia, and having boiled over in France, is already threatening Italy as well . . . But, my dear Jews, let's be clear. If the sky is stormy, whose fault is it? If a thunderbolt strikes your head, who provoked it? . . . We repeat: anti-Semitism, cease your blind furies. Yet at the same time, if it be true that there are some good men among the people of Israel, give us proof of it. Refuse to show any solidarity with the vampires of your caste, with those who suck human blood.[64]

With the Russian Revolution, Christian fear of the atheist-Jewish conspiracy reached fever pitch. As Communist militias threatened to take over Poland in the chaos after WWI, Papal envoy Achille Ratti (later

Pope Pius XI) reported ". . . we cannot deny the preponderant role that the Jews played in this movement . . . with the exception of Lenin, all the Bolshevik leaders are either Polish Jews or Lithuanian Jews." Ratti strongly suspected "they seek the formation of a Judaic Poland."[65] Soon, Fr. Enrico Rosa outlined the logic which would prevail through WWII: "We have tried . . . to demonstrate how much the Jews are to blame for the Russian revolution and how prevalent the corrupted generation of Jews has been in it, as they were previously in the French revolution . . . The result has been the collapse of the Muscovite Empire and the tyranny imposed by the Bolshevik takeover, which threatens Europe."[66] In Vienna, the correspondent for *Città cattolica* reported it was "the common opinion among Catholics . . . that behind Bolshevism and Communism is none other than Jewish Masonry which, by means of the total confiscation of Christians' wealth, is moving toward Judaism's absolute rule."[67] To defeat such a threat, Polish priest Józef Kruszynski wrote "If the world is to be rid of the Jewish scourge, it would be necessary to exterminate them down to the last one."[68]

With the theory so often repeated, it grew impossible to disprove that all things godless and anti-national were hydra-heads of a greater Jewish-Satanic conspiracy. Speaking after attempted communist revolutions in Germany and Poland, the young Adolf Hitler said (in April 1922), "My feeling as a Christian points me to my Lord and Saviour as a fighter. It points me to the man who once in loneliness, surrounded by a few followers, recognized these Jews for what they were and summoned men to fight against them . . . How terrific was His fight for the world against the Jewish poison . . . as a Christian I have also a duty to my people."[69]

For Nazi propagandists like Hanns Oberlindober, Jews were behind the decadence of modern art which threatened to destroy social morality. His 1937 article, sarcastically titled "The Decent Jew," targeted a Jewish researcher on sexual life named Magnus Hirschfield, claiming that he was "one of a legion of Jewish corrupters of the youth, sexual criminals, pseudo-scientists, playwrights and novelists, painters and sculptors . . . making easier the work of their racial comrades seeking to dominate an unnerved and powerless people rendered susceptible by such 'art.' "[70]

By 1939, Italian Fascist leader Roberto Farinacci reasoned, "We Fascist Catholics consider the Jewish problem from a strictly political point of view . . . But it comforts our soul to know that if, as Catholics, we become anti-Semites, we owe it to the teachings that the Church has promulgated over the past twenty centuries."[71] From this it was only a few steps to Joseph Goebbels' statement at the height of Nazi Germany's "anti-Communist-Jew" crusade: ". . . no compassion and certainly no sorrow is called for over the fate of the Jews . . . Every Jew is our enemy."[72]

Even after the Holocaust, in 1950, Pope Pius XII wrote in an unpublished encyclical, explaining that the Jews had brought suffering to themselves by killing Christ. "Blinded by their dream of worldly gain and material success," they had brought "worldly and spiritual ruin." Pius warned of ongoing "spiritual dangers" from "exposure to the Jews, so long as their unbelief and enmity to Christianity continue." The Church was still obligated "to warn and help those threatened by revolutionary movements which these unfortunate and misguided Jews have joined with a view to overthrowing the social order."[73]

As the 21st century began in America, echoes of this vilification of Jesus' religion could still be heard, sometimes from think-tank intellectuals. As the conservative Howard Institute explained to Christian families and policy makers, "Two European Jews, Karl Marx and Sigmund Freud, played a major role in the secularization of culture, launching major assaults on the God of the Bible and leading countless Jews and Gentiles into skepticism and unbelief."[74] Recently, Bailey Smith, an elected head of the Southern Baptist Convention came on CNN's Larry King Live show to tell King, whose family is Jewish, "God Almighty does not hear the prayers of a Jew."[75] Ultra-fundamentalist Christians still taught that the Messiah the Jews look for will be the Anti-Christ, who will try to establish a global anti-Christian order, and whose godless followers will be justly exterminated by Jesus in a final battle of ethnic cleansing on Armageddon Day. As the "Left Behind" novel *Tribulation Force* explained, "God's chosen people, who planned to rebuild the temple and reinstitute the system of sacrifices until the coming of the Messiah, had signed a deal with the devil."[76]

Fortunately, in the 1960s Pope John XXIII led a large part of Christianity in rejecting this whole war on Jesus' religion, praying "Forgive us for the curse we have falsely attached to their name as Jews. Forgive us for crucifying Thee a second time in their flesh. For we knew not what we did."[77]

3. Correcting Forgiveness

As a kid, I thought Jesus' main message about forgiveness was that it's a nice thing. At church we repeatedly heard the Good News that our sins were forgiven. But we were still in danger of hell if we sinned, so maybe Jesus meant we'd be forgiven if we did nothing wrong. As an instructor at the Coral Ridge Presbyterian Church in Ft. Lauderdale put it, "Because He is a just judge, He must punish our sins; His law declares that our sins must be punished and that He 'will by no means clear the guilty'. There is no doubt about this!"[1] But Jesus went around during his life telling people, "Your sins are forgiven." Did that mean he had a special authority to forgive crimes? Or did he mean that those people were going to be forgiven later, after he sacrificed himself to pay the penalty for their sins? Surely, I figured, he wasn't just failing to take offense at people, like the pagan Greek who advised, "If a man is reported to have spoken ill of you, make no defense, but say, 'He did not know the rest of my faults, else he would not have mentioned only these.' "[2]

We heard that when Jesus told people their sins were forgiven, the priests and Pharisees got angry. For them, religion required making people pay the proper penalties for each misdeed. The Pharisees thought Jesus was arrogantly presuming to cancel God's judgments, such as "rest on the Sabbath, for it is holy . . . anyone who does any work on that day shall be killed." (Exodus 31:14–15) Some Christians in my town basically agreed with the Pharisees, that forgiving wrongs was a sin. Others felt that Christianity required contrition for sin, and made praying for forgiveness their main spiritual practice. They seemed to think that the worse they felt about their sins, the better. It could become an endless petition to God, which is why Bishop John Spong asked, "What kind of human being constantly begs for mercy?"[3]

Since the history of Christianity is strewn with violent intolerance, lots of my friends think it's a religion of merciless bigotry. When I hear about Christian forgiveness and universal love, I remember threats of eternal damnation, in which forgiveness seems totally out of the question. My grandmother, for example, was a Catholic from Ireland, who ran off and married a Protestant. And she believed that marrying a heretic was a cardinal sin, which meant she could never be forgiven. Her only escape from eternal damnation was to get divorced, but divorce was also a cardinal sin. It was a moral dilemma, which Graham Greene explored in several novels, about how people live after losing all hope of being forgiven.

After hearing a lot of confusing debate in church, I was surprised to notice that Jesus' actual words on forgiveness were fairly simple. Basically, ". . . if you forgive others the wrongs they have done, your heavenly Father will also forgive you. But if you do not forgive others, then the wrongs you have done will not be forgiven by your Father." (Matthew 6:14–15) By this logic, people had to forgive others before they could ask forgiveness for themselves. (Matthew 5:23–24) So, the way to get forgiveness is to forgive? Is that all? Is that realistic?

A primitive text from the second-century expressed literal, simplistic faith in this teaching: "You . . . must love those who hate you, and you will not have a single enemy." (Didache I:3) But was that true? Jesus had a lot of enemies, and they killed him. Also, there's the case of King Sigeberht of Essex, who was murdered by his relatives in the 600s because he felt it his Christian duty to forgive enemies. The relatives felt he was betraying his duty to defend them.[4] If Jesus and Sigeberht forgave their killers, the killers certainly didn't forgive them back. So it didn't work, did it? If we judge an idea by its results, isn't forgiveness obviously ineffective? Or was Jesus talking about the effect on the forgiver?

Comparing Gospel Accounts with Church Doctrines

I knew forgiveness was a main theme for Jesus. He spoke of it often, and even got threatening about it. He told the surprisingly sadistic tale of a man deep in debt, who was mercifully forgiven all he owed by the king. Yet this man still used force in demanding repayment of what others owed him. On hearing of this, the king hauled him into court saying, "You scoundrel! I remitted the whole of your debt when you appealed to me. Were you not bound to show your fellow-servant the same pity as I showed you?" The king was so furious he re-imposed the man's debts, and condemned him to be tortured in jail till he paid in full. This, Jesus threatened, "is how my heavenly Father will deal with you, unless you each forgive your brother from your hearts." (Matthew 18:23–35) Like I said, it was graphic and thought provoking, but I didn't consider it relevant to modern economics.

To compare what Jesus said about forgiveness with the words of later church leaders, I'll first spend a few pages reviewing his responses to various sorts of unforgiven or unforgiving people, such as "unclean" folks, criminals, debtors, traitors, or self-righteous accusers. Then I'll go through various changes in church doctrine down the centuries, which in many cases turned forgiveness from a good thing into a crime.

Judging Innocent Victims as Innocent

In several gospel stories, Jesus told sick people that their sins were forgiven. And while the sick were apparently amazed to hear this, the local religious leaders were furious. They replied, "This is blasphemy! Who but God alone can forgive sins?" (Mark 2:7) All this made no sense to me for a long time. What did forgiveness have to do with sickness? Why was it amazing to "forgive" handicapped people? Why was it blasphemy? Later, I got a clue about this when my city was hit by a hurricane, and I heard people asking "What did we do to deserve it?" It was like the questions

43

Job's friends asked him after he lost his flocks, his family, and his body was covered in boils. I started to realize how common it is for people to believe that suffering is the wage of sin. A retreat facilitator at the Cornerstone Church in San Antonio put it this way: "Why do alcoholics give birth to alcoholics? Why do the fatherless give birth to the fatherless? There are some people out there who will tell you it's genetics. It's in our genes, they say. Well, I tell you it's not genetics. It's a generational curse!"[5] It sounds judgmental, but don't we generally suspect that bad things are the fruits of bad deeds?

All the way back to the earliest records of Near Eastern civilization, this was the prevailing common sense. As archaeologist Samuel Kramer explained, "The Sumerian sages believed and taught the doctrine that man's misfortunes are the result of his sins and misdeeds, and that no man is without guilt. They argued there are no cases of unjust and undeserving human suffering; it is always man who is to blame, not the gods."[6] Even down to 1979, the Episcopal Church Prayer Book still referred to sickness as a punishment for sin.[7] When Jesus met a blind man, it was totally normal that the onlookers asked, "Rabbi, who sinned, this man or his parents that he was born blind?" Obviously someone sinned to deserve it.

So it was then natural for sick people to assume they were suffering for their sins. Likewise, rape victims commonly believed they had done something to deserve rape. Conquered people felt they were suffering for their nation's sins. Since God made the realities of might, right, wealth, and health, those realities represented God's will. It would be impious to deny it. Yet Jesus did deny it, saying "Neither this man nor his parents sinned . . ." (John 9:2–3) Where most people automatically blamed the victims, Jesus insisted they were innocent. He "forgave" them in the sense of claiming there was nothing to forgive. For him, innocent suffering was an injury to be healed, or a challenge to be overcome. But what about people who actually were guilty of crime or abuse? Did "forgive and you will be forgiven" apply to abusers?

Forgiving People Who Were Guilty as Sin

For most ancient people, fighting evil was the main purpose of religion. They assumed that "forgiving" evil meant accepting it. And probably most ancient Palestinians had seen cruelty we would find unforgivable. For Palestine's dispossessed villagers, conquered patriots, or beaten wives, "forgiveness" seemed to basically mean abject submission to an abuser. Rather than accept the outrage of domination by foreign infidels, some of Jesus' neighbors rallied for God and country to Judas the Galilean. They formed the terrorist party of Zealots, whose bands lurked in the hills throughout Jesus' life.[8] Other contemporaries rejected their society's corruption, and lived in monastic isolation with the Essenes. According to the Essene "Manual of Discipline" these people took a holy vow to "love all that [God] has chosen and hate all that [God] has rejected."[9] For traditional moralists, the notion of forgiving evil was simply ridiculous.

So what did Jesus actually advise for coping with crime and evil? Was it just "try to be nice"? I assumed that forgiving seventy times seven times meant abandoning any effort to hold people accountable for anything. Also, a pious instruction to forgive abusers sounded remarkably different than Moses' words to the slaves in Egypt. But on actually reading the gospel accounts, I noticed that Jesus' response to crime was quite confrontational:

> *If your brother commits a sin [or crime], go and take the matter up with him strictly between yourselves, and if he listens to you, you have won your brother over. If he will not listen, take one or two others with you, so that all facts may be duly established on the evidence of two or three witnesses. If he refuses to listen to them, report the matter to the community; and if he will not listen even to the community, you must then treat him as you would a pagan*

or a tax gatherer. (Matthew 18:15–17)

This was not infinite acceptance for abusers, but advice to confront them openly. And to actually do this took courage. It was a challenge to meet abusers face to face, and that confrontation would probably be painful. In this kind of discussion, the abusers would have to face the pain they caused, and the victims would face the ones who caused it. For the abusers, repairing their harm would be the price of re-admission to their community. To "forgive" in this case meant demanding the offenders' repentance, rather than their destruction. And this seemed unusual because, in that culture, traditional justice meant revenge, and taking revenge was deemed a sacred duty. The vengeance might be limited to "an eye for an eye," or the aggrieved parties might go for the maximum possible damage as in modern war. Jesus advised dropping the threat of revenge attacks, in hopes it would make a discussion of repentance possible, as in the lines, "If your brother wrongs you, reprove him; and if he repents, forgive him." (Luke 17:3)

Did this work? Clearly it didn't save Jesus from his killers. But he still preferred it to the usual revenge and intimidation contests. Surely he supported the Hebrew law's intent to stop cruelty. He just thought the real solution to abuse was changing the abusers.

Rebuking Hypocrites Who Refused to Forgive

So how did Jesus go about changing abusers? In the gospel accounts he constantly confronted people, but the ones he confronted were usually lawyers and priests, not criminals or prostitutes. And the offense he attacked most repeatedly was hypocrisy. These rebukes to hypocrites were so heated, that the lines in Matthew 23 rank among the most furious anti-clerical rants in recorded history:

The doctors of the law and the Pharisees sit in the chair of Moses; therefore do what they tell you; pay attention to their words. But do not follow their practice; for they say one thing and do another. (Matthew 23:3)

Alas, alas for you, lawyers and Pharisees, hypocrites that you are! You shut the door of the Kingdom of Heaven in men's faces; you do not enter yourselves, and when others are entering you stop them. (23:13)

Alas for you, lawyers and Pharisees, hypocrites! You travel over sea and land to make one convert; and when you have won him you make him twice as fit for hell as you yourselves! (23:15)

You snakes, you viper's brood! How can you escape being condemned to hell? (23:33)

Hypocrisy, it seems, was Jesus' biggest concern. Why? Maybe it was the biggest block to forgiveness. Hypocrites typically excuse their own flaws while demonizing those of others. We might recall the Bible repeatedly calls the Devil "the accuser," and hypocrites specialized in condemning other people for "unforgivable" sins. While assuming their own self-interest was God's will, they claimed other people were driven by greed and hate. While their own violence was heroic, that of their enemies' was cowardly and cruel. This sort of self-righteousness could easily grow to a point of zero tolerance for other people's evil. And in that case, forgiveness would seem so immoral, stupid, and counter-productive that it would be out of the question.

For hypocrites, the usual solution to evil was for righteous people to control sinners. So, Augustus Caesar supposedly established world peace by eliminating all rivals for power, uniting everyone under his own command, and claiming to represent the gods' will on earth. By comparison with the lawyers and priests who Jesus rebuked, this Emperor was the supreme hypocrite. Lesser hypocrites simply wished to follow his example within their smaller realms. But rather than encouraging the self-righteous to control others, Jesus ridiculed their arrogance. What did he advise to these hypocrites? Some of the remarks were:

> *Alas for you, lawyers and Pharisees, hypocrites! You clean the outside of cup and dish, which you have filled the inside by robbery and self-indulgence! Blind Pharisee! Clean the inside of the cup first; then the outside will be clean as well.* (Matthew 23:23-24)
>
> *Why do you look at the speck of sawdust in your brother's eye, with never a thought for the great plank in your own? You hypocrites! First take the plank out of your own eye, and then you will see clearly to take the speck out of your brother's.* (Matthew 7:3-5)
>
> *Pass no judgment, and you will not be judged. For as you judge others, so you will yourselves be judged, and whatever measure you deal out to others will be dealt back to you.* (Matthew 7:1-2)
>
> *Let the one of you who has not sinned throw the first stone.* (John 8:7)

Apparently, Jesus felt it was human beings who labeled each other as evil, and then treated each other accordingly. And this vilification of others was the cause, not the solution to abuse. As Garry Wills translates Jesus' warning in Matthew 5:22, "anyone who labels his brother 'idiot!' will be subject to the Sanhedrin. But anyone who calls his brother 'subhuman!' will be subject to Ghenna's fire."[10] Of course this didn't stop judgmental hypocrites of the future from claiming to be the godliest Christians.

Forgiving Debt

Besides dealing with guilt and crime, Jesus touched on the problem of debt, as in "forgive us our debts, as we forgive our debtors." He didn't give detailed instructions on this, but threw out challenging suggestions. For example he asked, "What do you think, Simon? From whom do the kings of the earth take toll or tribute? From their children or from others?" When Peter said "From others," Jesus said, "Then the children are free." (Matthew 17:25–26) He said the Kingdom of God was like an estate where the Lord was willing to cancel all debts owed by his tenants, provided they also forgave each other's debts. Many early Christians took this as a call to restore the Old Testament law requiring forgiveness of debts every seventh year (Deuteronomy 15:1–11). They also cited Exodus 22:25 against collecting interest on loans from the poor. But failing legal reform of the empire, these people still made general claims that God rewards forgiving debt. No doubt many early Christians were in danger of losing their lands and freedom over arrears.

Naturally, forgiveness of debt was most popular among people too poor to pay it. And cancelling loan repayment has always tended to kill future options for credit. But among relatives and close friends, it was normal to give without expecting any return. To "forgive" in those cases tended to cement ties of cooperation for the future. To track and collect debt with interest was the way one treated an "outsider," and many early Christians insisted that charging interest to a "brother" was immoral. At least some well-off Christians practiced forgiving their debtors or freeing debt slaves. They hoped for a social rather than economic reward, and often received considerable fame for their compassion. But as for turning a profit, how did "forgiving" work with customers, suppliers, and competitors? Perhaps it involved taking baby steps towards business arrangements of mutual benefit. And maybe this actually made sense, as in the old Middle Eastern saying, "the honest and loyal person is a partner in the property of others."

Over the centuries, people have twisted the notion of debt forgiveness in several directions. Many socialistic movements drew partly on Jesus' words, to demand debt forgiveness by force. That tended to destroy the economy. On the other hand, the Roman Church showed market awareness, and quietly stopped observing its own canon laws against collecting interest on debt, which allowed the Vatican to become a major money-lending operation. In this case, the church showed mercy for bankers. But the search for mercy on debtors also produced certain practical changes over time. Century by century, the rights of creditors over debtors grew slowly less draconian. Eventually it seemed more a matter of prudence than bleeding-heart charity, to ban debt slavery, and to allow legal bankruptcy instead of supporting debtors' prisons.

In modern America, a Christian organization recently appeared called "Jubilee USA," to revive the biblical notion of a "Jubilee year" for debt forgiveness. The group promoted pardoning debts owed by the world's most impoverished nations, especially debts run up by previous corrupt regimes. Of course other Christian leaders like Jerry Falwell also spoke of "Jubilee years" in the life of their congregations. But this often had nothing to do with forgiving debts for the sake of mercy, and was basically a campaign slogan for church membership drives.[11]

Forgiving Disloyalty

A third problem Jesus tried to solve with "forgiveness" was treason. In Jesus' world, religion was mainly a matter of loyalty, so that asking which religion you followed was like asking "Which Lord do you obey?" Since treason to lords or superiors was the ultimate sin, the common penalty was death, as in "Whoever reviles his father or mother shall be put to death." (Exodus 21:17) And in ancient times, many families really practiced such lethal discipline to enforce loyalty. Also, the most common objects of such enforcement were women. Since women's disobedience made men look weak, it could destroy their respectability, and many family heads felt they had to prevent this by any means necessary. As a Maronite Christian man in Syria recently put it, "I would murder my daughter rather than see her marry a Muslim."[12]

In response to all this, Jesus urged his followers to renounce threats, and try to win a more willing loyalty through forgiveness. The classical world was scandalized that many early Christians responded to the treason of adultery as Jesus did, by simply telling those involved to "go and sin no more." Later of course, many Christians repented of this "lax" willingness to confront, forgive, and talk. They reverted to a stricter, more vengeful "Christian" morality, like the Maronite man. But over centuries to come, most semi-Christianized societies came to see it as depravity rather than morality, for family members to control each other by violence. Even in the political arena it would eventually seem barbaric for politicians to enforce loyalty by force, rather than by trying to earn their citizens' trust.

From Requiring Mercy to Requiring Sacrifice

For around three centuries, the Christian movement was famous for forgiveness, as many followers pointedly forgave their enemies, and even their killers. Whether we respect the "martyrs" of those centuries, or see them as pathetic victims of brainwashing, it seems undeniable they took forgiveness seriously. In hindsight, something absolutely counter-intuitive seems clear. If the early Christians had practiced revenge attacks against their enemies, they never would have prevailed in the Roman world. But then over centuries to follow, most Christians moved toward a different attitude. Maybe they slowly got realistic. Their revisions concerning forgiveness came a step at a time, and in many cases ended up reversing what Jesus advised.

Changing Jesus' Protest against Sacrifice for Sin

Like several prophets before him, Jesus attacked the notion of offering blood sacrifice to get forgiveness. Like John the Baptist, he believed in baptism, but not in sacrifice or killing to buy freedom from guilt.[13] Instead he claimed forgiveness was free for all who forgave others. As he quoted Hosea against the temple priests: "Therefore I have lashed you through my prophets and torn you to shreds with my words; I desire mercy not sacrifice." (Hosea 6:5–6) Referring to Jeremiah (7:6–11), he accused the priesthood of making the Temple a robbers' den, where God's mercy was bought through offerings to priests. (Mark 11:15–18) Concerning the huge business of sacrificial offerings in the Temple, Jesus believed in the prophecy of Zechariah: "there shall never again be a trader in the sanctuary of the Lord of hosts at that time."[14] He would endorse Isaiah's words wholeheartedly:

> *Your countless sacrifices, what are they to me? says the Lord.*
> *I am sated with whole offerings of rams and the fat of buffaloes;*
> *I have no desire for the blood of bulls, of sheep and of he goats.*
> *Whenever you come to enter my presence — who asked you for this?*
> *No more shall you trample my courts.*
> *The offer of your gifts is useless,*
> *the reek of sacrifice is abhorrent to me.* (Isaiah 1:11–13)

Here we see something that might shock most later Christians — that Jesus was almost violently opposed to making his religion a cult of sacrifice for sin. It's striking, because after his execution, his followers increasingly taught that Jesus was himself a human sacrifice for sin. And despite celebrating this as the ultimate sacrifice to redeem all sin, many church leaders still held that each new sin created a fresh debt to God, which still required fresh sacrificial atonement.

The Traditional Arguments for Sacrifice

The logic of sacrifice was very pervasive in Jesus' world, and Judaism was quite typical in this. Its priests held that God established a divine law, and required sacrifice for all violations of that law. As the book of Leviticus ruled, "If any person among the common people unwittingly incurs guilt by doing any of the things which by the Lord's commandments ought not to be done . . . he shall bring a female goat without blemish as his offering for the sin of which he is guilty." (4:27–28)

A sacrifice was a sin offering, made to appease an offended superior being. And such sacrifice was the main business of the second Jewish Temple. The priestly caste lived off the income of legally required sacrifices, as the book of Exodus said, "Aaron and his sons [the hereditary priesthood] shall eat the ram's flesh and the bread left in the basket, at the entrance to the tent of the Presence [later the Temple at Jerusalem]. They shall eat the things with which expiation was made . . . No unqualified person [layman] may eat them, for they are holy." (29:32–33) So the vocation of ancient priests and lawyers in West Asia was to uphold their codes of sacred law, and to determine the sacrificial offerings necessary to compensate God for each violation.

Of course may Jews ignored the requirements for expensive sacrifices. And several prophets — including Isaiah, Hosea, Micah, and Jesus — rejected the whole logic of sacrifice. As Micah protested, "Will the Lord be pleased with thousands of rams, with ten thousand rivers of oil? Shall I give my first-born for my transgression, the fruit of my body for the sin of my soul? He has shown you, O man, what is good; and what does the Lord require of you but to do justice, and to love kindness, and to walk humbly with your God?" (6:7–8)

In response to such criticism, "orthodox" Jewish leaders upheld blood sacrifice as the required means of making peace with the Lord. They claimed that sacrifices to God were a greater religious duty than helping other people, arguing, as Shalom Spiegel explains, "Certainly what we owe to creatures can never compare to what we owe the Creator. If neglect of man be a sin, neglect of God is sacrilege."[15] Beyond this, some Jews took belief in sacrifice so far as to literally treat their own lives as a sacrifice. So in the book of Maccabees, the hero Eleazer was recorded praying as he died, "You know, God, I could have saved myself. I am dying in these fiery torments for the sake of the law. Be merciful to our people and let our punishment be a satisfaction in their behalf. Make my blood their purification and take my life as a ransom for theirs." (4 Maccabees 6:27–29)

Jesus repeatedly contradicted this logic, but it reappears in the accounts written after his death. The gospel writers explained that Jesus gave himself up to the executioners as a sacrifice for sin. But they also said he was a wanted man, and the authorities in Jerusalem argued, "This man is performing many signs. If we leave him alone like this the whole population will believe in him. Then the Romans will come and sweep away our temple and our nation . . . it is more expedient for one man to die than for the whole nation to be destroyed." (John 11: 48–50)

This logic was also very traditional. The local authorities were accountable to higher overlords, and if they could not keep their people under control, the overlords would step in to do it for them. If they allowed alternative leaders to arise, they would all be subject to collective punishment, so the wanted man must be eliminated lest the entire community suffer on his account. Perhaps, as Albert Nolan suggests, this was the real sense in which Jesus was "a sacrifice for the people." Possibly it was this threat of punishment from imperial overlords which was later ascribed to God — so that it was God who had Jesus die rather than make all of humanity suffer.[16] It was a notion of God quite different than Jesus described in his tale of the prodigal son.

From Forgiveness to Re-Directed Punishment

At first, Paul reflected what Jesus said about forgiveness and hypocrisy, advising "Let us therefore cease judging one another . . . I am absolutely convinced as a Christian, that nothing is impure in itself; only if a man considers a particular thing impure, then to him it is impure." (Romans

14:13–14) From this, Paul seemed convinced that offense is in the eye of the beholder, and it's the beholder who resents others. This seemed to be a moral standard as relative as any Greek Skeptic philosopher's. With such a view, Paul was able to respect non-Jews, without trying to remake them in his own image. This is what he claimed to learn from Jesus, and he announced it as if the equality of souls and cultures was a previously unknown revelation: "Gentiles and Jews, he has made the two one, and in his own body of flesh and blood has broken down the enmity which stood like a dividing wall between them: for he annulled the law with its rules and regulations [requiring division], so as to create out of the two a single new humanity in himself, thereby making peace. This was his purpose, to reconcile the two in a single body to God on the cross, on which he killed enmity." (Ephesians 2:14–16)

But when Paul spoke of forgiving resentments, he did it for different reasons than Jesus. And his reasons lead in different directions. We start to see this in his letter to Romans, where Paul begins almost ranting against certain people who disgust him:

> *For we see divine retribution revealed from heaven and falling upon all the godless wickedness of men . . . There is therefore no possible defense for their conduct: . . . In consequence, I say, God has given them up to shameful passions. Their women have exchanged natural intercourse for unnatural, and their men in turn, giving up natural relations with women, burn with lust for one another; males behave indecently with males, and are paid in their own persons the fitting wage of such perversion . . . Thus, because they have not seen fit to acknowledge God, he has given them up to their own depraved reason. This leads them to break all rules of conduct. They are filled with every kind of injustice, mischief, rapacity and malice; they are one mass of envy, murder, rivalry, treachery, and malevolence; whisperers and scandal-mongers, hateful to God . . . (Romans 1:18–30)*

If the same person actually wrote both these messages, we might assume he was a hypocrite. On one hand Paul felt that all human judgments were groundless before God, in which case to "forgive" might simply be a matter of recognizing reality, as if to say, "I forgive you, that I wrongly resented you." But Paul the ex-Pharisee also believed that God does make laws for humans, judges the violations, and punishes every sin. Paul simply felt that mortal humans must leave that judging and punishing to God. Why? Because we humans are all sinners ourselves, and we all deserve to be judged and punished rather than to judge. So, continuing his letter to Romans, Paul switched from condemning others to say:

> *You therefore have no defense — you who sit in judgment, whoever you may be — for in judging your fellow man you condemn yourself, since you, the judge, are equally guilty. It is admitted that God's judgment is rightly passed upon all who commit such crimes as these; and do you imagine — you who pass judgment on the guilty while committing the same crimes yourself — do you imagine that you, any more than they, will escape the judgment of God?* (Romans 2:1–3)

So in Paul's eyes, all of us were criminals against God's law. All of us deserved even the death penalty. But the good news was this: though we all deserved capital punishment, our penalty was redirected. God's son Jesus took our death penalty upon himself: "For all alike have sinned, and are deprived of the divine splendor, and all are justified by God's free grace alone, through his act of liberation in the person of Christ Jesus. For God designed him to be the means of expiating sin by his sacrificial death . . ." (Romans 3:23–25) So when Jesus suffered horribly on the Romans' cross, he took the punishment we richly deserved. His death penalty paid our debt to God. The burden of guilt, which God had justly placed upon us, was lifted away. We were pronounced free to go — and sin no more, lest fresh crimes cancel God's pardon.

During his time as a Pharisee, Paul had believed that every deviation from the Jewish law was an offense against God, which required compensation. The compensation could be paid voluntarily by sacrifice, or else God would make the sinner pay in the end. Later as a Christian, Paul applied similar logic to explain the importance of Jesus' life. We can wonder how this interpretation — that Jesus died as substitute victim for the sins of others — sounded to the Galileans who actually knew Jesus. And Paul's letters mention critics who claimed his teaching differed from that of the original disciples. The criticisms probably had some validity, because Paul imposed several themes onto Jesus' life. According to Will Durant, "Paul created a theology of which none but the vaguest warrants can be found in the words of Christ: that every man born of woman inherits the guilt of Adam, and can be saved from eternal damnation only by the atoning death of the son of God."[17]

In the 50 or so years between Jesus' death and the various written gospel accounts, it seems his Jewish followers interpreted his life in terms of Jewish traditions. They associated Jesus with the Passover lamb, which was sacrificed to put blood on the doorposts of Jewish people, so God's angel of death would pass over them, and kill only the firstborn child of every non-believer Egyptian family. They also associated Jesus with the animals sacrificed at Yom Kippur — both the lamb sacrificed to God, and the "scapegoat" lamb, who was made to "carry" all the sins of the people, and be driven into the desert with the cry "Here is the lamb of God who takes away the sins of the world!"[18] Such images reinterpreted Jesus, not as a protester against the old cult of sacrifice, but as a fulfillment of it. And if even Paul remained typically legalistic about God's requirement for sacrifice, other writers of the New Testament waxed even more passionate on the need for sacrificial blood to remove sin. In the letter to Hebrews we read:

> *. . . the blood of his sacrifice is his own blood, not the blood of goats and calves; and thus he has entered the sanctuary once and for all and secured an eternal deliverance. For if the blood of goats and bulls and the sprinkled ashes of a heifer have the power to hallow those who have been defiled and restore their external purity, how much greater is the power of the blood of Christ; he offered himself without blemish to God, a spiritual and eternal sacrifice; and his blood will cleanse our conscience from the deadness of our former ways and fit us for the service of the living God . . . it might almost be said, everything is cleansed by blood and without the shedding of blood there is no forgiveness. (*Hebrews 9:12–22)*

Did this imply that God forbade people to forgive each other without requiring sacrifice? Did it suggest we must never expect forgiveness without punishment? If Jesus believed sacrifice was required for sin, then why did he urge his followers to say "forgive us our sins, as we forgive those who trespass against us"?

Making Jesus Himself a Sacrifice for Sin

In some early accounts of Jesus such as the Gospel of Thomas, there was no mention of how he died. Apparently the writers of Thomas didn't see it as important. And in the Didache, written in second-century Syria, we have instructions for observing the Lord's Supper which also neglect to mention his death. In this rite, the "sacrifice" was simply the food offered to others. The participants gave thanks for the food and for Jesus' teaching. And this could be the earliest form of the Eucharist, as observed by Jewish Christians near Galilee.

As tends to happen in popular folklore, the accounts of Jesus' final meal grew more detailed with time. Mark's account gave a brief sketch of it, and then Luke and Matthew filled it out in richer detail. According to these accounts, Jesus knew he was about to die, and told the disciples that this was his last meal. His executioners were due to arrive shortly, and he had agreed to let himself be sacrificed. He urged his followers to re-enact this last meal in the future, taking the bread and wine as his own body and blood, which he was offering to pay for the world's sins.

The next account, John's gospel, was written around 100 AD, and takes this theme further. Even long before his fatal trip to Jerusalem, John's Jesus proclaims to the crowds,

> *In truth, in very truth I tell you, unless you eat the flesh of the Son of Man and drink his blood you can have no life in you. Whoever eats my flesh and drinks my blood possesses eternal life, and I will raise him on the last day. My flesh is real food; my blood is real drink . . . Many of the disciples on hearing it exclaimed, "This is more than we can stomach! Why listen to such talk? . . . From that time on, many of his disciples withdrew and no longer went about with him. So Jesus asked the Twelve, "Do you also want to leave me?"*
> (John 6:53–67)

Concerning these accounts, Rev. Bruce Chilton asks: "What Jew would tell another to drink blood, even symbolic blood?" The Torah forbids it in several places such as Genesis 9:4, and the Mishnah records horror at the very thought.[19] Yet the gospel accounts suggest that Jesus violated these sentiments, and spoke of his own body and blood as a sacrificial meal. The later Gentile churches commonly took these accounts in the most literal way possible — as a promise that the bread and wine of their ritual meals would actually become Jesus' own flesh and blood.

In pondering Jesus' words at the Last Supper, Chilton proposes a different understanding. In speaking of "his flesh" and "his blood," Jesus was likely comparing his ritual meals with the sacrificial rites of the temple priests. The priests had their burnt offerings of flesh, but Jesus' offering was his shared bread. The priests made blood sacrifices, but Jesus' equivalent was his wine. His offering, Jesus implied, was more simple and holy than the costly sacrifices of the high priests.[20] His ritual should replace the old one.

A claim like this, Chilton feels, would be as shocking to the priests as Jesus' earlier attack on the Temple itself. It would imply that Jesus considered himself the true high priest, with authority to proclaim a new ritual in place of the old. By his example, Jesus suggested a new priesthood. His followers would not call for sacrifices from the people, but offer service at the table of fellowship. Then, as foretold in the book of Zechariah, people would gather from the east and the west to feast with Abraham, Isaac, and Jacob in the Kingdom of God. (Zechariah 8:7–23) Later, in memory of Jesus' ritual meals, his first apostles called themselves *diakonai* [deacons] which meant "servants at the table." It was a conventionally female role, but Jesus took it proudly, washing the guests' feet and serving the food. If this is what Jesus meant by his wine for blood and bread for flesh, it would accord with what he said against blood sacrifice during his life. It would accord with his vandalizing protest against the Temple's sacrifice business, which is probably what the authorities were coming to kill him for.

As Jesus surely hoped, his teaching about sacrifice and ritual meals prevailed in later Judaism. After the Temple of Jerusalem was destroyed, Rabbi Yohanan ben Zakkai told his fellow rabbis that the Temple didn't matter. If that had been the place where the nations' sins were atoned through sacrifice, Rabbi Yohanan said "be not grieved. We have another atonement as effective as this. And what is it? It is acts of loving kindness, as it is said, 'I desire mercy and not sacrifice.' "[21] At Jewish Sabbath meals since then, the candlesticks, loaves, and wine were set out in a manner recalling the Temple, but these offerings were simply shared among family and friends. Each Jewish mother acted the part of Sophia, the Woman of

Wisdom, as she says in Proverbs 9:5: "Come, eat of my bread and drink of the wine I have mixed."

But another interpretation soon prevailed among the Gentile Christians, in which the ancient priestly concept of sacrifice for sin gained a huge new lease on life.

The Future Christian Doctrine of Forgiveness through Blood Sacrifice

Some early non-canonical scriptures expressed views on sacrifice that might strike us as shockingly primitive. The Gospel of Philip explained of Christ's death, "God is a man-eater. For this reason men are [sacrificed] to him. Before men were sacrificed, animals were being sacrificed — since those to whom they were sacrificed were not gods." (62:35–63:5)[22] Around the year 95, Bishop Clement of Rome compared Jesus' death to the ancient traditions of sacrificing kings: "In times of plague, many kings and rulers, in response to oracles, have given themselves up to death so that their people might be rescued through their blood."[23] We may object that these writings were excluded from the New Testament, with good reason. But some of the canonized writings endorsed similar beliefs about sacrifice. In Romans we hear, "Therefore, my brothers, I implore you by God's mercy to offer your very selves to him: a living sacrifice, dedicated and fit for his acceptance. . ." (12:1) What exactly did that mean, and how far would various readers take it?

The literal way some early church leaders taught the virtues of self-sacrifice can be seen in the *Acts of the Christian Martyrs*. Here were accounts of Christians killed by the Roman state, like Jesus was killed, because the rulers feared people who refused to promise blind obedience. In the modern world, we would say these martyrs died for objecting to tyranny. But as in Jesus' case, many contemporary observers explained these deaths as sacrifices to God, made to purchase redemption from sin. The early bishop Polycarp praised people for what we might call suicidal fanaticism: "Through the suffering of one hour they purchase for themselves eternal life."[24] Tertullian interpreted the martyrs' deaths, not as tragedies or cases of heroic civil disobedience, but as atonements for guilt. He wrote that he also longed to be killed for his beliefs, "that he may obtain from God complete forgiveness, by giving in exchange his blood."[25] Many later Christians bought this notion of atoning for misdeeds by mortifications of the flesh. When the Black Death struck Europe in the 1300s, vast numbers of people assumed it was a punishment from God for sin. The flagellants tried to take the punishment on themselves with whips and chains, hoping to win forgiveness by shedding their blood. The clergy denounced them for trying to take both punishment and forgiveness into their own hands, rather than dealing with these things through ministrations of the designated priesthood.[26]

Some early Christians objected that this whole idea of sacrificial blood was barbaric and offensive to God. Concerning innocent victims sacrificed for the sins of others, Ezekiel claimed it was an abomination that anyone should suffer for the crimes of another. (18:19–20) The law in Deuteronomy said, "Fathers shall not be put to death for their children, nor children for their fathers." (24:16) The early Jewish-Christians, in their Gospel of the Ebionites, rendered Matthew 5:17 as "I have come to annul sacrifice, and if you will not cease to sacrifice, the wrath will not turn from you."[27] Most Jews also soon abandoned the whole temple cult of blood sacrifice. The new rabbinic Judaism focused on learning, prayer, and service as its spiritual practices. Later, St. Antony described Jesus, not as a sacrificial offering for others' sins, but as a divine physician who showed the way to healing.[28] For many other early Christians, Jesus was a prophet in the lineage of Moses, who aimed to liberate peoples' spirits, not just atone for past misdeeds.

In general, sacrifice has always implied giving up a lesser good for the sake of a greater good. But if we say that ordinary people should sacrifice themselves for something more important, what are we assuming is more important than they are? Perhaps all Christians have been torn between viewing self-sacrifice as a great ideal, and their actual experience of making causes, churches, nations, or leaders more important than the people who serve them. But Jesus asked what it meant to care for self and others *equally*. And Paul also said "There is no question of relieving others at the cost of hardship to yourselves; it is a question of equality." (II Corinthians 8:13)

Most bishops of the rising institutional church, however, upheld Tertullian's understanding of sacrifice as orthodox, and condemned other views as heretical. For many later church leaders, the cult of sacrifice for guilt became the centerpiece of Christianity. So Augustine argued around the year 400: "By his death, which is indeed the one and most true sacrifice offered for us, he purged, abolished and extinguished whatever guilt there was by which the principalities and powers lawfully detained us to pay the penalty . . ."[29] Many have joyfully proclaimed that Christ paid the price of forgiveness for all. And if the point of this story was overcoming chronic guilt, then it often seemed to work. As a young man in Chile recently testified, "I heard a voice say to me: "Your sins are forgiven," and in the same instant my life completely changed; the streets, the trees were different. It was a very poor neighborhood, old houses, unpaved streets. But for me, everything was new, everything was changed."[30] But for this experience, was the theology of sacrifice necessary?

The Universalist or Unitarian churches of New England thought not. For them, Jesus was an inspiration to uplift the world, not a sacrifice to take its punishment. Pastor William Ellery Channing (1780–1842) challenged any other Christian in America to point out a clear passage in the Bible teaching the "orthodox" doctrine "that man, having sinned against an infinite Being, has contracted infinite guilt, and is consequently exposed to an infinite penalty." On receiving no response to this challenge, he concluded such doctrines were "the fictions of theologians."[31] Likewise, the modern religious historian René Girard abhorred the notion that God needed his Son to die for our sins. As Garry Wills explains, Girard's "most radical assertion is that Jesus is not a sacrifice. His Father is not the one whose aggressions need to be bought off. Jesus is not an item of barter in the exchange system set up by sacrifice; God does not accept victims. He sides with the victim against the slayers, reversing the whole logic of placation."[32] Marcus Borg agreed, saying that the claim "Jesus died for our sins" involves interpreting his death according to the priestly logic of sacrifice for sin, which Jesus rejected.[33]

But over centuries the doctrine of Jesus' "substitutionary atonement" grew firmly established, and sometimes reached fascinatingly sadistic conclusions. For example, in the 1400s Archbishop Antonius of Florence argued from the pulpit, "Had no one been prepared to carry out the crucifixion through which the world was redeemed, Mary would have been ready to nail her son to the cross by herself. We may not assume that she was inferior in perfection and obedience to Abraham, who offered his only son as a sacrifice."[34]

This concerned a man who told his nation's overlords, "If you had known what that text means, 'I require mercy, not sacrifice', you would not have condemned the innocent." (Matthew 12:7) But as modern evangelist Jerry Falwell insisted, "The entire message of the Gospel centered on the death, burial, and resurrection of Christ. If he did not die for sin as God's substitute for Man and if he were not literally raised from the dead, then there would be no Good News to proclaim to the world." For Falwell, anything else was beside the point: "Where Modernism was content to proclaim the moral message of Christ as summarized in the Sermon on the Mount, Fundamentalists were committed to the Gospel itself."[35]

64

From Welcoming to Expelling Sinners

Jesus' followers said that some people had "entered" God's kingdom, and basically, these were people who treated others as they would be treated themselves. Of course nowadays we tend to see such virtue as no big deal — just common civility, or willingness to leave each other alone. The world has changed so much over 2,000 years, we can hardly imagine a time when it was amazing to treat "outsiders" as potential friends. But in Jesus' time it was alarmingly controversial to befriend an outcaste or outsider. When we hear of the Samaritan woman at the well, we may have no sense how shocking it was for Jesus to ask her for water. The text of John explains for Greek ears, "Jews and Samaritans, it should be noted, do not use vessels in common." (John 4:9) In other words they saw each other as ethnic pollutants. There was a social wall, where ancient traditions required holy apartheid: ". . . at the public reading from the book of Moses, it was found to be laid down that no Ammonite or Moabite should ever enter the assembly of the Lord, because they did not meet the Israelites with food and water, but hired Balaam to curse them, though our God turned the curse into a blessing. When the people heard the law, they separated from Israel all who were of mixed blood." (Nehemiah 13:1–3)

Ancient Middle Eastern society was commonly this divided between insider and outsider groups, and we still see it modern Israel and Palestine, or recently in Iraq. In Jesus' time, to address an "outsider" as "sister" could seem an act of treason against your own people. When he suggested that some Samaritans were better neighbors than many fellow Jews, some of his listeners considered killing him on the spot. His critics knew the Bible recorded old demands for rejection of other people. For example the book of Deuteronomy said: "He whose testicles are crushed or whose penis is cut off shall not be admitted to the house of the Lord. No descendant of an irregular union, even down to the tenth generation, shall become a member of the assembly of the Lord. No Ammonite or Moabite, even down to the tenth generation, shall become a member of the assembly of the Lord." (23:1–3)

Jesus and his followers broke all these rules, for example when Philip the Deacon baptized a castrated Ethiopian. (Acts 8) Naturally, many people were disgusted with Jesus for mixing with thieves, prostitutes, Samaritans, and agents of the occupation. They said "This fellow welcomes sinners and eats with them," or "Look, a glutton and a drunkard, a friend of tax collectors and sinners!" (Luke 15:2, 7:34) With seemingly total amorality Jesus explained, "Tax collectors and prostitutes are going into the Kingdom of God ahead of you." (Mathew 21:31) Since he thought everybody was a sinner, he treated them all the same. As Donald Spoto says, "If you don't approve of that, you don't approve of Jesus."[36]

Raising Hell Over Open Borders

At first, Jesus' followers took it as a mission to break down social walls. And in that socially divided world, they needed only simple acts to proclaim their Kingdom of "forgiveness." If they invited an outsider to eat with them, it might be the talk of the village. Jesus' story of inviting people to dinner, being refused, and turning to invite the local outcastes probably came from his own experience.[37] Meals made the lines of inclusion clear, demonstrating who would eat with whom. It was more controversial than in 1960s America, when civil rights protesters broke taboos against Blacks and Whites eating together in public.

As many historians explain, ancient table manners usually meant observing all distinctions of rank between participants — in terms of seating arrangements, who was served first, who could eat in the same room, and the quality of food each person got. Elder men generally ate first and got the best food. Women commonly served, then ate in another room, and got the leftovers. These were "proper table manners" in a ranked society, and most people were ashamed or afraid to violate them. But the New Testament makes casual reference to men and women eating together. It shows men taking the female roles of serving and washing feet. Other early texts speak of women presiding at ritual meals. All this violated the greatest social barrier of all, leading to accusations that the Christians had abandoned all standards of decorum between the sexes. Their early experiments with open social borders sometimes led directly to scandal — as people of different ranks and sexes became friends, and the relatives raised an uproar over disloyalty and indecency.

Naturally, some early Christians were more inclusive than others. Many hoped only to unite the chosen people of Israel, which would be a big step. Even healing a feud between two family members might take a lifetime. But to those who felt it was God's will to *build* and *defend* walls of segregation between the pure and impure, or between high and low, the first Christians seemed to be pushing the wrong way. For them, the Christians' efforts to join what God had set apart were counterproductive, offensive, and in clear violation of sacred tradition: "do not follow the practices of the nations whom I am driving out before you . . . I am the Lord your God who has separated you from all nations. You shall therefore mark a distinction between clean and unclean . . ." (Leviticus 20:23–26)

For conventional religion, it made sense that good people must separate themselves from bad. Jesus' critics said he was only "polluting" himself by mixing with outcasts and outsiders. But Jesus apparently felt his inclusiveness was a better direction than the alternatives. If Israel went on trying to exclude sinners and foreigners as pollutants or enemies, then he saw a looming catastrophe. His various apocalyptic warnings suggested divine wrath against all who ignored his authority. But maybe those warnings simply described the practical consequences of living life as a contest for domination between good insiders and bad outsiders. The following warning to Jerusalem likely concerned a clear and present danger, which actually came to pass within 40 years: "A time is coming when your enemies will raise fortifications all around you and hem you in on every side; they will dash you and the children inside your walls to the ground; they will leave not one stone standing on another within you — and all because you did not recognize your opportunity [for forgiving enemies?] when God offered it." (Luke 19:43–44)

Obviously the primitive Christians made enemies, and didn't always love them. Even Jesus snapped that his critics were a "viper's brood." If the Christians were an "open community," they were highly conscious that many people stood deliberately outside it. The paradox then arose of a social barrier between those who would treat all people as fellow souls, and those who definitely would not. Later of course, those who would exclude others from God's Kingdom started claiming to be the real Christians.

Beating a Hasty Retreat to Respectable Living

Paul faced the same problems as Jesus, and his efforts to bridge divisions seemed healing to some. But many of Paul's critics said he simply relaxed all standards for separating good and bad people. His open communities suffered accusations of scandalous mixing between men and women, and Paul found such accusations intolerable. He felt an imperative fatherly need to defend the worldwide reputation of his church. As various rumors of impropriety surfaced, he wrote to Corinth in alarm: "I actually hear reports of sexual immorality among you, immorality such as even pagans do not tolerate: the union of a man with his father's wife. And you can still be proud of yourselves! You ought to have gone into mourning; a man who has done such a deed should have been rooted out of your company." (I Corinthians 5:1–2)

To deal with accusations of being an immoral cult, Paul grew zealous to cast out sinners from the community. Where Jesus made a point of inviting outcasts, Paul began pleading with his churches, ". . . not to associate with immoral men . . . not to associate with anyone who bears the name of brother if he is guilty of immorality or greed, or is an idolater, reviler, drunkard, or robber — not to even eat with such a one . . . Drive out the wicked person from among you." (I Corinthians, 1:10, 5:9–13)

In this spirit, many later churches adopted authoritarian methods to silence or expel any disreputable members. Around the year 100, Bishop Clement of Rome wrote the church at Corinth to rebuke the more rebellious members as "those of no reputation against those with reputation, the fools against the wise, the young against the old." Clement insisted that Christians owed obedience to official heads of the church, because God ruled all things, and He established the rulers of both churches and states. Any church members who refused to "bow the neck" were rebels against God. And then, for perhaps the first time in church history, Clement said that anyone guilty of insubordination "receives the death penalty."[38]

A hundred years later, Tertullian was busy denouncing Gnostic groups in North Africa for more improper social mixing: "they all have access equally, they listen equally, they pray equally — even with pagans who happen to come . . . they also share the kiss of peace with all who come."[39] For Tertullian it was obvious: the church would soon be a den of sin if it failed to cast out sinners. And this common sense appeared in alterations of the Bible text, in the way devout copyists treated the story of Jesus and the adulteress. In many manuscripts this story was omitted, or stuck in different locations. Most scholars feel the story is vintage Jesus, but as Raymond E. Brown explains, "The ease with which Jesus forgave the adulteress was hard to reconcile with the stern penitential discipline in vogue in the early church."[40] Surely, Tertullian would insist, everyone knew the test of a religion was its success in promoting virtue. And who, besides the hopelessly muddled Gnostic advocates of "free love," would dare disagree that life was a battle between morality and evil?

Over the next 1,500 years, probably most church leaders insisted it was God's will to enforce legal apartheid between various ethnic groups, and uphold strict segregation between the sexes. These leaders emphasized "fencing the altar" against "unworthy reception" of communion. Even Roger Williams, who founded Rhode Island as the first Christian state to recognize full religious freedom, sometimes lapsed into the old separatist language. As if sleepwalking while contradicting most of what he stood for in his life, Williams was heard preaching about the separation of "holy from the unholy, penitent from impenitent, godly from ungodly."[41] Of course the great American struggle over racism has mostly proved a victory for healing through inclusion and forgiveness. But long after the Civil War, preachers like A. C. Gaebelion kept the spirit of moral and social exclusivity burning bright. Drawing a fresh line in the sand against social pollution, Gaebelion insisted (in 1914) that "God's greatest call is separation" — probably from whoever or whatever he didn't respect.

In North America, such self-righteous rejection of other people fed a rise in schisms dividing churches, and an expansion of exclusive communities. In recent decades the security barrier industry boomed, perhaps modeled on the mother of all security fences in Israel, but applied to North American gated communities. Usually the ones buying the fences felt they were protecting virtuous people from low-life sinners. Concerning fundamentalists dedicated to separation rather than forgiveness, Pastor Elton Richards warned, "Take what they say, and in most cases, it's the exact opposite of Jesus' message. Jesus' message was one of inclusion. Theirs is exclusion."[42]

In Europe it got far worse, as Christians repeatedly supported ethnic cleansing of non-Christians. In the 1930s and 40s it was the Jews, and the 1990s saw attempted genocide against Muslims in Eastern Europe. The people who committed these atrocities were fairly normal. They made what Richard Rohr calls "that perennial, universal mistake that is happening probably every three minutes in most human hearts and minds — the instinct to destroy what we perceive as the source of the problem."[43] For example, there's a recent joke going around Germany: Question: What's the difference between a Jew and a [Muslim] Turk? Answer: The Jew has learned his lesson, and the Turk has yet to learn his.

From Teaching Forgiveness to Threatening Eternal Revenge

The early Christians' enthusiasm for forgiveness perhaps peaked with the non-orthodox teacher Marcion, who claimed (in the 130s) that Jesus' message was opposite to that of the Hebrew Bible. As already mentioned, Marcion said the God of the Christians was a forgiving Father-God, utterly unlike the wrathful Jewish God. And this revelation soon gained enormous popularity among non-Jewish Christians. Still, it raised a big concern for many church leaders. If Marcion wanted to cast aside all notion of a judging, punishing God, how would his followers behave? If Marcion trashed the image of the almighty king whose commands must be obeyed, which shepherd would the flock obey? Several bishops warned that Marcion's message invited total anarchy, and declared him one of the first heretics.

Around the year 200, the church elder Tertullian belatedly joined this attack, writing an essay called *Against Marcion*. In this, Tertullian blasted the notions of an all-loving God, or an all-accepting prophet, who would open the floodgates of sin:

Listen, you sinners; and you who have not yet come to this, hear, that you may attain to sinfulness! A better God has been discovered, who never takes offense, is never angry, never inflicts punishment, who has prepared no fire in hell, no gnashing of teeth in the outer darkness! He is purely and simply good. He indeed forbids all delinquency, but only in word . . . And so satisfied

71

are the Marcionites with such pretenses, that they have no fear of their God at all. They say it is only an evil being who is feared; a good one will be loved. Foolish man, do you say that he whom you call Lord ought not to be feared, whilst the very title you give him indicates a power which must itself be feared? . . . Come then, if you do not fear God . . . why do you not boil over into every kind of lust, and so realize that which is, I believe, the main enjoyment of life to all who fear not God? Why do you not frequent the maddening circus, the bloodthirsty arena, and the lascivious theatre? . . . God forbid, you say . . . So you do fear sin, and by your fear prove that He is an object of fear who forbids sin.[44]

To Tertullian's horror, Marcion's vision almost came true in the Roman church. With popular acclaim, the Christians of Rome elected an ex-slave named Callistus as bishop in 217. Callistus preached that no sin was unforgivable, and the clergy had power to forgive all. He admitted priests who had married twice or even three times, since he saw no crime in love. He let women of rank marry men of low birth, and even slaves — without being expelled from the church. Callistus offered second baptism for lapsed Christians who wished to return to the fold. To those horrified by this laxity, Callistus cited Paul's words: "Who are you to pass judgment on someone else's servant?" (Romans 14:4)[45]

Tertullian could certainly answer that question — he was an elder of God's true church, and he was required to condemn sin. With his tract *On Modesty*, Tertullian hurled his moral thunderbolt at "the bishop of bishops" in Rome:

Christian modesty is being shaken to its foundations . . . I hear that there has even been an edict set forth, and a pre-emptory one too. The Sovereign Pontiff [of Rome] — the Bishop of bishops — issues an edict: "I remit, to such as have discharged the requirements of repentance, the sins of adultery and fornication." O edict, on which cannot be inscribed "well done!" And where shall this liberality be posted up? On the very spot, I suppose, on the very gates of lust, beneath the very advertisement of lust.[46]

In 229, about a decade after Tertullian's argument with the Pope, the Egyptian teacher Origen raised this question of forgiving evil in a more theological way. While debating a Greek named Candidus, Origen claimed that the Devil himself would eventually be saved. Candidus gave a seemingly orthodox reply that the Devil was God's enemy, and with him there could be no forgiveness. God and his church could only wage war against Satan till the forces of evil were finally destroyed. But Origen claimed that Christian faith involved belief in free will. Every creature had a choice between right and wrong, or love and hate, and the Devil too had a choice. Origen cited Paul's argument in I Corinthians (15:28) that God brought everything into being with love, and in the end all would be restored to love.[47] By implication, even the Devil was a soul to be saved, and God would eventually win even his greatest enemy back to love.

Origen's bishop, Demetrius of Alexandria, had already complained of Origen's insubordinate attitude. But now Origen was publicly proclaiming his willingness to forgive God's enemy, as if this was a tenet of Christianity. And rather than put up with such pseudo-intellectual depravity any further, Demetrius threw Origen out of the Egyptian church. When Origen fled to Palestine, Demetrius sent letters to the regions' other bishops, demanding that none of them should allow this heretic into their churches. Instead of teaching that forgiveness can transform every life, the church leaders were now excommunicating people for uttering such foolishness. And taking the stand against immoral forgiveness a bit further, some copyists of the New Testament deleted the line from Luke, "Father forgive them, for they know not what they do."[48]

So the church gravitated back to common sense concerning

forgiveness. Clearly, Jesus had said the law's main point was love for others as oneself. But how should the church love a wrong-doer? If it simply forgave every violation of the social code, what would result? Surely to love sinners involved making them stop sinning. Obviously sinners had to repent their crimes before they could be forgiven. And surely repentance required taking punishment for wrongdoing. Jesus, of course, had treated sin as a sickness to be cured rather than a crime to be punished. But wasn't punishment itself the cure for sin? And wasn't the threat of punishment what made sinners want to change?

With such reasoning, a punitive version of Christian morality spread. Many clergymen felt that only the most savage threats of eternal punishments could hope to control a sinful world. Already in the second century, several writers of New Testament letters portrayed Jesus threatening destruction to all who disobeyed him. Where the gospels quoted him warning of "Ghenna," which was the name of the burning ground for garbage and executed criminals outside Jerusalem, some interpreters said Jesus was simply warning people against taking a path to suffering. This is how the Jehovah's Witnesses take it, and so they don't believe the doctrine of hell. But others have taken Jesus' warnings as threats that he was going to punish sinners himself. The writer of 2 Thessalonians picked this second interpretation and predicted, ". . . the Lord Jesus is revealed from heaven with his mighty angels in flaming fire, inflicting vengeance . . . on those who do not obey the gospel of our Lord Jesus. These will suffer the punishment of eternal destruction . . ." (1:7)

Over several centuries of persecution under classical Rome, the church's preachers of divine vengeance on their enemies grew more eloquent. They began teaching that their oppressors would suffer horribly after death, undergoing fiendish tortures for all eternity. Joseph Campbell confirms that belief in an *eternal* hell did not originate with the Jews, Greeks, or Persians, but with the early Christians in their period of persecution.[49] As Celsus complained of their emerging doctrine, "The Christians use sundry methods of persuasion, and invent a number of terrifying incentives. Above all, they have concocted an absolutely offensive doctrine of everlasting punishment and rewards, exceeding anything the philosophers (who have never denied the punishment of the unrighteous or the reward of the blessed) could have imagined."[50]

From claiming, as in the Didache, that "every sin will be forgiven," many Christians began to insist that God would *never* forgive their enemies. Tertullian rather gleefully predicted that in the hereafter, "What sight shall wake my wonder, what my laughter, my joy and exultation? As I see all those kings . . . along with Jove . . . groaning in the depths of darkness! And the magistrates who persecuted the name of Jesus, liquefying in fiercer flames than they kindled in rage against the Christians! . . . I believe things of greater joy than circuses, theatre . . . or any stadium."[51]

Of course pagan critics cleverly pointed out that these visions of hellfire seemed to depart from the Christian spirit of love and forgiveness.[52] But Tertullian and other veterans of the persecutions held that such visions were revealed from on high. For them, a doctrine of unlimited divine vengeance was fundamental to the Christian faith. Any Christian who doubted it would now be damned as well.

Over the centuries, Christian preachers often vied to outdo each other in imagining the tortures of hell. And recently, some have gone beyond just preaching about it, to utilizing the arts of mass media to convey the spectacle of God's wrath. In his mass-produced evangelical cartoon tracts, Jack Chick strove to instill the fear of God through sheer graphic horror. As Chick explained, "I want to shock people. I want to make them physically sick when they see this."[53]

The modern development of "Hell House" drama aims to warn the public of God's eternal wrath, usually against rather ordinary personal sins like extra-marital sex, homosexuality, abortion, drunk driving, or having the wrong religious ideas. In these productions, the Christian message seems stripped down to "The wage of sin is death." As in older morality plays, Satan often serves as God's chief enforcer, hounding sinners to their horrible fates. Some Hell Houses portray gay marriage ceremonies conducted by representatives of Satan, followed by AIDS deathbed scenes in which the sinners are dragged off for further agony in eternity. In one play a satanic professor indoctrinates hooded students to believe that people are "born gay." At one point he screams to the audience that they can learn more about being born gay by dialing "1-800-666-HOMO." Another production has Satan gleefully warning, "We've got your alternative lifestyle, all right — in Hell!" Compared to this level of eternally unforgiving hate, Jesus' warning to sinners in Matthew seems downright bland: "If any man . . . sets aside even the least of the Law's demands, and teaches others to do the same, he will have the lowest place in the kingdom of Heaven." (5:19) But in some Hell House productions Jesus does the torturing himself. A somewhat sad production shows a newly dead woman begging Jesus to forgive her unfaithful life. Jesus sternly replies, "I never knew you," and opens the trap door to send her plunging into eternal flames.[54]

Of course there were other innovations in imaging the afterworld. In medieval literature the notions of "Limbo" and Purgatory arose, both of them relatively charming. Limbo was created for innocent babies who died before baptism, because they were not authorized for admission to Heaven, but God would not have them suffer. And Purgatory was a vast improvement on the eternal torture favored by modern Protestants. It retained the notion that people had to pay for all sins through suffering despite Jesus' sacrificial atonement, but it at least retained hope of future release from pain. The various visions of heaven seemed strangely value-laden. Some writers placed Christians and those of other religions or nations in separate areas, organizing heaven by geographic divisions. Others pictured male monks in the highest reaches of heaven, with female celibates slightly below, and then the incontinent. Mechthild of Magdeburg (1200s) filled her Hell with rich and powerful men of her age.[55]

Best of all were visions of the Virgin Mary as the granter of mercy despite God's judgments. Beyond appealing to Jesus on behalf of sinners, she was shown negating debts of sin, using her own power to pardon dead sinners from Hell. As Ildefonsus of Toledo praised Mary's powers, "We cannot find anyone more powerful in merits than thou art for placating the wrath of the Judge."[56] But as people imagined and painted icons of Mary forgiving all on her own power, it seemed to suggest that her mercy could cancel God's laws. As the Pharisees corrected Jesus for presuming to overrule God, so the Council of Trent in the 1500s corrected such presumptuous views of Mary's power to forgive. Temporarily, the Council banned her iconography.[57]

Until recent centuries, perhaps most pastors and priests still saw themselves as enforcers of holy law, like a mixture of watch-dogs and police officers over their flocks. Many clerics relied almost completely on threats of divine punishment to influence others. And if their threats of torture in the next world failed to sufficiently intimidate sinners, then they endorsed the local authorities applying tortures of hell to the living. So in much of early modern Germany, the town authorities ruled that petty thieves must have their ears cut off. Blasphemers had their tongues cut out. Exiles returning illegally to Nuremberg had their eyes gouged out.[58] The Calvinist leaders of Geneva and Scotland temporarily reinstated the Old Testament death penalty for adultery.[59] And in 1548, the English Parliament required that homeless beggars be branded with a hot iron on the forehead, with a "V" for "vagrant." That would teach them permanent consequences. As in the period's religious wars, enforcing obedience from subordinates seemed to require ever-greater violence.

Only in the 1700s would seemingly unorthodox Christians like Cesare Bonesana or Voltaire start to sell a different realism. Bonesana made it sound like common sense: ferocious punishments made their victims into ferocious lifelong outcastes. Torture was counterproductive because it forced false accusations. If the laws were cruel, then they promoted cruelty in society. Nations would reduce crime better by investing in education than by building more prisons.[60] As notions like this grew popular, within a few decades, even the Papal States stopped punishing people by breaking them on the wheel, or by life sentences to slavery in the galley ships.

In modern America, the confession of sin followed by proclamation of forgiveness was the most common feature of worship. And the law theoretically followed merciful principles like those of Cesare Bonesana. But numerous religious leaders still insisted that Christianity forbade forgiveness for whatever sins they hated most. As R. J. Rushdoony demanded in *The Institutes of Biblical Law* (1973), the full book must be applied without mercy. A Christian America must impose the death penalty for adultery, blasphemy, homosexuality, incest, striking a parent, incorrigible delinquency, and for women, "unchastity before marriage."[61] For some reason, America was both the most generally Christian nation in the world, and the one with the highest rate of prison incarceration on the planet. The more traditionally "Bible belt" a state was, the higher its jailed population tended to be.[62]

Recasting Jesus as the Avenging Horseman of the Apocalypse

Jesus didn't live up to traditional expectations of a messiah. According to traditional dualistic religion, God's hero must play a two-fold role: he must uplift the good, while paying the evil their just deserts. Jesus did the first job in spades, but he neglected the last. Surely, many felt, if Jesus was truly the Messiah, he would have to come back a second time and finish the job.

John of Patmos, the author of Revelation, was probably a refugee from Roman massacres of the rebel Jewish population. His feelings toward Rome were probably similar to survivors of the Nazi holocaust. In his book, John declared a vision of Jesus' second coming, this time as a ferocious horseman of the sixth apocalypse: "He was called the Word of God, and the armies of heaven followed him on white horses, clothed in fine linen, clean and shining. From his mouth there went a sharp sword with which to smite the nations; for it is he who shall rule them with an iron rod, and tread the winepress of wrath and retribution of God the sovereign Lord. And on his robe and on his thigh there was written the name: 'King of Kings and Lord of Lords.'" (Revelation 19:11–16)

In this book, a Christianized vision of the apocalypse grafted Jewish legends from Exodus or Ezekiel onto dreams of a wrathful Jesus. It proclaimed a Day of Judgment in which the evil world order of "Babylon" would be cast down, and the righteous raised to sit at God's table. As in the Passover night, God's chosen people would be marked for salvation from the general slaughter. And the punishment to fall on the rest of humanity was an uncanny repetition of the plagues of Egypt, save that these plagues would devastate the whole world. In this vision, God repented of his post-flood promise to never again destroy his creation. And despite Jesus reportedly forgiving or redeeming the sins of the world, this version of Christianity clung to the Bible's voices of indiscriminate revenge: "I punish the children for the sins of the fathers to the third or fourth generations of those who hate me." (Exodus 20:5)

What crimes would this avenge? From all of Middle Eastern history we see a similar popular thirst for vengeance against unjust rulers. The ancient people of these countries, especially the ethnic or religious minorities, were often subject to savage repression. Their smoldering rage built to explosions of almost random vengeance, to which the rulers reacted with wholesale slaughter. In these conflicts, both rulers and rebels dreamed of wielding the sword of God to chastise or obliterate their enemies. Each side attributed its genocidal rage to God. In Jesus' time the authorities' demands and the villagers' anger were close to exploding into a war of mutual extermination. And that's just what happened within a few decades. A Jewish poem of that period foretold the utter destruction of the Roman world, saying "God shall burn up the whole earth and consume the whole race of man. He shall burn everything up and there will remain sooty dust."[63] It took people consumed by bitterness and contempt for the world as they knew it, to seriously proclaim a world-destroying Christ to come.

In recent times of uncertainty, we've seen a leap in popular demand for the apocalyptic solution to evil. Rather than predicting that Jesus will somehow establish justice and mercy on the earth, apocalyptic believers foretold that Jesus' true believers will be raptured off the earth, and everyone left behind will be exterminated. Carl McIntyre seemed like he could hardly wait: "Thank God, I will get a view of the Battle of Armageddon from the grand stand seats of the skies." Jerry Falwell also confidently predicted, "The Tribulation will result in such bloodshed and destruction that any war up to that time will seem insignificant." And Charles Jones reasoned, "Some day we may blow ourselves up with all the bombs . . . But I still believe God will be in control . . . If he chooses to use nuclear war, then who am I to argue with that?"[64]

In the stupendously popular *Left Behind* series, Tim LaHaye and Jerry Jenkins described the Armageddon "Tribulation Force," battling on the plain of Jezreel. Chief pilot Montgomery "Mac" McCallum asked, "Isn't Jesus' hometown up there somewhere? Nazareth?" His colleague Abdullah Smith relied, "On the north side of the valley." McCallum empathized with Jesus in this moment of ultimate war: "Imagine how it will feel for Him to fight an entire army that close to home."[65]

The battle itself lived up to expectations: "Men and women, soldiers and horses, seemed to explode where they stood. It was as if the very words of the Lord had superheated their blood, causing it to burst through their veins and skin . . . Their innards and entrails gushed to the desert floor, and as those around them turned to run, they too were slain, their blood pooling and rising in the unforgiving brightness of the glory of Christ."[66]

Instead of telling people "You are judges by worldly standards, but I am no one's judge" (John 8:15), Jesus in the *Left Behind* novels declared, "Like my Father with whom I am one, I have no pleasure in the death of the wicked, but that is justice, and that is your sentence."[67]

In addition to the *Left Behind* books, there were popular military apocalypse novels like Mel Odom's *Apocalypse Down*, *Apocalypse Crucible*, and *Apocalypse Burning*, plus a *Left Behind* kid's series including *Through the Flames*, and a *Left Behind: Eternal Consequences* video game.[68] Most of this popular apocalyptic literature was, as John Kloppenborg put it, "a virtual avalanche of images concerning the judgment and destruction of the impenitent."[69] A 15-year-old fan said, "The best thing about the *Left Behind* books is the way the non-Christians get their guts pulled out by God."[70] The authors of these productions seemed to imagine the second coming as a day of divine ethnic cleansing, to weed out all life-forms we don't respect, or simple religious cosmicide. Where in all this, Kloppenborg asked, was the positive outcome of God's coming? God would slaughter all "my enemies" — and then what?

For many Christians, the re-making of Jesus into a terrible swordsman of the apocalypse seemed utterly incompatible with the actual Jesus. They simply didn't see Jesus avenging wrongs or imposing punishments in the gospel accounts. In Luke, the disciples urged Jesus to call down fire from heaven to destroy his critics, but Jesus "turned and rebuked them." (9:55–56) The Gospel of John said, "God did not send the Son into the world to condemn the world." (3:17) In Luke, Jesus said, "The Kingdom of God is not coming with things that can be observed, nor will they say 'Look, here it is!' or 'There it is!' For in fact the Kingdom of God is within you." (17:20–21) The Gospel of Thomas had Jesus claim that the Kingdom of God has already come: "It is already spread upon the earth, but people fail to see it." (3:51, 99:16–18) For many Christians who stressed these verses, the Day of the Lord was not a day of universal destruction, but of inner transformation. Jesus described the Kingdom as a growing community, spreading like scattered seeds or leaven in dough. In 1917, Baptist preacher Shailer Mathews criticized apocalyptic preaching in a tract called "Will Christ Come Again?" His answer was that Jesus had already come, and his influence was already changing the world by spiritual power. But preachers of the apocalypse seemed to think spiritual means were inadequate. They seemed to assume that, "In order to succeed He has to resort to physical brutality . . . [and] miraculous militarism."[71]

In the Bible, there were two main visions for the solution to evil in the world. One was people's conversion to forgiveness and peace, as described by several Old Testament prophets and Jesus in his "first coming." The other vision was obliteration of the world, as in Noah, Revelation,[72] or 2 Peter, which put it this way: "For God did not spare angels when they sinned, but sent them to hell . . . he did not spare the world from the Flood, or Sodom and Gomorrah from total destruction." (2:4–7) Evidently, Bible writers and readers both got to choose which ending they liked best. And for Pastor John Hagee, of the Cornerstone Church in San Antonio, the apocalyptic Jesus of the second coming was infinitely preferable: "In Matthew he is a lamb being led to slaughter. In Revelation he is the LION OF JUDAH! He is going to rule with a rod of iron!"[73]

4. Correcting Respect
for Women

It was dangerous and shocking in the ancient Middle East, if a woman left her family to go wandering with men who weren't her relatives. That sort of behavior could get people killed. But the gospel accounts say that as Jesus "went journeying from town to town and village to village . . . With him were the Twelve and a number of women . . . Mary of Magdala . . . Joanna, the wife of Chuza, a steward of Herod's, Susanna, and many others. These women provided for them out of their own resources." (Luke 8:1–3) So the wife of Chuza left her husband to follow Jesus, and like many other women, shared her family wealth with him. Later at the crucifixion, after all the male disciples ran away, "Many women were also there, looking on from a distance; they had followed Jesus from Galilee and had provided for him." (Matthew 27:55)

What did all these women do besides "provide"? In the Mary-Martha passage (Luke 10) Jesus encourages female students to leave off serving others and give their whole attention to his teaching. Was he expecting them to learn to do what the male students learned and did? Most male leaders of the later church would say, of course not. But that would dismiss a lot of lines in the Gospels, Acts, and Paul's letters. If traveling around Palestine with Jesus while paying for his mission made one a disciple, then the gospels describe a flock of female disciples. They also show Jesus gratefully accepting devotion and help from these women. But by around year 95, a letter attributed to Clement, the bishop of Rome, contradicted Jesus' behavior almost point by point:

> With God's help this is what we do: We do not live with virgins and have nothing to do with them. We do not eat and drink with virgins, and where a virgin sleeps there we do not sleep. Women do not wash our feet, nor do

they anoint us. [Where we spend the night, t]here may not be any female,
neither unmarried girl nor married woman, neither old woman nor one
consecrated to God, neither Christian nor pagan maidservant, but only
men may be with men.[1]

How Jesus Behaved with Women

What did Jesus say to women? Was it any different from what he said to
men? To crowds of both sexes he asked: "Who is my mother? Who are
my brothers? . . . Whoever does the will of God is my brother, my sister,
my mother." (Mark 3:33–35) Where many listeners felt that their main
duty was to family heads, Jesus showed surprising hostility to such family
values: "If anyone comes to me and does not hate his father and mother,
wife and children, brothers and sisters, even his own life, he cannot be a
disciple of mine." (Luke 14:25–26) For him, blind submission to family
heads was idolatry: "Do not call any man on earth 'father'; for you have
one Father, and he is in heaven." (Matthew 23:9) To women, this suggested
there were more important things than serving fathers and husbands. And
some of the women who believed him left their families behind.

We have no direct record of Jesus inviting women to join his traveling
road show — only record of them coming and staying. But in that sexually
segregated world, how did he win female followers? It seems he was
totally open in talking to women, just like he was with men. But in that
culture this was shocking: "his disciples returned, and were astonished to
find him talking with a woman; but none of them said . . . 'Why are you
talking to her?' " (John 4:27)

When women followed Jesus, how did their families' men respond?
We should recall that most people in that age assumed that any woman
traveling without an escort of male relatives would almost inevitably be
raped. What else could possibly result? What else could she possibly be
seeking? As Bat Ye'or explains their reality, "The sources make abundant
mention of this fear which prevented women from going out and men

from venturing into the fields unarmed, and which necessitated collective traveling accompanied by armed guards — a situation which remained the norm till the twentieth-century in countries overrun by nomads, particularly in Palestine, Syria, and Iraq."[2]

If a woman ran away from home, most people assumed she must be inviting other men to take her. She had to be a whore. And in the gospels we hear this accusation: Jesus "eats with whores" (Mark 2:13–20). Later, the Western church clergy seem to have believed such slander about Mary Magdala.[3] And over the next three centuries there were numerous written accounts of female preachers being pursued, threatened or killed either by offended male relatives or rapists. Among these then-popular accounts we have the heroes Thecla in *The Acts of Thecla*, Drusiana in *The Acts of John*, Maximilla in *The Acts of Andrew*, or the martyr Perpetua in her published diary. During various state persecutions of Christians, we also hear of male preachers being killed for putting insubordinate ideas into women's heads. Perhaps Jesus' strange outbursts against family loyalty ("From now on, five members of a family will be divided, three against two and two against three . . ." (Luke 12:52)), were responses to such pressure on his female disciples.

Jesus on Marriage

If Christian law was based on the Bible, its "original" rules for marriage seem starkly unequal. In the earliest books of the Old Testament, men owned their women as property and sold their daughters to the best bidders. The father's blessing made a marriage legal, and if a daughter had objections, her father's will was binding. If women chose their own lovers independently, they could be stoned to death. (Deuteronomy 22:13–29) It's unclear if the Torah pronounced these things to be God's will, or simply recorded that this was the way of the world. With either sadness or conviction, the authors of Deuteronomy described how "A man takes a wife and possesses her. She fails to please him because he finds something obnoxious about her, and he writes her a bill of divorcement, and sends her away from his home . . ." (24:1) The book mentioned no right of a woman to reject her owner.

Many Jews insisted that such standards were eternal. But actually, the rules of Jewish life were slowly changing, and the Jews of Jesus' day were divided over family values. Some claimed the ancient rules must be enforced, such as ". . . both adulterer and adulteress shall be put to death." (Leviticus 20:10) Others believed that gentler ways were an improvement over the past. In this shifting environment, Jesus was probably the first prophet to teach full equality in marriage. His romantic ideal was mutual love between equal partners, which if it was the real thing, would know no cause for division. He dismissed the old unequal laws of marriage in the scriptures, claiming these were written because the ancient Hebrews weren't yet ready to understand real love. Now, he believed, they were ready. But actually they weren't, because the male disciple's immediate response was, "If that is the position between husband and wife, it is better not to marry." And at this, Jesus had to admit that obviously not everyone was ready for his ideal: "That is something which not everyone can accept . . . Let those accept it who can." (Matthew 19:3–12)

Later, most bishops took Jesus' words on marriage in Matthew 19 as the male disciples did. They assumed that Jesus' main points were (a) that the Law of Moses should be revised to forbid all divorce, and (b) that it is indeed better for people not to marry at all. When Jesus said "Let those accept it who can," they claimed "it" referred not to equality in marriage, but to rejection of any such thing. And toward those who did get married, the later bishops took Jesus' words on real marriage, not as an ideal to strive toward, but as a legal requirement to be enforced even on victims of spousal abuse.

The later church made it an article of faith that Jesus shunned marriage, which suggests he viewed it as spiritually degrading. But in that case, why did he teach romantic ideals about marriage? Why did he celebrate the wedding at Cana? Was it an alteration of Jesus' teaching to say he taught celibacy? Was he the only rabbi in recorded history to treat marriage as a corruption? If so, why did Paul say, "On the question of celibacy I have no instruction from the Lord"? (I Corinthians 7:25)

In answering that, we should recall the importance of marriage in ancient Jewish culture. In first century Palestine, as in the modern Middle East, it was an expected mark of maturity for adults to be married. This was especially true for men acting as leaders, which is why almost all Jewish rabbis, Muslim mullahs, and most Eastern Orthodox priests have been married. In surveying the hundreds of recorded Jewish rabbis living in the first centuries of the Christian era, historian Schalom Ben-Chorin finds only one, a certain Ben-Asai in the 100s AD, who was not married. And this one unmarried rabbi was constantly badgered as to why he avoided the responsibilities of family life. Ben-Asai said his devotion to the scriptures left him no time for a family, but the people of his community were unimpressed. Their attitude, Ben-Chorin believes, prevailed among all first century Jews, including the first Christians: "This needs to be kept in mind when we look at Jesus' career . . . If he scorned marriage, then his opponents among the Pharisees would have reproached him with that, and his disciples would have asked him about this sin of omission." Since no one is recorded asking Jesus any such question, Ben-Chorin feels it probable that Jesus was married like the other rabbis.[4]

If Jesus got married at the usual age of budding adulthood, and later church officials wanted to purge all relations with women from his record, this would give a plausible reason why the gospel accounts omit everything about his life between ages twelve and around thirty. One possibility is that he was married for some time, then his wife died, and later he devoted himself completely to his religious quest.

88

According to the second-century "Gospel of Mary," Mary of Magdala was not Jesus' wife, but a close disciple. The story shows the male and female disciples reflecting after Jesus' death, and Peter asking Mary "Sister, we know that the Savior loved you more than all other women. Tell us the words of the Savior that you remember . . ." (6:1–4) Then, rather than idealizing the people in this picture, the text shows serious discord. The gospel accounts had recorded disagreements over women between Jesus and his male disciples, but this story shows direct clashes between the men and women of Jesus' circle. After hearing Mary give her own interpretations of Jesus' teaching, Peter demands to know, "Did he, then, speak with a woman in private without our knowing about it? Are we to turn around and listen to her? Did he choose her over us?" (10:3–4)[5] These words may be "historical fiction," but the tensions they described grew very real in church history.

The "Sister-Brother" Teams

In the synoptic gospels, Jesus commissions a "further" seventy or seventy-two disciples, who go out teaching "two by two." Were Jesus' many female followers among them? Many scholars feel it's likely that some or all of these two-person teams were male/female pairs. Paul suggests it in asking, "Have I no right to take a Christian wife about with me, like the rest of the apostles and the Lord's brothers, and Cephas [St. Peter]?" (I Corinthians 9:5) Later, Bishop Clement of Alexandria (c. 150–215) said the first preachers went out two by two, as male-female pairs, so that the women could speak to women, while the men spoke to other men.[6] Since early Christianity was often called a cult of women, and since the society was highly segregated by sex, it seems there was a lot of woman to woman teaching going on. And since it was dangerous for women to travel alone, it was logical and traditional for them to go with "brothers" or "husbands in Christ." The book of Acts suggests these male-female teams by using the term "brothers and sisters" 32 times, interchangeably with the word "disciples."[7] One of these women, Tabitha, is directly named as a disciple (9:36–42), which should end the question of whether there were female disciples.

Paul named five male-female teaching teams: Prisca and Aquila (Romans 16:3), Andronicus and Junia (16:7), Philologus and Julia (16:15), Nereus and his sister (16:15), and Peter with his wife (I Corinthians 9:5). He introduced Prisca and Aquila as "fellow workers in Christ, who risked their necks for my life, to whom not only I but also all the churches of the Gentiles give thanks." Junia and Andronicus "shared my background and my imprisonment, highly distinguished apostles who came before me to Christ."[8] Later churchmen denied the implications of Paul's letter. They claimed that Peter's wife could not have shared in his teaching role because she was female. Some copyists also corrected Paul for describing a woman as "distinguished apostle," by changing Junia's name to "Junius." A more subtle modification concerned Acts 17:4. The earliest texts say that in Thessalonica "a great number of God-fearing Gentiles and a good many influential women" joined with Paul and Silas. But some later manuscripts modified this to say, "a great number of pious Greeks, along with a large number of wives of prominent men."[9]

Concerning female priests, Paul's letters addressed a series of women leading the first house-churches. In Philippi, Paul's first European convert was a businesswoman named Lydia, who made her home into a local church. (Acts 15) In Colossians the church was Nympha's house (4:15); in Corinth it was Chloe's house (I Corinthians 1:11); in Philemon's town it was Appia's home. (Philemon 1:2) In Philippians, Paul urged an end to rivalry between two female church leaders named Euodia and Syntyche. (4:2) In all these cases we hear of women opening their houses to a new religious sect, and serving as its local leaders. We hear no mention of what the men of their families thought about it.

So the scriptures mention female apostles, female priests, apostles' wives, and priests' wives. But later the Roman church rejected all these kinds of holy women as abominations to God. The notion of male-female teaching teams grew unthinkable. In the early 300s, the Council of Nicea banned a tradition of "spiritual marriage" between monks and nuns, as if such partnership was impossible between people of different sexes. St. Jerome would pour contempt on it: "From what source has this plague of "dearly beloved sisters" found its way into the church? Whence come these unwedded wives? These novel concubines, these one-man harlots? They live in the same house with their male friends; they occupy the same room, often the same bed; yet they call us suspicious if we think anything is wrong?"[10]

Making Church Women Respectable

At first, many primitive churches were proud of setting gender segregation aside. When he first came to Corinth Paul waxed passionate on the equality of sexes.[11] But probably a large majority of Greek and Roman men thought such talk was dangerously idiotic. Men were legally accountable for controlling their female subordinates. If they didn't, it would be an abdication of responsibility leading directly to personal disgrace and social anarchy. For a taste of traditional Roman attitudes, we have Cato's defense of a law to restrict conspicuous consumption by females:

This is the least of the things enjoined upon women by custom or law and to which they submit with a feeling of injustice. It is complete liberty or rather, if we wish to speak the truth, complete license that they desire. If they win in this, what will they not attempt? Review all the laws in which your forefathers restrained their license and made them subject to their husbands; even with all these bonds you can scarcely control them. What of this? If you suffer them to seize these bonds one by one and wrench themselves free and finally to be placed on a parity with their husbands, do you think that you will be able to endure them? The moment they begin to be your equals, they will be your superiors.[12]

Some critics of the church already dismissed it as a cult of women. There were rumors that the movements' real leaders were Jesus' female followers, such as Salome, Mary Magdala, Marcellina, Helen of Samaria, and Martha, the sister of Lazarus. Later, Hippolytus of Rome (early 200s) repeated the claim that Mary Magdala had been "The apostle to the apostles."[13] Of course many male church leaders hotly rejected such claims, as if the church's respectability depended on proving them false. And even Paul found his female church leaders taking more equality than he could handle. It seems some of them scandalized Corinth by seeking divorces, so they could pursue their religion more freely.[14] Some of these women became rivals in church leadership, with some aspiring, like Paul, to be among the greatest apostles.[15] What if they succeeded, and emerged as the most charismatic church leaders in Greece? What if they drew a mainly female following, and made Paul's churches look like a cult of women? What could be more shameful for the church, than its growing reputation as a cult where men had no control over women?

To most Greco-Romans and Middle Easterners, it seemed obvious that any community attempting "sexual equality" would lose all means of controlling immorality. So why would Christians speak of sexual equality unless their real desire was sexual permissiveness? The Roman writer Juvenal claimed that all women's participation in religious cults was nothing but a pretext for sexual escapades. What more plausible excuse, he asked, could women contrive to get out of the house, out of men's sight, and out of all control?[16] Later, the Christian "apologist" Minucius Felix would denounce church members who "know one another by secret signs and signals, and they make love together before they know one another —

for there is a certain amount of lust mixed up with their religion, and they promiscuously call themselves brothers and sisters . . ."[17]

Paul's personal morals as a Pharisee were very strict. Like any Middle Eastern father of his people, he felt personally responsible for any scandals among them. To eliminate grounds for damning rumors, he called for increasingly restrictive rules for church women: "As in all congregations of God's people, women should not address the meeting. They have no license to speak, but should keep their place as the law directs. If there is something they want to know, they can ask their own husbands at home. It is a shocking thing that a woman should address the congregation." (I Corinthians 14:26, 34–35) Paul's phrase "as the law directs" (14:34), likely referred to Corinthian law, since many Greco-Roman towns outlawed rites that involved ecstatic speech, dancing, or loss of self-control by women.[18] To avoid accusations that Christians engaged in such things, Paul needed a show of strict sobriety. Where Jesus had been heedless of accusations that he ate with prostitutes, or was a glutton and a drunkard, Paul now called his churches to renounce all "reveling and drunkenness" (Romans 13:13). The fragility of the church's reputation required a display of conventional virtue.

By this point, Paul seems to have stopped praising female church founders. His concern for the organization's public image outweighed his respect for women.[19] Probably he felt his requests for female modesty, veiling, etc., were only temporary tactical moves. In the coming Kingdom, all would be equal. But for the time being, if church women agreed to a subordinate role, it would make Jesus' message more widely acceptable to men of influence across the empire. If women raised their voices in church, it would only feed degrading rumors. Rather than encouraging freedom from "the ways of the world," the new party line was cautious conformity to social norms. Perhaps it was best for the movement if Christian women showed the world that their faith posed no threat to patriarchal traditions.

This trend intensified with time. Where the first evangelists praised women for following Jesus despite their men's objections, later ones re-emphasized Genesis 3:16: "Your orientation will be toward your husband and he will rule over you." Someone writing in Peter's name enshrined this demand as a revised gospel for women: ". . . you women must accept the authority of your husbands . . . Such was Sarah, who obeyed Abraham and called him 'my master.' " (1 Peter 3:6) While starting to claim that a Christian "new covenant" transcended "the old law," the emerging clergy also taught that the past's unequal laws remained in force for women.

To make Christianity respectable, leaders like Paul or Luke needed to show that strong moralistic men were in charge. So in 1 Timothy congregations were advised to choose the most conventional father-figures as their leaders: "Our leader . . . or bishop, must be above reproach . . . He must be one who manages his own household well and wins obedience from his children and a man of the highest principles. If a man does not know how to control his own family, how can he look after a congregation of God's people?" (3:2–5) Such leading males felt accountable for keeping both their emotions and their women under control. Increasingly they claimed their religion stood for a new sexual segregation, which was actually stricter than that of traditional Jews, Greeks, or Roman Stoics.[20] Around AD 200, Clement of Alexandria announced, "Women should be completely veiled, except when they are in the house. Veiling their faces assures that they will lure no one into sin. For this is the will of the Logos."[21] Clement was serious about proving Christianity was no "love cult." He claimed that Christian husbands loved their wives strictly as a matter of productive duty: "Like the farmer, the married man is permitted to sow his seed only when the season allows."[22] Of course no such idea could be found in the New Testament.[23]

Eliminating Female Leadership

Since the bishops increasingly discouraged women from teaching out in the streets, many women still served as "internal" church leaders. Inside these communities of trusted friends, women might have little to fear and much to offer. But even here there were rising objections to sharing any authority with women.

One reason for restricting women's influence was control over property. For the first several centuries, Christian women made a name for themselves as generous organizers of charities. But as the pagan emperor Julian chided Christian men in 363, "Every one of you allows his wife to carry everything out of his house to the Galileans."[24] The Christian women, it seems, were often too generous, and gave too much of their family fortunes away. If these women were church administrators, they might squander the incoming tide of donations by giving it away to the poor. The men of their families or churches would lose control of resources, and it was shameful for men to lose control. In the late 300s, Emperor Valentinian decided to eliminate the problem. Claiming to benevolently protect weak-minded women from unscrupulous fund-raisers, he banned the church from accepting any gift or legacy from a female. From now on, male household heads would approve all donations. And once the church received that income, male clerics would manage it responsibly. The famous armies of Christian women administering charities throughout the empire would then initiate nothing without approval from male supervisors. Fortunately, this law caused such a decline in church donations that 200 years later Emperor Justinian repealed it, so the churches could rake in donations from women again.

Another set of problems involved pre-Christian taboos surrounding sex. The Hebrew Bible recorded ancient beliefs that men are polluted by touching a menstruating woman, sitting on a seat where she sat, etc. Where women hosted the sacred meal, Bishop Dionysus of Alexandria

95

(200s) was concerned that their sexual fluids would desecrate the bread and wine. He insisted that menstruating women must not serve the meal, and shouldn't even receive it: ". . . pious devout women would never even think of touching the sacred table or the Body and Blood of the Lord [during their menstrual periods]."[25] But actually, it was the most devout women who were likely to lead sacred meals. And if male leaders tried to stop them, they could always hold their ceremonies for females only. In a Roman catacomb called the Cappella Greca, a fresco painting dating to the 200s seems to show this. The painting shows seven people gathered around a table, with one holding a loaf of bread aloft. The painting is labeled *fractio panis* (the breaking of the bread), and all seven people are women.[26] The church women of Salamis (in Asia Minor) also did this. We know because their Bishop, Epiphianus, insulted them for it: "They attempt to undertake a deed that is irreverent and blasphemous beyond measure — in her [Mary's] name they function as priests for women . . . For some women prepare a certain kind of little cake with four indentations, cover it with a fine linen veil on a solemn day of the year, and on certain days they set forth the bread and offer it in the name of Mary."[27]

As Christianity spread into Europe, these problems with female leadership continued, or increased. Many regions of Europe had ancient traditions involving local holy women. And in these areas, local priests often treated support from female leaders as a blessing. So, in 494, Pope Gelasius felt he must rebuke the overly permissive priests of Portugal: "As we have learned to our anger, such a contempt for the divine truths has set in that even women, it has been reported, serve at the holy altars. And everything that is exclusively entrusted to the service of men has been carried out by the sex that has no right to it."[28]

As the church gained state backing, these taboos which Jesus ignored gained a new purpose, of helping justify why men should get all paid positions in the church. But even a male monopoly on paid clerical roles didn't make voluntary female leaders disappear. Across Asia Minor and Greece, the female heads of traditional house-churches continued serving bread and wine, with no claim to pay for it. The Council of Nicea in 325 ruled "With regard to the deaconesses who hold this position we remind [church leaders] that they possess no ordination, but are to be reckoned among the laity in every respect."[29] Where Paul had boasted of his success inspiring female church leaders from Antioch to Rome, the Council of Laodicea in 364 banned them: "Presbytides, as they are called, or female presidents, are not to be appointed by the church" (Canon 11), and "Women may not go to the altar" (Canon 44).

Still with all these restrictions, Pelagius observed around the year 400 that "even today women deaconesses in the East are known to minister to their own sex in baptism, or in the ministry of the Word."[30] John Chrysostom (also around 400) admitted that the New Testament encouraged women to teach. Because obviously it took women to teach other women in their quarters. And if the church forbade females to instruct men, how could a Christian woman ever convert her male relatives?[31] But Chrysostom tried to draw a line against women serving the Lord's Supper. He no longer argued they would pollute the bread, but admitted it was a question of power. Women, he said, were already too powerful in the church: "Since they can effect nothing by themselves, they do all through the agency of others; and they have become invested with so much power that they can appoint or eject priests at their will."[32] If allowed priestly office, Chrysostom was afraid they would totally dominate everything.

In Ireland, the natives still assumed it was natural to have female priests, and respected Brigid of Kildare as one of the three greatest church leaders of her generation (400s). The Irish had always known religious roles for both wise men and wise women, and were amazed that the Roman Church insisted there must be only holy males. It took over 200 years till the Celtic Church gave in to pressure and dumped its female priests.[33] After that, only a few further restrictions were needed to totally eliminate women from any liturgical role. St. Boniface's synodal statutes in the 700s banned women from singing in church, lest their beautiful voices seem so sexual as to defile men's thoughts. For centuries the soprano parts had to be sung by boys.

We might assume that women needed only to be told to give up leadership, and they meekly obeyed. But perhaps it took more force to de-liberate these women. In a cave called the "Grotto of Saint Paul" near the old city of Ephesus, Turkey, an ancient fresco painting portrays three heroes of the early church. They are identified with labels as St. Paul, his co-evangelist Thecla, and Thecla's mother. Thecla was famous in early centuries, and her life recorded in a book called *The Acts of Thecla*. The book described her brave adventures in learning from Paul, her escape from death threats by family members and suitors, and her adventures as a major evangelist. In the painting, the figures of Paul and Thecla are both raising their right hands in the ancient gesture of teaching. But while Paul's image is untouched after so many centuries, Thecla's eyes are rubbed out and the paint of her teaching hand is burned off.[34]

All this denial of women's leadership in the Jesus movement left a lot of references in the New Testament, church council deliberations or writings of church fathers. Around the year 900, an Italian priest named Ambrose wrote to his bishop, Atto of Vercelli, asking why there were so many old references to women with titles like "presbytera," "diaconal," etc. Bishop Atto gave as honest a reply as he was able:

> . . . *since your wisdom has determined that we ought to decide whether to understand "priestess" or "deaconess" in the canons; it seems to me that since in the primitive church according to the holy word, "Many are the crops and few are the laborers," for the helping of men even religious women were ordained caretakers in the early church. This is something that blessed Paul*

points out in his epistle to the Romans when he says, "I commend to you my sister Phoebe, who is in the ministry of the church that is in Cenchreae." One understands this because then not only men, but also women were in charge of the churches . . . This practice C[anon]. 11 of the Laodicean council later prohibits . . .[35]

Thomas Aquinas would explain it more bluntly and learnedly in the *Summa Theologica*: "Since any supremacy of rank cannot be expressed in the female sex, which has the status of an inferior, that sex cannot receive ordination."[36] Only in recent centuries did various churches return to using their talent pools of female supporters. The Southern Baptist Church in the USA started ordaining women in 1964, and by the early 1980s had over 400 female pastors. But then in 1984, the Baptist annual convention voted to strip these women of authority to preach, to "preserve a submission God requires because the man was first in creation and the woman was first in the Edenic fall." Retracing the path taken by the early church, the Convention next voted (in 1986) to cut funding to any missionary service around the world employing a female pastor. And in 1988 it tried to require sexual inequality within private homes, declaring that wives must practice "gracious" submission to their husband's leadership.[37]

Meanwhile the Roman Church made its reversal of Jesus' respect for women into an eternal requirement. Like the old Hindu caste system, it insisted God's will disallowed vocations from the wrong birth-groups. Though over 60% of American Catholics felt their Church would be improved by ordaining qualified women, the Church's 1977 "Declaration on the Question of Admission of Women to the Ministerial Priesthood" overrode Jesus' challenge to Mary and Martha, plus all biblical references to female disciples, apostles, house church leaders etc., by flatly denying there was any evidence that Jesus ever intended his ministry to include women.[38] In 1994, Pope John Paul II finally issued an infallible ban on women serving as priests in Jesus' religion. As this ruling was elevated to canonical status in 1998, the Toronto *Catholic Register* gave the news a front page headline: "Pope Changes Canon Law in Defense of Faith."[39] As one result, in 1998 the Vatican ordered the Liturgical Press of Collegeville, Minnesota to destroy all stocks of the book *Woman at the Altar*, by Sister Lavinia Byrne. After 20 years of service with the Institute of the Blessed Virgin Mary, the silenced Dr. Byrne resigned and took her skills in teaching, broadcasting, writing and public speaking, elsewhere.[40] After several years as a journalist, author, and international public speaker, she added a job as City Councillor for Wells, England.

Making a Separate Holy Law for Women

The early bishops often considered themselves governors over their flocks, like Jewish high priests with a revised set of holy laws. Their canon rules evolved over centuries, mainly through a series of all-male church councils, which met like legislative assemblies. Most bishops at the early councils came from lands surrounding the Eastern Mediterranean, and to them it seemed obvious that Christianity stood on cultural foundations from that part of the world. As when most Islamic scholars accepted Arabian culture as their international standard, so the Christian bishops endorsed traditions from the regions around Jesus' homeland. They meant well. Like Middle Eastern fathers to their people, they felt responsible to protect their women and their community's reputation. To uphold their ancient family values, they supplemented the gospels with pre-Christian traditions, like those of the North African "founding father" Tertullian.

Tertullian greatly admired the courage of female evangelists, especially the ones who died in Roman persecutions around 200. But to women in his own church, he offered a more traditional message: "Put on the panoply of modesty; surround yourself with the stockade of bashfulness; rear a rampart for your sex, which must neither allow your own eyes egress nor ingress to other people's"[41] Instead of encouraging both male and female Christians to risk themselves in teaching others, Tertullian counseled fear and self-protection for the females. He felt his sisters must hide their beauty from the world. If they went out among wolves, they would only be raped, lose their virtue, and shame their families. Probably protecting their chastity was the highest goal they could achieve.

Some Middle Eastern fathers even felt that a woman's chastity was more important than her life, and in later centuries the church commonly upheld this priority. For example, in 1950, the Church canonized an 11-year old girl named Maria Goretti, who had been stabbed to death while resisting a rapist. It seemed the church preferred girls to die resisting attackers rather than submit and lose their virginity.[42] More recently, Reginald Finger, an evangelical Christian serving on the Center for Disease Control's Advisory Committee on Immunization Practices, considered opposing the use of an experimental HIV vaccine in Africa, because it might encourage premarital sex by making it less dangerous.[43]

With such traditional values in mind, the early church bishops began generating decrees in response to questions raised at the time. Should women be allowed to hold all-night prayer vigils at the tombs of martyred saints? The Council of Elvira (about 309) said no, since this could be a pretext for sexual escapades.[44] The Elvira council also ruled that Spanish women must not receive letters in their own names.[45] Any message to a woman must be addressed to her husband or father for his inspection. Should men and women worship together in church? The Apostolic Constitutions (380s) ruled that each sex should sit in separate areas with separate doorways. Should women wear the veil? The Council of Carthage in 394 said yes, until at least age 25.

Concerning dowry payment, arranged marriage, child marriage, the sale of women, or punishment for adultery, the church councils often accepted Hebrew or Roman standards with little change. In accordance with Roman attitudes, the council of Elvira set worse penalties for adultery than for slave killing.[46] Sometimes the bishops revised Hebrew tradition. Instead of allowing only men to initiate divorce, many bishops felt that both partners should be denied that right, save for cases of "unchastity." And sometimes the bishops were innovative. Though neither Jesus nor the Old Testament made any clear statement on abortion,[47] the council of Elvira decreed excommunication for life to any woman who aborted a fetus.[48] The Elvira council also voted to outlaw marriage between Christians and Jews or pagans, calling such love for outsiders "fornication."[49] Where Jesus had deliberately violated social barriers raised to prevent love between "enemy" groups, the church's legalists were once again trying to *limit* love.

Since women had no direct say in framing these laws, the bishops' councils slowly accumulated decisions to control women. The Apostolic Constitutions (c. 380) advised women they "should not wash all too frequently, not in the afternoon, nor every day. Let the tenth hour be assigned to her as the right time for bathing."[50] The Council of Chalcedon (451) threatened excommunication to anyone plotting to "carry off girls under pretext of cohabitation." This ruling made no distinction between kidnapping and elopement. For the bishops it was all the same crime of violating a father's will for his daughter.

Instead of proposing the same rights for women they would wish for themselves, most church leaders defended inequality as a fundamental Christian value. In recent centuries, some traditionalists even objected when anaesthesia was introduced for women in childbirth, because it violated the lines, "I will greatly multiply your pain in childbearing . . ." (Genesis 3:16) More recently, Pope John Paul II described the 1994 United Nations Cairo Conference on Women's rights as "the work of the devil." And to counter U.N. proposals for women's reproductive freedom, The Catholic Family and Human Rights Institute's director Austin Ruse announced "a new and very potent alliance between Catholic and Muslim countries." "Our enemies," he explained, "see all this as an unholy alliance. And so from their point of view it is,because it is from this alliance . . . that our victory will come."[51] And in El Salvador that victory arrived. While the church condemned birth control, the government banned all abortion, even in cases of rape or danger to the mother's life. Women coming to hospitals bleeding from back-alley abortions were shackled to their beds and charged with a felony. Some of these women received prison sentences for up to 30 years.[52]

Imposing Middle Eastern Standards on Europe

As Christianity spread north into Europe from the 300s to 800s, the clergy imported traditions from the ancient Middle East alongside Jesus' teaching. Since these customs came from the Holy Land, they seemed to be God's way. In European cultures where men and women had been roughly equal partners, many priests now taught that men must rule their wives. If local customs recognized women's property as separate from that of their husbands, the church held that all property belonged to male family heads. Where Emperor Diocletian (late 200s) had abolished male guardianship over adult women, ecclesiastical laws from the late 300s brought it back, except for within the Byzantine Empire after the 500s. Where homosexual love had been respected, the church taught Europeans to punish gay and lesbian lovers. Where couples had been free to choose or leave each other, later church laws drastically reduced both freedoms.[53] And where Europe's kings embraced an alliance of church and state, all these standards gained force of law. Naturally the authorities quoted the Bible to justify their rulings. But where many early evangelists stressed a message of equality for everyone, now both rulers and clergymen cited other verses to prove God's support for inequality. There were a series of major implications for family law in an officially Christian Europe.

Divorce and Remarriage

Until the 800s, the Roman Church was quite lax about divorce. But the clergy attempted to forbid remarriage after divorce or even the death of a lover — for the women. If remarriage for women was legal, it would allow half-brothers or sisters to be born, which could generate conflict over family estates. The church lent its moral authority to prevent any such thing. In 314 the synod of Arles decreed that women who remarried must be excommunicated for life. Hopefully that would prevent half-siblings from the female side, or at least cut off their right to inherit. The penalty for remarrying men was usually a verbal reprimand.[54]

Despite the threat of excommunication, remarriage was still common for centuries. As in previous ages, people continued rebuilding their lives, celebrating second or third marriages outside the church. But during the reign of King Louis the Pious (814–840), the bishops grew concerned to end this problem.[55] They agreed (with various exceptions for powerful people) to cut off the supply of divorcees seeking remarriage by banning all divorce in the first place. And here the Church of Rome started going its separate way. Because the Eastern Church councils were slowly expanding the recognized grounds for divorce, to include cruelty, incompatibility, impotence, or mental illness.

So long as European women could still initiate divorce, it made little sense for a father to give his daughter in an arranged marriage. If the daughter disliked the arrangement, she could reject it. But once a girl's right to divorce was abolished, her marriage could be more predictably arranged. And then a tradition from the Middle East grew popular in Europe, of arranging betrothals for child brides. Where this became a standard practice, women lost both the freedom to initiate marriage, and the legal option to end it. Marriage could then be a binding economic arrangement between male family heads, as it was in much of the holy land. The church imposed its seal of approval on the proceedings, and threatened any women who tried to escape with eternal damnation.[56]

Property Rights and Inheritance

On inheritance, Christian values could be better for women than some pagan traditions. The old Frankish Salic law was as unequal as any code in the old Middle East: "Of Salic land, no portion of the inheritance shall go to a woman."[57] We have record of one Frankish Christian convert in the 700s complaining of the Salic law, reasoning it was contrary to God's equal love for sons and daughters.[58] But later preachers stressed a different standard, and the supposedly Christian demand for male control gradually prevailed. Since ownership of land was limited sovereignty, any division of property with women seemed to weaken the estate lords. And this concern grew more serious after 870, when the landlords of France forced Charles the Bald to recognize their royal grants of land as private property, which the fief-holders could will to their successors. To avoid further breakup of kingdoms and estates, the headmen moved toward a custom of inheritance through primogeniture to eldest sons only, which of course excluded younger sons and all daughters. The daughters then tended to inherit only movable goods — perhaps some money or a percentage of income from parts of the family land. In 1037, Holy Roman Emperor Konrad II tried to ban all women from inheriting land, though ordinary "semi-pagan" villagers often ignored the rule. In Scotland, women's rights to own property in their own names survived down to 1366. And across Northern Europe women continued owning property despite the supposedly Christian laws.

Dowries for Marriage

Where women were increasingly restricted from owning property, the ancient traditions of dowry payments tended to change. In most pagan traditions a groom paid dowry to his bride's family. But to many early preachers, this seemed un-Christian. The Christianized Danish King Knut (1000s) rebuked the practice in terms worthy of Jesus: "No woman or maiden shall ever be forced to marry a man whom she dislikes, nor shall she ever be given for money unless the suitor wishes to give something of his own free will."[59] But as Christian tradition developed, another twist emerged; the tradition of paying dowry was simply reversed. Instead of the groom paying for a bride, it was the bride's family that had to pay.

The older custom of dowry to brides involved compensating her family for losing a productive member. But under laws where women could not directly gain property, females seemed to count as expenses to men's resources. In that view, the groom's family was taking on the expense of a woman. Where Moses had to pay Sarah's father with seven years labor, now a father had to pay to unload his daughter — as in India. The question now was how much the father had to pay. If his girl remained a virgin, a father could probably marry her off for less. So controlling his daughters' virginity grew more financially important. With that in mind, medieval Europe saw a rise of veiling restrictions and confinement to female quarters. In France, upper class fathers commonly sent their girls to live in nunneries till their marriages were arranged. Then the brides might be escorted directly from the convent to the altar, perhaps under armed guard.[60] The poorer girls were increasingly sent out to work for other families, so they could earn their own dowry. It commonly took them over a decade working as a maid to do it.

Since the church passed so many rules to govern women, we might assume these rules existed to teach certain moral lessons. But what did these rules teach? Clearly the point was not about learning to make "right" moral choices, because these restrictions implied that females should not make decisions at all. Morality for them lay in accepting whatever their male guardians decided for them. And although this may strike us as complete abdication of personal morality, it fit the accepted doctrines that ordinary men and women (especially women) were infected by inborn sin, and must not trust their own minds. And if this was Christian, we have evidence that it wasn't good for women. Surveying records of medieval communities, Emily Coleman estimates that Christendom suffered an imbalanced death rate for females. Due to a combination of factors including female infanticide, lower nutrition, and general subordinate status, Coleman calculates the ratio of females to males fell over the course of the Middle Ages. Her figures suggest, that in 801, Western Europe had around 156 males for every 100 females. By 1391 she estimates the population imbalance had risen to 172 males per 100 females.[61]

Eliminating Women from the Family of the Church

In the early church, most clergymen still believed that having wives was a good thing. As the Jews expected their rabbis to be married, so most Christians expected it of their priests. Marriage was a school of life, and if a priest wasn't married, people would think there was something wrong with him. As earlier mentioned quotes suggest, probably all the original apostles were married. But when the early church faced accusations of being a free love cult, the leaders' fear of sexual scandal sometimes grew extreme. In refuting allegations of sexual mixing in church, some clerics began preaching not just sexual discretion, but complete chastity. These clerics increasingly insisted that virginity was a primary Christian value. John of Patmos claimed it was a vision from the Lord that a mere 144,000 souls would be saved from an upcoming Apocalypse, and these would be pure males "who have not defiled themselves with women, for they are virgins . . ." (Revelation 14:4)

To promote claims of sexual innocence for their church, some scribes or translators of New Testament texts altered the words of scripture. Translation errors like St. Jerome's use of "virgin" for "young woman" reflected a certain agenda, as when Jerome insisted that heroes of the Old Testament like Daniel or Miriam were also celibates, though the book didn't say so. A worse change happened to I Corinthians, to make Paul say "It is a good thing for a man to have nothing to do with a woman . . ." (7:1–2) The *New English Bible's* footnote to this verse says that earlier versions of the text were written as follows (with the later omitted elements in bold):

> **You [Corinthians] say,** "*It is a good thing for a man to have nothing to do with a woman,*" *but because there is so much immorality, let each man have his own wife, and each woman her own husband.*

In the original version, Paul criticized other people for advocating sexual segregation in the church. He urged church members to work as couples, the way he claimed the apostles did. But his defense of families working together seemed to disappear in a puff of smoke, with the simple deletion of a phrase. And in its place stood a corrected statement of naked contempt for all women. As St. Jerome then explained, "If it is good not to touch a woman, it is bad to touch one, for there is no opposite of goodness but badness."[62]

In a holier-than-thou competition for higher church office, growing numbers of bishops began claiming that *all* contact between men and women was corrupting, and such pollution was especially serious for a priest. With a pious ashamed-to-have-a-penis attitude, Saint Ambrose (d. 397) argued that all priests who loved their wives "pray for others with unclean minds as well as unclean bodies."[63] Ambrose's disciple Augustine bemoaned that, "Nothing is so powerful in drawing the spirit of man downwards as the caresses of a woman and that physical intercourse which is part of marriage."[64] Ambrose, Jerome, and Augustine all managed to interpret the story in Mark 4 (of the seed which fell on barren ground compared to the seed which fell on fertile ground) to mean that celibates were the good soil, and loving couples the barren ground.

In 388, a cleric called Jovian tried to argue that family people were just as spiritual as celibate ones. He asked pro-celibates, "Are you better than Sarah, Susanna, Anna, and many of the holy women and men in the Bible?" But for arguing like that, Pope Siricius threw Jovian out of the church.[66] Another cleric named Helvidius (also 380s) tried to defend wives and mothers, claiming that Mary was holy as a virgin when she bore Jesus, and equally holy as a wife and mother of additional children after that. Saint Jerome hotly replied that Mary never had sex in her life, and any reference to Jesus' "brothers" and "sisters" (Matthew 13:55–56) had to mean "cousins." Women, Jerome wrote, could only be holy if they "cease to be married women [and] imitate the chastity of virgins within the very intimacy of marriage."[67] With that understanding of the Bible's "real" message, Jerome left the flesh pots of Rome to live with anti-worldly monks in the Palestinian desert. From there, he wrote that priests who had wives and children were "no longer any different from pigs."[68]

Augustine was less insulting towards lovers. He was simply perplexed as to what women were created for. Aside from the somewhat lamentable function of reproduction, he saw no benefits to their existence. Later this became the orthodox view of the Roman clergy:

I don't see what sort of help woman was created to provide man with, if one excludes the purpose of procreation. If woman is not given to man for help in bearing children, for what help could she be? To till the earth together? If help were needed for that, man would have been better help for man. The same goes for comfort in solitude. How much more pleasure is it for life

109

and conversation when two friends live together than when man and woman cohabitate.[69]

Still, all was not lost. When Pope Sixtus III (430s) was brought to trial for seducing a nun, he said "Let him who is without sin throw the first stone."[70]

The Rising Celibate Party

As the Christian community developed, it divided into three main orders, namely a) the lay people, b) the all-male clergy, and c) the celibate "religious." Then argument arose of which order ranked highest, as in those arguments over status among the first disciples. At first the lay people were most important, since they chose and supported all church leaders. Later the professional clergy gained state backing as supervisors over the laity. But by early medieval times, the celibate monks emerged as the Christians of highest rank. With their isolation from the world and from sex, they seemed to be holier than either the local clergy (who were still mainly married), or lay families. In both the West and East, higher clerics were increasingly drawn from the ranks of monks. It was an important change. As Robert Markus explains, "The ascetic take-over [roughly in the time of Pope Gregory the Great (590–604)] signals the end of ancient Christianity."[71]

In the Greek, Russian, Egyptian, or Ethiopian churches, things remained at roughly this stage down to the present. Most common priests remained married, and the rules of celibacy applied only to monks, nuns, and sometimes higher clergy. For local priests, marriage remained the standard. As Demetrios Constantelos explained of Greek Orthodox tradition, "The fact that the Church has not made an official pronouncement placing celibacy above marriage indicates that the conscience of the Church has accepted marriage as a more courageous state of being."[72]

But in the Latin West, the ascetic takeover went one big step further. There, the monastic leaders managed to impose their celibacy onto the common priests, forcing them to divorce their wives en masse. And this struggle between celibates and clerical families involved the longest, bitterest struggle in church history. In 1074, after about 700 years of theological warfare, the pro-celibate hierarchy managed to impose a sort of sacramental apartheid between the priesthood and womankind. They not only reserved priestly roles for men alone, they also made the sanctity of priests depend on isolation from females. Since the other churches of Eastern Europe, Asia, or Africa retained marriage for ordinary priests, we have to wonder: why did this great divorce of all clerical wives happen in the West?

The War on Sex in Clerical Families

One of the first efforts to enshrine anti-family policy came in at the Council of Elvira (about 309), where a majority of bishops called for priests to give up sex with their wives. This ruling came under review at the Council of Nicea in 325, and there the majority of bishops rejected it. Though Bishop Paphnutius of Egypt was a celibate monk himself, he successfully defended marriage as honorable according to all the scriptures. He said the church would commit a great wrong to force separation on married families.[73] The Eastern churches upheld this Nicean ruling ever afterward. And this became their most important conflict with the Roman Church. Because while the Eastern churches continued affirming family life for priests down to the present, many leaders of the Roman Church embarked on a long campaign to ban it as a crime.

We can imagine how clerical families felt as church council after council debated the validity of their marriages for over seven centuries. In 340–41 the Synod of Gangra defended married priests and denounced fanatics for asceticism. It also condemned celibate fanatics who called for

111

public boycotts on services by married priests. The Apostolic Constitutions (ca. 380) ruled that any priest who repudiated his wife on pretext of piety should be cast out of the church. But then the councils at Carthage (in 390 and 401) insisted that priests must be pure from pollution and stop having sex with their wives. In the mid-400s Pope Leo I endorsed this, ordering that "in order to make their carnal marriage a spiritual one, while they may not dismiss their wives, they must however possess them as if they did not possess them . . ."[74] If the married priests did not obey, this only confirmed Leo's conviction that the priests' wives were seducing them to impurity. And as if family love was a diabolical plot, Pope Gregory I (d. 604) warned his priests to "love their wives as if they were sisters and beware of them as if they were enemies."[75]

By the 500s, the notion that sex was pollution for priests grew dominant among bishops in the Western Church. But most common priests still loved their wives despite all official correction. In 567, the council of Tours threatened to excommunicate any cleric found in bed with his wife. It said: "The Bishop may look upon his wife only as his sister. Wherever he stays, he must always be surrounded by clerics, and his and his wife's dwelling must be separated from one another, so that the clerics in his service never come into contact with the women serving their bishop's wife."[76] This was a proposal of sexual segregation more drastic than any invented in Arabia. The council, however, admitted that if it enforced this rule, the Western Church would lose almost all its priests. Since it wouldn't do to leave the churches empty, the bishops compromised. When they caught a priest loving his wife, the most common penalty was 100 lashes for the wife.[77]

How could the church actually catch clerical families having sex? The council of Toledo in 633 advised watchdogs in the bedroom: "Since the clergy have caused not a little scandal on account of their way of life, the bishops should have witnesses in their rooms, so that all evil suspicions may be removed from the minds of the laity."[78] Some fanatics wanted to castrate priests who loved their wives.

In the 700s, St. Boniface wrote to Pope Zachary, requesting help in forcing celibacy on the married priests of Germany. But on checking the scriptures, Zachary said he could see no such instruction from the Lord. Near as he could tell, the scriptures just said that husbands should love and be loyal to their wives, rather than throwing them out in the street. Many church leaders complained that the real problem was "celibates" in the church who furtively had several concubines.

In reporting the endless lapses in priestly continence, most church officials expressed dismay at the clergy's moral depravity. But the Eastern Orthodox clergy upheld traditional family values, and in 867, Patriarch Photius of Constantinople accused the Roman Church of heresy for repeatedly ordering celibacy in church families. For Photius, the Roman Church had succumbed to a Manichaean belief that matter and flesh were evil.[79] And this was probably the flash point that formally split the Greek and Latin churches in 1054. Because by then, Pope Leo IX was determined to stamp out sex in clerical marriages by any means necessary. His ambassador to Constantinople, Cardinal Humbert, berated the Orthodox leaders, accusing them of sexual depravity: "Young husbands, just now exhausted from carnal lust, serve at the altar. And immediately afterward they again embrace their wives with hands that have been hallowed by the immaculate body of Christ. That is not the mark of true faith, but an invention of Satan!"[80] Photius said it was sad that forced celibacy resulted in "so many children who do not know their own fathers."[81]

And still the drive to stamp out love in church families was getting nowhere. As Bernard of Clairvaux admitted in the 1100s, "To be always with a woman and not to have intercourse with her is more difficult than to raise the dead."[82] If that was the case, then either the whole idea of policing clerical bedrooms was futile, or else the priest's wives had to go. Maybe

Bernard sympathized with first solution. Because when the Albigensian heretics claimed that God calls his elect to renounce marriage, Bernard thundered back prophetically, "Take from the Church an honorable marriage and an immaculate marriage bed, and do you not fill it with concubinage, incest, homosexuality, and every kind of uncleanness?"[83]

If this war on love in church families was so hard to win, what was the problem it was supposed to solve?

Controlling Church Property through Childlessness?

According to some church historians, the rule of priestly chastity arose to prevent any hereditary dynasties within the church. And Pope Gregory VII (1073–85) did argue that the political divisions and wars of Europe's history happened mainly due to squabbles over inheritance. If the church allowed its clergy to have babies, then the children would fight to own the church as well.

Contrary to the biblical record, Pope Gregory held that all the original apostles were celibates, and all their property was pooled in one commune. Since this commune supposedly had no children, its members were loyal to the movement alone. That, Gregory argued, was the true Christian way, to which his holy monks of Cluny had returned. Now, he insisted, all the local priests must also conform to that ideal.[84] All lands and wealth belonging to God's church would then remain under one corporate administration, without risk of being subdivided among heirs like landed estates.

But if this was the real reason for enforcing celibacy, why didn't Jews, Muslims, and Eastern Orthodox Christians outlaw clerical families? Was this measure not needed in Islam, Judaism, or Eastern Christianity? Even in the Roman Church, Pope Pelagius II (in 580) arranged to keep control of church wealth without destroying the staff's families. Pelagius simply ruled that no wives or children of priests could inherit any church property. To enforce this, he ordered each priest to make an inventory of all property in his care on taking office, and then account for it on his departure.[85] In the Greek Church, Justinian's Code of the 500s forbade any member of the clergy from giving or selling anything that belonged to the church. So it was possible to block inheritance to clerical families without destroying the families themselves. On the other hand, the rules against privatizing church wealth could still be violated even with all clerical families destroyed. Long after the great divorce of 1074, Pope Boniface VIII (1294–1303) channeled about a fourth of all church income to his extended relatives.[86] His subordinates felt they couldn't protest, due to the supposedly Christian principle of unquestioning obedience to superiors.

If the existence of church families was so irrelevant to managing church wealth, was this really the reason for destroying church families? After all, corruption existed everywhere. And if people were usually corrupt in order to favor their own families, few leaders in world history ever proposed to correct the problem by banning families. But that's just what the Roman Church did. Was it more concerned about eliminating women than controlling property?

Pope Gregory VII wanted his clergy totally loyal to the organization. The church of his dreams was a military-style task force under one commander-in-chief. But the priests who had wives were rooted to their homes. Their devotion to women competed with loyalty to the all-male church.[87] Maybe that competing influence from women was more of a problem in Western Europe than it was in the East.

Finding Strength through Avoiding Strong Western Women

In the old Near East, Jewish rabbis or Muslim mullahs were expected to uphold local traditions, including traditions of male authority over wives. In many cases, the more holy these men aspired to be, the more strictly they tried to control their women. The Near Easterners commonly controlled (or protected) females by imposing a segregation of women from public life, known in Arabic as *purdah*. And where men had long dictated the parameters of women's lives, this could work. But in Western Europe, the incoming Christian priesthood was in no position to dictate the boundaries of women's lives.

In Western Europe, women's traditional powers were a challenge to the church's imported Middle Eastern values. When European priests married Western European women, the traditional equality between partners often remained. Church doctrine might teach that a priest must be the family head, but their wives were often leaders as well. Where local people trusted the village wise women more than male priests, the wives could easily eclipse their husbands' influence. If a priest's wife had a stronger personality than her husband, she could shape his views. If she supported local women's traditions more than the all-male church, she would be subverting the parish to paganism. A compromised priest might stand aside to allow the women's festivals and oracles. He might tolerate their ministering to the villagers' spiritual and bodily health. But the church hierarchy claimed a monopoly on these services. It expected its priests to take charge and make no deals with the competition.

Either such challenges slowly grew over time, or they just showed no sign of fading away. But obviously, the church hierarchy's patience ran out. According to church historian Thomas Bokenkotter, the great Gregorian reform for priestly chastity gathered force because the hierarchy realized how strongly marriage assimilated its clerics to Western women's values.[88] In some exasperation, Pope Gregory VII declared, "The church cannot escape from the clutches of the laity unless priests first escape the clutches of their wives."[89]

To solve this problem, the church decreed a kind of *purdah* in reverse. Instead of trying to enforce a seclusion of women from public life, it segregated its priests from women. Evidently, having strong wives was not so big a problem for clerics in the East.

The Problems of Enacting Mass Divorce

Around the year 1000, the Roman hierarchy shifted from trying to end sex in clerical families, to a goal of ending the families period. But how to do it was still a practical and a moral question. Because speaking on the issue of divorce, Jesus said that if a man and woman really loved each other, they would never find cause to separate. Taking these words legalistically, the Roman Church had long taught that the only moral justification for divorce was adultery. But if that was its doctrine, how could the clergy justify divorcing their mainly loyal wives *en masse*?

Basically, the monastic popes tackled the means before clarifying the justification. They weren't, after all, accountable to any electorate of sinners. Pope Nicholas II aimed to make it impossible for married priests to operate. In 1059 he denounced all married priests as sinners, and threatened to excommunicate any parishioner who accepted communion from a married priest.[90] This, however, implied recognition of the old Donatist heresy — that the sacraments were invalid if served by a sinful priest. And at this, the "heretical" critics of church hypocrisy made such hay, that Nicholas withdrew his ruling.

It took a more determined celibate like Pope Gregory VII to make the divorce stick. Gregory renewed the bans on married priests in 1074, and this time there was no backing down. When high-ranking churchmen such as Bishop Otto of Constance refused to enforce the order, Gregory excommunicated them without hesitation. When parish priests ignored the order, Gregory ordered dukes and princes to use armed force or suffer excommunication from God themselves.[91] The married priests found themselves cut off by both their employers and their customers — unless they renounced the sin of loving a woman. By such tactics Gregory won an official victory, "sundering the commerce between the clergy and women through an eternal anathema."[92] With seeming papal approval, gangs of lay people publicly taunted priests' wives as whores. These women found that their men's employers presumed to banish them from their homes, as if they had no right to exist. Local officials were authorized to beat offending church wives till they fled for their lives. Some of the cast-out women killed themselves.

As many thousands of church women were driven out to the roads, a conclave of Italian bishops in 1076 tried to excommunicate Pope Gregory for the crime of destroying families.[93] Sigebert of Gembloux wrote, "Many have seen in the ban on attending mass of a married priest an open contradiction to the teaching of the fathers. This has led to such a great scandal that the church has never been split by a greater schism."[94] Again Gregory fired the protesting clerics. In real concern, the Eastern Church Patriarch Petros of Antioch suggested that the Pope must not know of the old Council of Nicea ruling on clerical marriage from 325, possibly due to general destruction of records when the Goths or Vandals sacked Rome.[95] That ruling from Nicea read in part, "Whatever presbyter or deacon shall put away his wife without the offense of fornication . . . and shall cast her out of doors . . . such a person shall be cast out of the clergy. . ."[96]

Many priests grew violent to defend their families. In the Paris Synod of 1074, Abbot Galter of Saint Martin demanded the flock follow its shepherd in celibacy. A mob of outraged priests beat him, spit on him, and threw him in the street. In the same year Archbishop John of Rouen threatened to excommunicate protesting priests, and had to flee for his life under a hail of stones. In furious debate, the celibate party denounced its opponents as fornicators trying to prostitute the church. Married priests hurled back accusations that their foes were sodomites, whose obvious preference for homosexuality made them hate married families.[97] For decades church synods regularly broke into fistfights, with monks and priests smashing each other's faces. In 1233, protesters murdered papal legate Conrad of Marburg, who was touring Germany partly to enforce chastity.[98] In England, furious priests locked their churches, hid their families, and tried to keep them in secret.[99]

Since many clerical couples clung to each other, the hierarchy applied stronger measures. In 1089, Pope Urban II ruled that if a priest did not dispose of his wife, the local prince could enslave the woman. A decade later, Archbishop Manasse II of Rheims asked the Count of Flanders to throw priest's wives into prison. In London, Archbishop Anselm said that any women found living with a priest would be taken as human property of the local bishop.[100] The enslavement orders suggest that higher clerics and lords took this opportunity to pick whatever exiled wives and children they wanted as servants, and sold others on the slave markets.

Some decades after the great divorce, the hierarchy gave a theological justification for it. The Second Lateran Council in 1139 re-defined ordination as automatically invalidating any previous marriage. It cursed all relations between priests and women as "fornication," and ruled that all children of priests were "sacrilegious bastards."[101] Pope Alexander III (1159–81) explained that holy vows were more important than marriage, and those called to serve the church could annul their marriages to meet a higher obligation.[102] The hierarchy was following a higher law than any words of Jesus in requiring that priests dump their wives and children.

Correcting Love among the Laity

How did the doctrine of celibacy affect the message of the church? If the official carriers of Jesus' teaching now practiced apartheid between the sexes, what message did that media convey?

After adopting a host of ancient rules for ranking of males over females, the church reached a point of viewing all contact between men and women as a sin. As Matfré Ermengaud put it in the 1200s, "Satan, in order to make men suffer bitterly, makes them adore women; for instead of loving as they should, the creator with fervent love, with all their heart, with all their mind . . . they sinfully love women."[103] It seemed that only males who had no part in such pollution could mediate forgiveness for it. If that was the Christian message, then it was natural for people like Abelard's lover Heloise to reply, "Woe that ever love was sin!"

The Western Church's banishment of women sent a message at which the popular mind recoiled. As the church ruled sexual love a depravity to be repressed, the public turned with growing appetite to love minstrels and legends of heroic knights and ladies. The church still held a monopoly on publishing and religious teaching, but popular oral culture escaped control. Most secular singers or legend tellers avoided directly criticizing the church, since the clerics might kill them. The folk artists just affirmed their own dreams and ideals, which were totally different. In a safely secular mode, Walther von Vogelweide sang "German ladies, fair as God's angels; anyone who defames them lies in his teeth."[104] And in the rounds of Arthurian legend such as Wolfram von Eschenbach's *Parzival*, the land's true heroes were strong men and women, inspired to glorious deeds by love for each other. Instead of portraying women as the sinful sex that men must control or rise above, these legends cast women as uplifters, initiators, and guides for all men of real heart. Sexual love and devotion were holy sacraments, more powerfully uplifting to the spirit than any priestly ritual.

How could the bishops respond to this? Some clerics tried to forbid street plays, secular festivals, love songs, and other forms of sin. Others tried a more positive approach, of co-opting secular art to make its message fit church teaching. Around the year 1220, a Cistercian monk wrote a revised version of the Grail myth, *La Queste del Saint Graal*. In this account, the winner of the grail quest was not a married man like Parzival. It was the chaste knight Galahad, who won the grail due to his innocence from all corruption, and his virtuous horror of women.[105] Both

Galahad and his equally chaste sister finished their quest by renouncing all desire for this world, shaking off their mortal coils, and ascending into heaven. It was not a wildly popular ending. Dante's adoration for Beatrice drew vastly more readers. As Will Durant explains, "a conflict arose between the morals of noble ladies and the ethics of the church; and in the feudal world, the ladies and the poets won."[106]

The problems of enforcing the great divorce were legion. Priests had to be trained in schools rather than raised to the profession by watching their clerical fathers. The average wife-less priest had less time for parish work because he had to do more cooking, gardening, cleaning, hauling water, chopping wood, going to market, etc. Many priests hired serving maids. And often the maids were their former wives, now demoted to servant status by the church of Jesus. And then there was the problem of sexually repressed priests. Most apparent was the rise of concubinage, which grew so prevalent that the church decided to impose a sin-tax on priests for each concubine.[107] In 1415, Cardinal Zabarella urged the church Council of Constance that if concubinage could not be suppressed, then clerical marriage should be restored. The Holy Roman Emperor Sigismund told the Council of Basil (1431) that restoring marriage in the church would improve public morals. In this period, the term "avaricious" entered common language, meaning "lecherous as a priest or a monk."[108] Even Pope Alexander VI (1492–1503) must have agreed that requiring clerical celibacy had been a mistake, because he openly fathered at least five children.[109]

Martin Luther's clerical rebellion rode partly on popular rejection of sexual apartheid. As he wrote in his address "To the Christian Nobility of the German Nation":

And now the see of Rome, out of its own wickedness, has come up with the idea of forbidding priests to marry. This it has done on orders from the

121

Devil, as Paul proclaims in 1Timothy, 4: "Teachers will come with teachings from the Devil and forbid people to marry." This has led to a great deal of misery, and was the reason why the Greek Church broke away. I advise that everyone be left free to get married or not get married.[110]

In response to such criticism, Papal Nuncio Morone wrote to the Archbishop of Brandenburg in 1542; "I know that all my priests are living in concubinage. But what should I do to stop it? If I forbid them concubines, they either want to have wives or to become Lutherans."[111]

Later generations of Catholics found more problems with banning sexuality in priests. As Canada's 1990 Winter Commission report on child abuse at the Mount Cashel orphanage said, "Compulsory celibacy is cited as a factor that has contributed to immature sexual development, which can lead to furtive and dysfunctional sexual relationships on the part of priests who cannot live up to this requirement."[112]

Many people accused the Church of teaching contempt for both marriage and women. And to cope with such concerns, the Catholic Council of Trent (1545–63) officially established marriage as a holy sacrament, for the first time in church history. This seemed to affirm love and women in a fresh way, almost like Jesus at the wedding in Cana. But the Catechism on the Sacrament of Marriage still instructed couples it would be better, ". . . that all would wish to strive after the virtue of continence, for believers can find nothing more blessed in this life than that their spirit, distracted by no worldly cares and after quieting and subduing every pleasure of the flesh, should rest solely in the zeal of godliness and in the contemplation of heavenly things."[113] For any who doubted this, the Trent Council warned, "If anyone says that it is not better and more godly to live in virginity or the unmarried state, let him be anathema."[114]

Humbling Women in the Wider Society

According to orthodox theory, no woman should ever serve as leader or manager for any man. In secular society, females were legal wards of their fathers, husbands, or grown sons. This supposedly left no occasion for female leaders, save in the case of widowed family heads. As Martin Luther gave the prevailing, remarkably Middle Eastern ideal, "The rule remains with the husband, and the wife is compelled to obey him by God's command. He rules at home and [in] the state, wages war, defends his possessions, tills the soil, plants, etc. The wife on the other hand, is like a nail driven into the wall. She sits at home."[115] Of course these standards for ordinary women didn't quite apply to all the Queens ruling Spain, England, Parma, Savoy or Austria, but every context has its limits.

To legally ban ordinary women from formal leadership was simple. As they were barred from clerical office and marriage to the clergy, so they were increasingly banned from joining guilds, owning land, etc. But controlling women's informal powers was a harder thing. Most women needed no official position to influence the people around them. Outside church they spoke in public and shaped opinions. They still ran businesses, drank in taverns, or lent money. Though a growing maze of regulations restricted their right to compete with male bakers, tailors, or butchers, they still practiced hundreds of necessary crafts. They organized charities, often doing more for their communities than the priests, monks, or nuns. Widows represented their families in local councils, and defended their interests vigorously. When feudal and church lords claimed rights to control their female serfs, the women could be uncontrollably defiant. It seemed to openly contradict advice from monks like St. Odo of Cluny that "the highest virtue in a woman is not to wish to be seen."[116]

Where medieval lawmakers tried to restrict women's powers, the women commonly fought back. If a man claimed legal rights over property held by his female relatives, the local women might gather to shame him for his greed. They might call down curses, uttering threats of magical castration. In Germany, Franciscan friar Berthold of Regensburg (mid-1200s) felt that women were notorious for illicit magic: ". . . spells for getting a husband, spells for the marriage, spells before the child is born, spells before the christening . . . it is a marvel that men lose not their wits for the monstrous witchcrafts that women practice upon them."[117] If a woman influenced others with her "charming" nature, this medieval term suggested she cast spells and charms. If she won people's hearts to a cause of her own, she was "bewitching."[118] So The Penitential Book of the bishop of Exeter cursed women "who profess to be able to change men's minds by sorcery and enchantments, as from hate to love or love to hate, or to bewitch and steal men's goods . . ."[119]

The Final Solution to Female Insubordination

Since women were banished from the family of the church, they seemed to be a separate camp, more opposed to the church and more prone to sin. Since all women stood outside the legitimate priesthood, any spiritual power they displayed had to be illegitimate. If Joan of Arc claimed visions and prophecies from God, but was clearly not a member of the clergy, then the bishops felt it obvious her gifts were not from God. Of course the same argument was used on Jesus by the priests of his day. In general, any initiative from inferiors was subversive to superiors, and subversion was the Devil's cause.

Obviously, many medieval people feared and believed in witches. But beliefs concerning black magic were ancient features of the cultural landscape, and had rarely caused widespread alarm in the past. Something had to shift in the nature of those beliefs to produce the witch hunts. For a taste of the older pre-witch hunt folklore, Raphael Patai described the underworld of ancient Jewish demonology:

At night, the female Liliths join men, and the male Lilin women, to generate demonic offspring. Once they succeed in attaching themselves to a human, they acquire rights of cohabitation, and therefore must be given a get, or letter of divorce, in order that they may be expelled. Jealous of the human mates of their bedfellows, they hate the children born of ordinary wedlock, attack them, plague them, suck their blood, and strangle them. The Liliths also manage to prevent the birth of children, causing barrenness, miscarriages, or complications during childbirth.[120]

This old myth suggested a certain equality of male and female evil spirits. The spirits were of both sexes, and they afflicted men and women equally. The human hosts of evil were innocent victims, who must be somehow saved from harm. This was roughly what Jesus believed about demonic possession. But in the late Middle Ages, this sense of equality among victims, and of compassion for their plight, tended to disappear. Increasingly, people "possessed" by bad spirits were deemed guilty of inviting evil into themselves. And those accused of conjuring evil were mainly women. By the late 1400s, a new handbook for investigating witches, the famous *Malleus Maleficarum*, seemed to presume that women themselves were evil spirits: "You do not know that woman is the Chimera, but it is good that you should know it; for that monster was of three forms; its face was that of a radiant and noble lion, it had the filthy belly of a goat and it was armed with the virulent tail of a viper. And he means that a woman is beautiful to look upon, contaminating to touch, and deadly to keep."[121]

Of course Jesus viewed such vilification of other people as simple inhumanity. But the Dominican friars who wrote the *Malleus Maleficarum* believed their frankly murderous hostility towards women was deeply religious. For them, the mission of Christ's church was to march through the sinful world destroying evil. And the primary evildoers, it seems, were those already excluded from the family of the church for their sinful nature. In these clerics' eyes, it was mainly women who hid rebellion against God in their hearts. Women were the ones accused of "whoring after other gods."

Already in 1326 Pope John XXII announced the threat of witchcraft was real, and told the Inquisition to seek it out. In Carcassonne and Toulouse, the prosecutors called for informers to accuse their neighbors, and interrogated the accused. Since Pope Innocent III had abolished trials by ordeal in 1215, the investigators felt they needed other means of extracting the truth. They used torture to secure confessions, and force more accusations against others. Until the system of trial by jury emerged, the legal systems required confessions to convict, and judges assumed no guilty party would confess unless tortured. In Carcassonne the tribunal investigated some 400 witchcraft suspects over a period of over ten years, found perhaps half of these guilty, and burned them to death.

Over the next 150 years, the reports of evil plots gathered under torture fed a slowly growing conspiracy theory. By 1484, Pope Innocent VIII officially confirmed that witches could fly, had sexual intercourse with the devil, held anti-Christian rites, and made pacts with Satan. With their powers they blighted crops to cause famine, cursed neighbors with plagues, or made children wither and die. Of course these were the dangers every villager feared most. When the Church named a cause behind these calamities, it seemed to take the lead in preventing them.

Pope Innocent's warning of 1484 brought a rapid widening of investigations. Within a year we hear of 167 people killed in Grenoble, 157 in Wurzburg, 41 in Como, Italy, and 100 or so in the Piedmont valley.[122] By the time the torturers were done, dozens of local people could be marched through the streets to be burned in huge bonfires. These events were like religious revivals in reverse. Instead of calling sinners to be saved and rejoicing in their repentance, they called for sinners to be denounced and executed so the community could be purged of evil. And almost everywhere, a solid majority of those executed were women.

Since the *Malleus Maleficarum* was one of the earliest mass-produced books, we can credit the printing press for spreading the witch hunts. And with such international publicity, the pressure to conduct investigations increased across whole regions. In the course of interrogations, one accusation led to the next. According to trial records in Lorraine, Georgeatte Didier threatened that if she was accused, "she would accuse others whether they were good women or not." Chrestaille Wathot said if she was arrested, "I would accuse such important people of witchcraft that they would release me for the love of them."[123] The trial process handed accused witches the power to denounce anyone they wanted revenge on.

If ordinary villagers already feared being cursed by evil powers, the anti-witch inquisitions stoked those fears. They also escalated people's fears of being accused. And where both those fears took hold, some communities dissolved into panic attacks of accusations and counter-denunciations. By the time these seasons of terror ebbed, some villages in Germany had scarcely a female left alive. In some places even little girls were burned. Perhaps a little girl's fear of such deadly church discipline seemed to imply she had something to hide. But while these horrors unfolded in some communities, other nearby villages often went untouched, without any neighbor accusing another. The huge contrast highlights the importance of local people's choices. If the villagers refused to label each other as evil, the persecutors had no entry point.

According to some reports, the witch hunts targeted strong women who threatened the authorities in some way. Others claim the prosecuted were the weakest members of society. Father Pierre de Lancre described the devil's agents as desperate poor people: "For when people see themselves reduced to starvation, after the Devil has removed the fruits of the earth, they commit a thousand wickednesses to live, and Satan seeing them in this desperate need, forces them to beg for his help, and from beggars turns them finally into witches."[124] But whether the so-called witches were mainly weak or strong women, they were still people the church and local authorities feared. From our times we know how desperate people are often feared more than pitied. And church leaders would not persecute people unless they saw a threat to their interests. Quite possibly, poverty, desperation, and the threat of insubordinate women, all went together quite naturally.

Recent historians have tried to cut through various legends surrounding the witch hunts. Their surveys of records indicate a sporadic, very spotty series of persecutions. The total numbers killed were probably "only" several tens of thousands over a span of some 300 years. The vast majority of victims died in Northwestern Europe, and many of these in a handful of the worst episodes, such as Trier and Scotland in the 1590s, or Bamberg and Cologne in the 1620s to 30s. In Spain, the Inquisition generally regarded fear of witches as utter foolishness.

Perhaps in Spain and Italy the authorities were confident that no conspiracy of women could seriously threaten their world. But in Peru, the Spanish authorities were quite concerned over the powers of native women. The Peruvian Incas had traditional religious "societies of the sun" for men, and "societies of the moon" for women. The Spanish conquerors immediately assumed that societies of the moon were covens of witches. Wherever the missionary churchmen of that age found females in religious power, they tried to correct the mistake.

Controlling Religious Women

We might assume that so much abuse would turn women against the Church. But actually, the clergy had the opposite problem. Too many women wanted to be better Christians than their priests. Even the wives dumped in the great divorce commonly wished to outdo their former husbands in living like Jesus. The former wives often demanded admission to a nunnery. And bowing to pressure, Abbot Hugh of Cluny opened a convent for wives abandoned by his monks. He evidently felt that if these women had to be divorced, then they too should have a place to live in chastity. Of course the nuns had to be strictly enclosed, as Hugh explained, lest "in appearing in the world they either made others desire them, or saw things which they themselves desired."[125] Perhaps Hugh wished these overly desirable creatures could be somehow delivered to heaven directly, without posing any further risks to anyone's salvation.

But cloistered nuns were almost as big a problem as wives for the male hierarchy. A convent near a monastery was both an expense and a spiritual peril to male monks. Many orders found their patience with both problems wearing thin. Shortly before 1200, the General Chapter of the Premonstratensians decided on budget cuts for nunneries. The cuts were so severe that many women took to the roads as begging nuns. Abbot Conrad of Marchtal insisted that no more females be admitted. He explained,

> *We and our whole community of canons, recognizing that the wickedness of women is greater than all the other wickedness of the world, and that there is no anger like that of women, and that the poison of asps and dragons is more curable and less dangerous to men than the familiarity of women, have unanimously decreed for the safety of our souls, no less than that of our bodies and goods, that we will on no account receive any more sisters to the increase of our perdition, but will avoid them like poisonous animals.*[126]

Still, some nuns like Hildegard of Bingen made their convents islands of female-controlled community in a male-controlled world. Inside their convent walls, women could be fairly free to pursue their own spiritual goals. But as for playing any role in the outside world, they were generally no freer than inmates in a Middle Eastern harem. That seemed to be the official Christian vision for women's highest potential, and the male church heads seemed zealous to enforce it as any Middle Eastern patriarchs. So inside their cloisters, what did these brides of Jesus hope to achieve? Were they creating ideal communities to heal the world, or basically hiding from worldly sin? As ex-nun Karen Armstrong asked, "What was a virgin to do inside this fortress which saw enemies everywhere?"[127] Much to their male superiors' concern, many of them wished to be of service to the world.

The Female Reformation

By the late Middle Ages, popular religious art began portraying simple "acts of mercy" as suggested in the Gospel of Matthew: "As you did it for one of these, the least of my brethren, you did it for me." The pictures showed deeds which anyone might do, like feeding the hungry, giving water to the thirsty, welcoming strangers, tending the sick, visiting prisoners.[128] Anybody might do these things, but if cloistered nuns did them, they would have to go outside. And if they went out, they would be virgins among male wolves. They would only endanger their virginity, bring shame on the church, and disgrace themselves.

Of course many religious women had greater concerns than their own chastity. Already in the 1100s, Clara Blassoni in Milan left her cloister to start public clinics for "lepers," and named her organization the Hospitallers of the Observance. In the 1200s, Franciscan sister Margaret of Cortona also opened a public clinic, then got involved stopping street gang wars. After that she rebuked the Bishop of Arezzo for abusing church funds. Very likely, the clergy were protecting more than Margaret's virginity in wishing her re-enclosed.

For several centuries nuns like this ventured out, and were soon chased off the streets by clerical morality police. In the early 1600s, the cat and mouse game was still on, as English nun Mary Ward (1585–1645) formed a group called the Institute of the Blessed Virgin, for educating children "in the world." The Board of Cardinals expressed doubt in "the power of women to do aught of good to any but themselves in a life consecrated to God." In 1631, Pope Urban VIII felt it best to suppress the order, though it had already spread through five nations, and engaged near 300 women teaching previously unschooled children. When the women resisted re-enclosure, the church disowned Ward's nuns as heretics. They sentenced Mary to a small locked cell in a convent of the Poor Clares. Finally her superiors "pardoned" her, and allowed her to live out her days in a traditional cloister.[129]

This rule of purdah for religious women slowly broke down as growing numbers of nuns insisted there was more to Christianity than sexual abstinence. From Saint Teresa of Avila (in the 1500s) we hear:

> *When thou wert in the world, Lord, thou didst not despise women, but did always help them and show them great compassion. Thou didst find more faith and no less love in them than in men . . . [Now however,] we can do nothing in public that is of any use to thee, nor dare we speak of some of the truths over which we weep in secret, lest thou shouldst not hear this, our petition. Yet, Lord, I cannot believe this of thy goodness and righteousness for thou art a righteous Judge, not like the judges of the world, who, being after all men and sons of Adam, refuse to consider any woman's virtue above suspicion. Yes, my King, but the day will come when all will be known.*[130]

Teresa was a pre-modern nun, who chafed at her bonds of enclosure.

She felt that living like Jesus must involve travel, teaching, service, and controversy. As one papal nuncio complained, Teresa was "a disobedient contumacious woman who promulgates pernicious doctrines under the pretense of devotion, who left her cloister against the orders of her superiors, who is ambitious, and teaches theology as though she were a doctor of the Church, in contempt of St. Paul, who forbade women to teach."[131] But to Teresa, it seemed that the requirements of self-denial and isolation did less to protect her chastity than to protect the world from her own caring hands: "It seemed to me that, considering what St. Paul says about women keeping at home (I have already been reminded of this and I had already heard it) that this might be God's will. But He said to me, "Tell them that they are not to be guided by one part of the Scripture alone, but to look at others; ask them if they suppose they will be able to tie my hands."[132]

The first international service order founded by a woman appeared in 1531, as Angela Merici formed her association of Ursulines. Her aim was to open schools for girls, an idea whose time had not quite come. She started by inviting unschooled girls into her home for classes, and then slowly recruited an "association of virgins" for teaching. Actually, the women who joined were mainly widows, not young virgins, and perhaps that helped ease clerical anxiety over the women's chastity on the job. While not teaching class, the Ursulines lived in their family homes, supposedly under protection of male relatives. That was also more acceptable than nuns leaving convents. The resulting "Ursuline order" was a religious society without communal living, whose unity was its vocation of service. Many prominent townsmen appreciated the Ursulines' work, and their own daughters often benefited. But lay approval couldn't prevent the Council of Trent (in 1562) from issuing another blanket ban on religious women operating outside convent walls. For most bishops, the issue still seemed to be creeping sexual laxity. By 1572 Cardinal Borromeo prevailed on the Ursulines to start living in cloistered nunneries, and have the students come to them there.

As in many things, the church seesawed back and forth on the enclosure issue. In 1605 a deadly plague swept Bordeaux, and Cistercian nun Jeanne de Lestonnac led her sisters into the streets to treat the sick. After the crisis passed, Jeanne formed her Company of Mary Our Lady to continue the work. And in 1607, the Pope apparently overruled the Council of Trent by approving Jeanne's new order.

The next re-enclosure decree of 1631 affected a growing host of service orders, including the Institute of the Blessed Virgin, the Ursulines, the Company of Mary Our Lady, the Visitandines, Elisabeth Strowen's sisters in Maastricht, and those of Isabel Roses of Barcelona. The church, it seemed, would close them all down rather than let women play a leadership role. In the past, a papal order might have done it. But now, the popular demand for education and health care services from these women was so great, that only two years passed before the church again (temporarily) dropped its re-enclosure orders.

Maybe it was now obvious that the nuns couldn't be restrained. Maybe the rapidly growing towns were crying out for caregivers, and the authorities finally accepted any help they could get, even from consecrated virgins. At any rate, by the mid-1600s the Ursulines had 255 houses offering education. The French Carmelite nuns also set up many schools and homes for girls, of which a supporter wrote, "The world is astonished to see us seek so eagerly for what the world recks so little of . . . that is the souls of females."[133] Around the same time, the Sisters of Charity began offering a program of health service the world can still learn from; their hospitals were centers for outreach care to poor people in their homes. They even went to war zones and got named "angels of the battlefield."

Nothing so revived the Catholic Church after the Protestant revolt as the female religious orders and their self-made new vocations. Their movement for a calling beyond chastity set the context for a new church, which increasingly saw itself as a caring servant, not a godly master of society. Where many priests formerly tried to hold their parishioners to obedience through threats of excommunication or worse, the socially active nuns were a magnet, representing an older version Christianity. Instead of mediating between the rulers of earth and heaven through cloistered prayer, the new wave of religious women aimed to serve the sick, hungry, uneducated and homeless, who filled the cities of early modern Europe. These women showed what the church would have been from the first, if women hadn't been forcefully barred from partnership in its mission. And while male monastic orders slowly declined, the female service orders grew with a new sense of purpose. In the 23 years between 1766 and 1789, the numbers of male monks in France slumped from 26,000 to 17,000, while the nuns increased to over 37,000. The Archbishop of Tours complained that "The Grey Friars are in a state of degeneration in this province; the bishops complain of their debaucheries and disorderly life."[134] After the French Revolution, the National Assembly voted to suppress all monasteries, take their long-accumulated wealth for the state, and pay off the monks with pensions. But in view of their services to public health, welfare, and education, the female orders, at least in France, went untouched.[135]

The Legitimate Vocations for Lay Women

In the Protestant revolts, many Western clergymen tried to recover the priestly family as known in the Old Testament. Instead of upholding celibacy as the proper ideal for all Christians, Luther distrusted it so much that he wished to ban monastic vows for anyone under age thirty. Other Protestants went further, to re-launch a culture war between monastic and "secular" clergy. Where the monks had imposed their celibacy on parish priests, now rebel clergymen encouraged their rulers to close the abbeys, turf out the monks or nuns, and confiscate the monastery lands. With hardly an afterthought, these reformers tried to abolish nunneries, which had been the only sites for women's religious leadership. And in lands which went officially Protestant, this was done. As the Protestant Augsburg town council justified its decision to destroy these communities in 1534, "How should it come to any good when women join themselves in a separate life, contrary to the ordinance of God, yes, against nature, they give themselves to obedience to a woman, who has neither reason nor the understanding to govern whether in spiritual or temporal matters, who ought not to govern but be governed?"[136]

Many new wives of pastors had been former nuns, such as Luther's wife Kate. Others were former mistresses of former priests. As befit the age in Germany, these wives almost invariably dressed in the self-effacing style of household servants, making female humility a point of religious pride.[137] But since Protestants had no religious orders, it seemed for a time their women's highest vocation was homemaking, plus part-time voluntary service to their congregations. And growing numbers of Protestant women felt this was insufficient. They wanted a vocation beyond homemaking, but without organizational backing they were mostly on their own. Besides, the burdens of family work were usually so great for women, that few could manage even a few hours of wider community service per week. If males could now combine religious vocation with family life, that still seemed an impossible dream for most females.

Only in the 1800s did Protestant women start to recover what they lost with the suppression of religious orders. In England during the 1840s a women's society arose offering full-time nursing, education, and care for the elderly. Almost automatically people called these women "the nuns." Florence Nightingale was another example of a Protestant clearly inspired by the Catholic Sisters of Charity.[138] In Germany a similar professional service association formed during the 1830s, and people dubbed them "the deaconesses." Groups like this seemed to open a floodgate.

Within a few decades, the numbers of women in public service vocations rose to surpass the numbers of clergymen or members of religious orders, at least in Western Europe and North America. By the 1880s and 90s their efforts generated whole new industries in previously unvalued "welfare" work — mother and child welfare, family welfare, campaigns to eradicate tuberculosis and venereal disease, to raise awareness about nutrition or implement standards for sanitation and housing. In Germany, *Fürsorge* (welfare) became a catchword for a hundred newly popular initiatives to "improve" people's lives and relations.[139] These were the kinds of priorities that gained ground as Christian women's values entered the public domain. As Rosemary Radford Ruether describes it, "Reform of working and social conditions and public sanitation was thereby defined as an extension of a woman's housekeeping role in the family."[140] Some of these activist women started to see themselves as the truest Christians, and even the spiritually superior sex, with a clear calling from Jesus to reform the world. In the United States, the Women's Christian Temperance Union attempted moral crusades against alcohol addiction, child labor, and even war. Of course other women rejected all this as clear a violation of Christian tradition. One woman wrote to *Catholic World* magazine in 1893 to correct all her activist sisters and insist it was "beyond question" that women were banned from any role in public life.[141]

5. Correcting Freedom

What, if anything, did Jesus say about freedom? In his first recorded speech he quoted Isaiah: "He has sent me to proclaim release to the captives and recovering of sight to the blind, to set at liberty those who are oppressed . . ." (Luke 4:18) Later, Paul claimed "Christ set us free, to be free men. Stand firm then, and refuse to be tied to the yoke of slavery again." (Galatians 5:1) Some of these lines sounded like Moses speaking to the slaves in Egypt, and naturally the Romans were concerned. Usually, talk like that led to revolt against the powers that were. So the Romans suspected Jesus and his followers of insubordination. And while some Christians defiantly confirmed their rejection of Roman values, others insisted they were loyal subjects. Some claimed that Jesus never advocated freedom from conquerors, slaveholders, or abusive husbands; he stood for some other kind of freedom, like freedom from sin, from God's wrath, or from stiff-necked Judaism.

Later, many church leaders described Jesus as the ultimate king, whose every command was universal law. In that spirit, a retreat facilitator for the Cornerstone Church in San Antonio recently explained, "You're either blessed because you're obedient or cursed because you're disobedient."[1] But if that was Jesus' point, how did he deal with disobedient followers? According to John, a number of disciples grew angry at Jesus: "From that time on, many of his disciples withdrew, and no longer went about with him." And rather than cursing these departing followers, Jesus asked the remaining ones, "Do you want to leave me too?" (6:66–67) It seems he assumed people were free to either follow him or not. Like other ancient teachers, he accepted that students chose their teachers, and if they found their teacher offensive, they were free to try another.

Some of Jesus' followers wanted more control over other people.

They wanted to restrict who could speak about him, reporting "Master . . . we saw a man driving out devils in your name, but as he is not one of us we tried to stop him." (Luke 9:49–50) Later his students fought over "who among them should rank highest." But he ridiculed the arrogance of such ambition: "In the world, kings lord it over their subjects; and those in authority are called their country's 'Benefactors.' " Real leaders, he said, were like servants, not superiors. (Luke 22:24–26) When people repeatedly asked him which authorities they should obey, he wondered "Why can't you decide for yourselves what is right?" (Luke 12:57)

Paul had more difficulty with these issues of freedom. He boldly proclaimed the equality of all, and then argued with the Greeks: "We are free to do anything you say, but is everything good for us?" (I Corinthians 10:23) He tried to stop his students from following other teachers, partly by claiming a divine appointment to authority. He made appeals to Roman magistrates, apparently hoping for endorsement from the government. Later evangelists would succeed at this, getting whole populations to convert by their rulers' decree. It was more efficient than plodding peasant to peasant. Confucianists in China used a similar strategy: "Correct what is wrong in the prince's mind, and the kingdom will be settled."[2]

If "forgiveness" was the biggest controversy for first-century Christians, probably freedom has been a bigger issue ever since. From ancient Rome forward, church teaching about freedom has wandered all over the moral map. By around AD 400 it became church doctrine that faith required blind obedience to superiors. The kings of Christendom claimed their dictatorial powers by divine right, and supposedly received their mantles of authority from Jesus' hands. To most subjects of the Holy Roman Empire, it would appear simply inaccurate of Jesus to say that real leaders were servants, not masters. In medieval times many clerics took their authority so seriously, that they felt it was their holy duty to kill people who rejected their leadership. For over 1,500 years it passed for heresy against Jesus' religion to use the story of Exodus as an appeal for freeing slaves. As far as the parishioners were told, Christianity regarded freedom as a sin.

In recent centuries many Christians assumed that the French Revolutionary slogan of "liberty, equality, fraternity," was diametrically opposed to everything Jesus stood for. Yet in the American Revolution, similar values were seen as Christian. And both sides in the great conflicts over slavery claimed to defend Jesus' values. In England, the devoutly Catholic Lord Acton rejected Protestant prejudice that his church was an enemy of freedom, saying, "Liberty is so holy a thing, that God was forced to permit Evil, that it might exist."[3] We might suppose that all modern American Christians would agree. But recently Senator Rick Santorum discounted the liberation message of many Black churches, saying "When you take a salvation story and turn it into a liberation story you've abandoned Christendom, and I don't think you have a right to claim it."[4] On no subject has Christian "orthodoxy" been more explosively changeable.

The Powers of Church Members

Of course primitive Christianity was never a democracy as we know it. Jesus and the first apostles chose their most promising students to continue their work. This resembled Buddhist teaching lineages, where master teachers choose their best students to succeed them. But the students in both these traditions were still free to choose which teachers to learn from, and free to leave at any time. Many early preachers claimed themselves chosen to lead by the successors of an apostle. But they still had no means of making others follow them, or stopping people from following anyone else. Like Jesus, they had only their personal powers of persuasion. Before the 300s, if two preachers both claimed to lead a community, it was not inevitable that one must lose. Nothing stopped them from operating different house-churches, and letting the local Christians decide who to patronize. It wasn't an election system, but the teachers chose what students to accept, and the locals chose what leaders to follow.

In the Didache, we find a record of deliberations by second-century churches in Syria. And one set of issues they discussed was the selection and accountability of leaders. At the time, various preachers were traveling through the area, and these local churches discussed how to handle visiting "prophets." The recommendations they made showed no concern for establishing rank among leaders, but only for testing their authenticity. They were willing to help a visitor, but refused to be anyone's fool:

> And concerning the apostles and prophets . . . let every apostle that cometh unto you be received as the Lord. And he shall stay one day, and, if need be, the next also, but if he stay three, he is a false prophet. And when an apostle goes forth, let him take nothing save bread, till he reacheth his lodging, but if he asks for money he is a false prophet. And every prophet that speaketh in the spirit ye shall not judge: for every sin shall be forgiven. But not everyone that speaketh in the spirit is a prophet, but if he have the ways of the Lord, by their ways then shall the false prophet and the prophet be known. And any prophet that orders a table [or ritual meal] in the spirit shall not eat of it; else he is a false prophet. And every prophet that teaches the truth, if he does not what he teaches is a false prophet . . . but, if he bid you give for others that are in need, let no one judge him . . . (Didache 11:3–12)[5]

This was roughly how village synagogues received Jesus' traveling road show, and these were the kinds of communities he left behind. Their standards for judging leaders may seem commonsensical, but their differences from later orthodoxy are striking. These Didache communities apparently followed synagogue tradition, in which any member could play the rabbi's or prophet's role. Then the locals decided who they respected most. The community recognized positions of leadership, but they chose the leaders: "You yourselves must lay hands on bishops and deacons that are worthy of the Lord." (Didache 15:1) The letters to Timothy and Titus also suggested guidelines for electing church leaders, but this assumed the churches did the choosing. As yet, no "higher" authority could overturn their elections, condemn their beliefs, or expel them from the Jesus movement.

In the days before any centralized organization, this was the usual picture of a local church. Few communities had an educated priest. For administration they had committees of elders or presbyters, like those who wrote the Didache. In Carthage during the 250s, we hear of such lay committees presuming to hire or fire priests, much to Bishop Cyprian's concern. The lay leaders were usually confident that their decisions reflected God's will. Nobody had yet convinced them otherwise.

Down to the early 400s, leaders like Archbishop John Chrysostom still emphasized this tradition of mutual accountability and respect for other people's freedom. From his great cathedral in Constantinople he argued, "We do not have "authority" over your faith, beloved, nor do we command these things as your lords and masters . . . the counselor speaks his own opinions, not forcing his listener, but leaving him to his choice . . ."[6] In this, Chrysostom stood squarely on church tradition as he knew it. Like Jesus and Paul, he spoke of "God's commands" and sometimes said bigoted things, but he didn't try to act as an enforcer.

Of course some church leaders managed to make themselves oppressive long before the clergy gained state-backed authority. Only about 100 years after Jesus, the Didache was already advising churches how to deal with "Christ-hustlers." In Egypt's first monastic communities, Pachomius appointed the superiors over each house, but also advised the monks how to challenge and displace an abusive superior: "If the one who is the judge of all sins abandon the truth, because of the perversity of his heart or out of negligence, he shall be judged by twenty holy and God-fearing men, or ten or even only five about whom all bear witness. They shall sit and judge him, and degrade him to the lowest place until he amends."[7]

Such informal checks on power were sometimes effective and sometimes not. But when Christianity became the official cult of state, the very idea of mutual accountability between leaders and followers grew much harder to uphold.

Supporting Freedom, Even for Slaves

On slavery, we don't have a direct record of Jesus' opinion. But as a Jewish prophet, his attitude was probably similar to Moses'. Some of Paul's claims on behalf of Jesus suggest it: "There is no question here of . . . slave and freeman; but Christ is all, and is in all" (Colossians 3:11); "the man who as a slave received the call to be a Christian, is the Lord's freedman." (Corinthians 7:22) The Romans noticed that such lines made Christianity popular with slaves. And everybody knew that words like this could easily spin out of control. In the wrong mouths they could inspire explosive slave revolts, murderous repression by the army, or both. The early Christians faced a dangerous dilemma in relating to each slave they met.

Loyalty to Rome was legally required, and involved accepting a slave economy. In Jesus' time, Italy alone had around 1.5 million slaves, and this included near half the people in the city of Rome. These millions of slaves were mainly prisoners of war, or their descendents who inherited slave status. Any objection to their enslavement involved questioning Rome's right to conquer and rule, which was the basis of the Empire. Of course some Jewish groups did question it. The Torah demanded the death penalty for those who kidnapped others and sold them into slavery (Exodus 21:16), which is basically what Rome did to all its prisoners-of-war. Both the Essenes and the "Therapeutics" of Alexandria rejected slave holding, claiming it was as a violation of holy law. As Philo of Alexandria explained the Therapeutics' somewhat communist views, "They do not use the ministrations of slaves, looking upon the possession of servants or slaves to be a thing absolutely and wholly contrary to nature, for nature has created all men free, but the injustice and covetousness of some men who prefer inequality, that cause of all evil, . . . has given to the more powerful authority over those who are weaker."[8]

What could a law-abiding church safely say to slaves? In Paul's letter to Philemon, we have an appeal to a Christian slave owner concerning his runaway Christian slave. The slave, named Onesimus, had fled to Paul, and placed the apostle in a moral quandary. We should note the Torah specifically states, "You shall not surrender to his master a slave who has taken refuge with you." (Deuteronomy 23:15) After difficult discussions, Paul said the young man had become like a son to him. But no such personal love could take priority over the fate of the church, and Paul had convinced Onesimus to return to his master. He couldn't support slaves to break the law without rendering his church an outlaw organization. All he could do was appeal to voluntary mercy, ask that Philemon treat Onesimus as a son, or even free him in the future. But that had to be a matter of free consent on the slave owner's part. We can imagine Paul's powers of persuasion if he got Onesimus to return with this letter. Apparently the young man was convinced he should return to slavery, as this would be best for the faith.

As Roman suspicions of the Christian movement grew, the later pastoral letters went further to subordinate slaves' rights to the church's safety. 1 Timothy said, "All [Christians] who wear the yoke of slavery must count their own masters worthy of all respect, so that the name of God and the Christian teaching are not brought into disrepute." (6:1) The letter to Titus gave a whole string of appeals for full obedience from slaves.

1 Peter said Christian slaves should honor their masters as if serving God himself, to the point of accepting cruelty: "Servants, accept the authority of your masters with all due submission, not only when they are kind and considerate, but even when they are perverse" (2:18). We should mention that many slave owners demanded sexual service from slaves.

These letters probably date to the second century, well after Rome crushed the Jewish homeland. Their cautious wording urged slaves to love and obey their masters, usually without mentioning similar demands for the owners.[9] The instructions to love and obey were aimed at the subordinate members in every relationship. Subjects must obey rulers, slaves their masters, children their parents, and women their men. I Peter at least attempted balance, urging that "all of you should wrap yourselves in the garment of humility towards each other, because God sets his face against the arrogant but favors the humble." (I Peter 5:5) That was probably as close as most church leaders dared go in telling superiors how to treat their subordinates. These churches were clearly walking a tightrope. They might talk of equal relations between slave and free people as a private virtue. But if they spoke to slaves of freedom like Moses, Roman troops would appear with their swords drawn.

This was the dilemma for Christians down to the 1800s, wherever it was illegal to help a slave escape. But after the 300s, the church itself generally helped the state to control slaves, selectively quoting lines from slave holders in the Bible. As American pastor Richard Fuller declared prior to the Civil War, "What God sanctioned in the Old Testament, cannot be a sin."[10] Still, there were many Christians who tried to bend the rules for slaves without breaking the laws. In North Carolina, a community of Moravian settlers at least invited slaves to attend the same church with free folks. One of the slaves was moved to declare "After death, we will be with God, and there we will be equal."[11]

Chaos in the Primitive Church

For the first 200 years or so, there was no prevailing church orthodoxy, or official version of Jesus' story. There was only a growing body of folklore, spreading and changing like the tales of Krishna or King Arthur. In some stories, the baby Jesus gave solemn sermons from his cradle. In others he played happily with lions as a toddler. Some "infant gospels" made young Jesus a fearsomely omnipotent lad, who killed offensive playmates with a glance. Nobody could control the content or audience for these stories, any more than the popular legends of Greece or India could be brought under central control. Basically, the early churches were chaotic. When they met in private homes, anyone might stand and speak. Any speaker might claim a prophecy from God. The Roman officer Celsus was moved to contempt:

> There are countless in that region [of Phoenicia and Palestine] who will "prophesy" at the drop of a hat, in or out of the temples. Others go about begging and claim to be oracles of God, plying their trade in the cities or in military posts. They make a show of being "inspired" to utter their predictions. These habitually claim to be more than prophets, and say such things as "I am God," or even "I am the Holy Spirit," and "I have come for the world is coming to an end as I speak . . . I shall save you; you will yet see me, for I am coming again armed with heavenly powers. So blessed is he who worships me now. Those who refuse, whole cities and nations, will be cast into the flames."[12]

Some Christians proclaimed forgiveness for every sin, and said all social rules were merely human inventions. Others insisted their Hebrew or Greek traditions came from God, and following those ethnic customs was essential for salvation. A few became authorities unto themselves, rejecting anyone's right to judge another's conscience.[13]

Paul's Problems with Freedom

After saying that Jesus brought freedom, even from the Jewish law, Paul immediately faced a series of controversies over the limits of freedom. And for all his talk of liberty, he was still an ex-Pharisee and an agent of the national Sanhedrin. Now he claimed authority equal to Jesus' original disciples. But in dealing with the issues of freedom, how did he compare to Jesus?

At first Paul encouraged his new communities to experiment freely in building a new kind of community. He praised the initiative of female leaders and the mixing of ethnic traditions. He famously declared that human beings have no right to judge one another, and believed this realization could establish freedom while banishing strife from the world. But at the same time he felt responsible to ensure that these experiments produced the right results. When the church in Corinth made choices he found offensive, he argued like an elder brother, "'We are free to do anything,' you say. Yes . . . but does everything help build the community? Each of you must regard not his own interests, but the other man's." (I Corinthians 10:23–24) And Paul sometimes presumed to act like a Pharisee governor, in which case he could completely repudiate Jesus' attitude toward sinners: "Make no mistake; no fornicator or idolater, none who are guilty either of adultery or of homosexual perversion, no thieves or grabbers or drunkards or slanderers or swindlers, will possess the Kingdom of God." (I Corinthians 6:9–10)

Obviously, Paul had his own image of what community the Corinthians should be building. And if their dreams for the church differed from his, Paul suggested they distrust their own sentiments — in favor of "the other man's." It sounded selfless and responsible; church officials never tired of repeating it. But which other men should these people trust more than themselves?

As his churches grew, Paul's priorities shifted. From trying to change individual lives, he focused more on building the organization. For example, he increasingly judged spiritual practices more by their effects on the community than by their effects on individual practitioners. We can see this in his remarks about speaking in tongues: "When a man is using the language of ecstasy he is talking with God, not with men, for no man understands him. He is no doubt inspired, but he speaks mysteries. On the other hand, when a man prophesies, he is talking to men, and his words have the power to build; they stimulate and they encourage [others]. The language of ecstasy is good for the speaker himself, but it is prophecy that builds up a Christian community." (1 Corinthians 14:2–4)

If the wider community found ecstatic speaking offensive, Paul would presumably ask the speakers to restrain their practice. That's why he called for constraint of women when their leadership drew public resentment. He seemed to be saying that free Christians should subordinate their own interests to those of the church organization. If so, how subordinate?

Not all Christians agreed with this shift in priorities. Some wanted to focus on their own inner growth, not on strengthening the organization. For Paul the best Christian was the one who sacrificed the most time, energy, and wealth in building the church. But he also spoke of his own inner visions as the primary inspiration for all he did. How much of these inner experiences was it helpful for him share? Some things, Paul felt, should be shared only with those who were ready to understand:

And yet I do speak words of wisdom to those who are ripe for it, not a wisdom belonging to this passing age, nor to any of its governing powers, which are declining to their end; I speak God's hidden wisdom, his secret purpose framed from the very beginning to bring us to our full glory. The powers that rule the world have never known it; if they had they would not have crucified the Lord of glory. But in the words of scripture, "Things beyond our seeing, things beyond our hearing, things beyond our imagining, all prepared by

God for those who love him", these it is that God has revealed to [some of]
us through the Spirit. (1 Corinthians 2:6–10)

If his own inner visions would only confuse or offend others, Paul
judged he should keep them hidden. It was a matter of what would help
the church's public image. So was the individual or the organization the
primary concern? In a conflict of interests, which should overrule the
other? Jesus seemed willing to either defend or reject traditions based
on what seemed more compassionate for particular people. But Paul and
later church officers increasingly treated the organization as the higher
authority. Where Jesus held a creative tension between person and
community, Paul's priorities made it more of an either/or question. Those
who made the organization primary soon claimed the label of "Orthodox."
And those who put personal experience or individual authority first were
soon labeled heretics or "Gnostics." The term meant "knowers," especially
ones who claimed to know more than the clergy.

The Gnostic Discipline Problem

Around 70 years after Paul died, a Christian called Valentinus began
teaching Paul's "hidden wisdom," which he reportedly learned from
Paul's disciple Theudas.[14] In this teaching, the priority of institutional
over personal growth was reversed. According to Valentinus, the true
church was not a particular organization; it was the portion of humanity
that recognized its divine origin. It was not an institution set down from
on high, but a human means of self-discovery.[15] And Valentinus claimed
he had achieved this self-discovery. Now he offered teachings "beyond"
the rules and beliefs stressed by most priests, to "those ripe for it." But
when Valentinus tried to present his wisdom, he came under growing
attack from the professional clergy. One of the first signs of an emerging
international orthodoxy was an agreement among many regional bishops,

that Valentinus was an unauthorized Gnostic teacher who should be chased from the church.

What was the problem? Jesus had simply debated whoever he disagreed with, and it was "the orthodox" who treated him as a discipline problem. But now the Christian movement's officers had their own discipline problems over who should follow who. The dispute involved an emerging professional clergy, whose members were starting to act like governors of their flocks. Where other church members presumed to compete in teaching and acting the prophet, there were struggles over who could speak for Jesus. These "Gnostic-Orthodox" conflicts led to a first round of restrictions on freedom in church.

According to Tertullian (early 200s), the Gnostics favorite saying was "Seek and you shall find." But what, he asked, were they seeking, and who were they seeking it from? If the church already offered every truth and sacrament needed for salvation, what else did the Gnostics want? Hippolytus raised a similar question in his *Refutation of All Heresies* (ca. 230), and answered partly by quoting a Gnostic teacher named Monoimus: "Abandon the search for God and the creation and other matters of a similar sort. Look for him by taking yourself as the starting point. Learn who it is within you who makes everything his own and says, 'My God, my mind, my thought, my soul, my body.' Learn the sources of sorrow, joy, love, hate. . . If you carefully investigate these matters you will find them in yourself."[16]

Apparently, this Monoimus wanted people to learn about salvation from themselves, instead of from Jesus and his church. Hippolytus was concerned. What would sinners learn if they tried to teach themselves? Wouldn't the proud learn arrogance, and the hateful teach hate? Hippolytus felt it was fine for Christians to ask deep questions. He just accused the Gnostics of taking their answers from the wrong authorities.

To Tertullian, these Gnostics were guilty of a monstrous sin: they took

149

their own inner experiences as more important than the word of God's community. Of course there was a biblical tradition of people having visions and speaking as prophets. But Bishop Irenaeus (ca. 130–ca. 202) accused these lay people of simply making up religion from their own private psychoses: "They are to be blamed for . . . describing human feelings, passions, and mental tendencies . . . and ascribing these things . . . to the divine Word."[17] Irenaeus found their arrogance astounding: "They imagine that they themselves have discovered more than the apostles, and . . . they themselves are wiser and more intelligent than the apostles."[18]

Sure enough, some Gnostics went about claiming to have realized their own inner divinity, calling themselves "royal sons" of the Lord. Referring to Jesus' saying that people are more important than the Sabbath, some Egyptian Gnostics called themselves "Lords of the Sabbath." Comparing their souls' freedom to the power of absolute monarchs, they said "For a king, the law is unwritten."[19] Irenaeus, found their self-importance frightfully silly: "If anyone yields himself to them like little sheep, and follows out their practice and their redemption, such a person becomes so puffed up that . . . he walks with a strutting gait and a supercilious countenance, possessing all the pompous air of a strutting cock!"[20]

For Gnostics, no teaching or authority seemed to be final. If the bishops claimed to teach the final received truth, the Gnostics said it was only a prelude to greater things. The Gnostics of Irenaeus's church didn't reject their bishop's sermons or rites; they just regarded these as "elementary teachings" on the path to more advanced knowledge.[21] When Irenaeus tried to correct these people they replied, "We alone know the necessity of birth and the ways by which a man enters the world. And being so fully instructed, we alone are able to pass through and beyond decay."[22] We can imagine how modern pastors would feel if members of their congregations announced such wisdom.

Clearly the Gnostics were an endless headache. How were the designated priests supposed to handle laypeople who claimed "higher" teachings than those of the bishop? What if they claimed to receive new revelations directly from God or Jesus, and said those insights should supersede earlier teachings? The followers of these new revelations formed associations within churches. They often regarded themselves as a spiritual elite, and looked down on other members and clergy as less evolved souls. Irenaeus sensed a danger of division as a Gnostic group in his church conducted its own special rites. In their services they drew lots for playing roles of "prophet" or "priest," and both women and men played these parts. They taught that the Old Testament God, who demanded blind obedience, was a false deity; the true path to enlightenment required learning independence from authority. What was this, Irenaeus asked, other than license to "overthrow discipline"?

Discussions between Orthodox and Gnostic Christians tended to go nowhere. The Gnostics could always claim their critics were too spiritually immature to understand them. They could even quote scripture on this, since Paul had made the same potentially infuriating argument: "A man who is unspiritual refuses what belongs to the spirit of God; it is folly to him; he cannot grasp it, because it needs to be judged in the light of the Spirit. A man gifted with the Spirit can judge the worth of everything, but is not himself subject to judgment by his fellow men. For (in the words of Scripture) 'Who knows the mind of the Lord? Who can advise him?' We, however, possess the mind of Christ." (1 Corinthians 2:14–16)

Surely, though, some line had to be drawn on who could speak for God. Irenaeus warned that the Gnostics, ". . . put forth their own compositions, while boasting that they have more gospels than there really are . . . They really have no gospel which is not full of blasphemy. For what they have published . . . is totally unlike what has been handed down to us from the apostles."[23] If every Christian's inner vision had the status of divine revelation, wouldn't Jesus' teaching grow subordinate to every lesser person's "insight"?

No doubt many Gnostic practices and teachers were less than helpful. As Jesus said, "by their fruits you will know them." And most clergymen claimed the Gnostic's fruits were foolishness, division, and collapse of authority. But the Gnostics judged their spiritual practices by the effects on themselves. With a somewhat experimental attitude they asked what worked in lifting the pain of fear and despair. They said all experience was a learning process, and they were "on the path." But their path was a subjective, personal experience. It was not the usual focus of civic-minded Christians who would build a moral majority. As the Christian community grew, its bishops increasingly turned to issues of administration. With so many souls to lead, they grew concerned to establish guidelines for all, and enforce them. The church started to resemble a state within a state — often more concerned to govern its flock than inspire it. Where many Gnostics spoke of personal paths of "growth to the stature of Christ," Orthodox leaders like Tertullian seemed bent on setting an upper limit to growth: "Away with all attempts to produce a mixed Christianity of Stoic, Platonic, or dialectic composition! We want no curious disputation after possessing Jesus Christ, no inquiring after enjoying the gospel! With our faith we desire no further belief."[24]

In reply, the Gnostic "seekers" accused the clergy of throwing out the goal of religion. Their *Apocalypse of Peter* called orthodox bishops "waterless canals." The *Testimony of Truth* accused, "They say, '[Even if] an [angel] comes from heaven, and preaches to you beyond what we preach to you, let him be accursed!' "[25] Some Gnostics threw Jesus' words against the clergy: "Alas, alas for you, lawyers and Pharisees, hypocrites that you are! You shut the door of the Kingdom in men's faces; you do not enter yourselves, and when others are entering, you stop them." (Matthew 23:13) How could the clergy win this debate?

Where Paul had revised his original ideals of community to limit the challenge of female leaders, now the later clergy shifted things further, to discourage initiative from non-ordained men. Rather than allowing "their" churches to be further corrupted by other people's foolishness, the bishops increasingly agreed to "excommunicate" insubordinate members and unapproved books. It did eliminate a thousand ambiguities.

Building a Christian Chain of Command

If the church was divided over who possessed the mind of Christ, how could it settle the matter? Bishop Ignatius of Antioch (ca. 100) was perhaps the first to establish a structural solution. Rather than letting the whole community argue, and hope for a wise agreement, Ignatius hoped to determine who among them should rank highest. He divided his followers into four administrative levels, of lay people, deacons, priests, and himself as the bishop. As in the structure of Roman government, each level would settle its disputes by appeal to the level above it. The parishioners could "seek" by asking questions, but the priests must give the answers. The priests and deacons in turn, would get their answers from the bishop. And to avoid division at the top, Ignatius argued there must be only one bishop over each see. As the bishop obeyed God above him, so each lower order of Christians must obey their bishop "as if he were God."[26] With the chain of command so clarified, Ignatius could hope that the chaos of competition among teachers would cease.

In Ignatius' time most priests were still chosen, in some fashion or other, by their communities. The priests, in turn, were starting to name bishops above themselves. It was a basically bottom-up flow of rising leaders. But as administrators strove for better control, the bishops increasingly appointed priests below them. And in that case, the organization started telling local people who their religious leaders would be. The church now appointed "fathers" to guide the seekers, though Jesus advised, "Call no man on earth your father." (Matthew 23:9) Questions of *what* was right, were now being settled by deciding *who* was higher. And if God meant to rule through this chain of command, it would be unfaithful to oppose a higher church official. Ignatius felt it safest if lay Christians left all initiative to their superiors and all religious functions to professional clerics: "Let no man do aught pertaining to the church apart from the bishop. Let that Eucharist be considered valid which is under the bishop or to him whom he commits it . . . It is not lawful apart from the bishops, either to baptize, or to hold a love feast. But whatsoever he approves, that also will be well pleasing to God, that everything which you do may be secure and valid."[27]

A century later, Tertullian even insisted that laypeople stop discussing the scriptures lest they fall into "false exegesis." He said parishioners should let the clergy tell them what the scriptures said, and believe what they were told. Patriarch Demetrius of Alexandria certainly wanted such a rule for Origen, who presumed to teach without being ordained. And when Demetrius kicked Origen out of his church, he wished everyone to know that the Patriarch held the keys to heaven. Whoever disobeyed him would be cut off from communion by every other bishop as well. As Irenaeus had argued, "One must obey the priests who are in the church — that is . . . those who possess the succession from the apostles. For they receive simultaneously with the episcopal succession the sure gift of truth."[28]

The next level of hierarchy arose because the bishops of different sees disagreed, on matters including the excommunication of Origen. They tried meeting in regional councils to decide common rules and beliefs for their people to follow. And above this, the bishops of the Empire's greatest cities began acting as ultimate courts of appeal. Many Christians opposed or tried to limit this demand for ever-higher levels of authority. Bishop Cyprian of Carthage argued (in 256) that no one should set himself up as a "bishop of bishops" — "nor . . . compel his colleague to the necessity of obedience."[29] Cyprian meant to defend his own authority over the local churches of Carthage, but he opposed the emergence of yet higher officials, such as the patriarch of Rome.

This ranking of Christians brought a semblance of order from chaos. If those in higher office determined what was right, then any question of lower ranking Christians having "higher awareness" should not arise. Any allegations of common Christians surpassing their superiors in holiness could be dismissed as blasphemy or delusion. Perhaps the dream of most bishops was a church of perfectly obedient parishioners who believed what they were taught, did as they were told, and asked for nothing more. If that was their vision for human development, then official Christianity might become a static set of rules to be followed, beliefs to be accepted, and rewards or punishments according to the degree of compliance. That would be all there was to the human journey. Apart from choosing obedience, freedom would have no positive role in the Christianity.

But of course the challenge of innovative subordinates never went away. The world never ran out of fools, dreamers, or rebels who claimed to find a better way. And most of these people came from somewhere down the proper chain of command. These innovators might conclude that lending money at interest carried more benefits than evils for society. They might insist that women should be free to choose their own husbands. They could decide a layman like St. Francis was wiser than his bishop. How should the hierarchy respond? However final the clergy claimed their authority to be, they could never stem the flow of potential reformers claiming a "higher" vision.

Refusing Oaths of Blind Obedience to the Emperor

If most modern people reduce religion to a matter of personal morals, the Romans generally reduced it to a matter of loyalty. For them, the greatest question was which master they served above all. It was both a religious and a political question, because each lord in the ancient world tended to say "You shall put no other lords before me." It seemed to be a law of life that people had to choose which master to obey. On joining the Roman army, men took an oath of loyalty. It was a binding vow of unconditional obedience to the ruler, basically like the oath Adolf Hitler required. That was the traditional demand rulers made of their subjects. The Romans required a similar oath from all civilians, even non-citizens of the conquered colonies. They had to promise to place devotion to Rome above any other loyalty, be it to tribe, religious sect, or even family. Anyone who refused to swear this oath was guilty of treason, which was a capital offense even for children. Basically, disloyal subjects had no right to exist.

The main persecutions of disloyal Christians came in brief waves during periods of danger to the Empire, when the rulers grew anxious to weed out traitors. The government would then summon whole suspect populations to give the loyalty oath, and make a terrible example of any who refused. During the Jewish wars around 70 and 135, these investigations targeted Christians as suspected Jewish sympathizers. Later there were several more periods, mainly around the years 175, 200, 250, and 303, when the loyalty tests focused heavily on Christians. No doubt most church members simply said the oath to save their skins and get on with their lives. But large numbers refused, despite the threat of horrific punishments. In later persecution periods, suspicion sometimes grew so great that Christians were collectively declared a disloyal sect. In that case, proving loyalty to Rome also involved renouncing church membership.

Probably for most modern people, the whole age of martyrs seems pointlessly insane. How could the Romans have been so stupid as to force people to choose between *either* loyalty to the state, *or* loyalty to God? Why would the martyrs meekly submit to be killed, seemingly over a point of verbal correctitude like the distinction between loyalty and worship for the ruler? I always thought the word "martyr" was completely derogatory, meaning someone who wants to suffer. We tend to forget that these martyrs were refuseniks against a cult of state, who insisted on limits to a state's power over people. And this is still relevant, because we still have serious, even deadly struggles over demands on our ultimate loyalties, as seen in the Nuremberg and other modern war crimes trials. In North America we might recall that in 1940, the U.S. Supreme Court ruled on a case where two school children refused to say the pledge of allegiance in class. The kids were Jehovah's Witnesses, who claimed that the pledge was idolatry. The court denied their right to refuse the oath, claiming national unity was more important than religious scruples. Later, in 1943, the court reversed this decision in a similar case, ruling that freedom of conscience was more important than unity. In these cases, the Witnesses pointed out that since 1933, numerous members of their church in Germany had faced prison or death for refusing the required pledge of obedience to Adolf Hitler.[30] By the time WWII ended, over 90% of German Jehovah's Witnesses had paid those penalties.

Back in Rome, once Christianity was established as a state cult in the 300s, all political controversy over the martyrs' protests soon faded from memory. Instead of recalling their defiance of state power, church leaders piously extolled the martyrs' saintliness. Like Shia Muslim mullahs, they praised the glorious martyrs of times past, whose bloody deaths were so endlessly inspiring. But during the time of the persecutions, the protesting martyrs were a small fanatical minority of all Christians. Most members of the early churches responded to imperial rule somewhat like

St. Paul, pleading that they were loyal people who posed no threat to the Empire. The martyrs followed Jesus in a frightfully literal way. But those who wished to avoid all suspicion were actually the mainstream, which prevailed as the orthodox party of Christians. In seeking to win the rulers' acceptance, many of these "apologists" tried to outdo Roman society in its own virtues of loyalty, obedience, or male control over women. And perhaps this was the main outcome of the persecutions. As Professor Gordon Zahn explained of a later persecution on German Catholics in the 1870s, "The intensity of Bismarck's *Kulturkampf* against the [Catholic] Church burdened it with something of an inferiority complex, which continued long afterward to manifest itself in a compulsive drive to prove that Catholics could be good and loyal Germans . . . that in fact they would be the best and most loyal Germans of all."[31]

Getting into Bed with the Emperor

Before Constantine made Christianity a new imperial cult, the average congregation had no church building and its priest got no pay. For the Eucharist they had potlucks of bread and wine, which the neighbors passed around as an "agape feast."[32] Without paid clergy there were few distinctions between lay and religious people.[33] Some priests were slaves. Jonas of Orleans wrote, "There are priests so poor and so deprived of human dignity, and so scorned by some laymen, that they are used not only as stewards and accountants but as domestic servants, and are not allowed to eat at their lord's table."[34]

But when Constantine put the clergy on government pay, this in itself raised them high above other believers. A great distinction arose between the state-employed clerics and other Christians. It was like the difference in status between state employed Confucian scholars, and the rest. Before getting such patronage, most Christians divided their world into two realms — the sacred realm of their church community, and the profane world outside it. Now the professional priests increasingly saw themselves as the true Christian community, and drew a firm line between themselves and profane laity.[35]

Like all other emperors, General Constantine assumed that religion existed to help the ruler rule. Rome had always hired its priests to invoke divine help from above, and inspire popular loyalty from below. That's what emperors paid them for. When Constantine patronized the clergy, he expected their help in uniting the empire. When he became their pay-master, it changed the whole purpose of the church. From being voluntary leaders in an independent peoples' movement, the clergy became agents of the emperor. The church became an arm of government, in league with the rulers to control the population. Its preaching shifted in tone. Instead of calling ordinary people to "live more abundantly," the clergy adopted a traditionally Stoic concern for social duty.

Many ordinary Christians opposed all this. In colonized regions like North Africa, probably most local Christians still hated the empire and its emperor. Now they learned he was their church's new patron. We might assume they would rejoice, and many did. But for at least a large minority, a bitter struggle began. It was a struggle over who owned the church, who it served, and who decided these things. For example, if clergymen were now state-backed officials, who appointed those officials? Once appointed, who were they accountable to? What could the state-backed clergy require of other people? What could the rulers require the clergy to do? How would the imperial clerics deal with disobedience or criticism from lay people? What should a clergyman do if "his" people simply followed someone else? All these questions involved issues of freedom. And what, after all, did Christianity teach about freedom?

Especially in North Africa and Egypt, this conflict over who controlled the church grew violent. And that struggle was the turning point where the official church rejected freedom as a Christian value. After nearly 100 years of resistance from defiant, independent, anti-colonial church leaders in North Africa, Augustine and other loyalist bishops gained a series of legal rulings which banned lay Christians from choosing their own leaders. To justify this, the loyalist bishops established a doctrine of original sin, by which the population was disqualified from making its own decisions. Instead of encouraging people to think for themselves, the church actually outlawed any such thing. Men like Augustine did not come to this position lightly. They felt it was an inescapable necessity. Only extreme measures could cope with the crisis of loyalty, and the alternatives seemed even more terrible.

The events that led to this form a dramatic, ugly story. But maybe it's helpful to review the main blows which led the church to demonize freedom for over 1,000 years.

"What Has the Emperor to Do With the Church?"

The split which tore North Africa's churches started under the pagan emperors just before Constantine. It was a division imposed by imperial policy during the last persecutions between 303 and 311. The government tried to divide and rule by demanding that all clergymen must swear unconditional obedience to the emperor, and then prove it by closing their churches, and handing over their scriptures to be burned. This seemed to present each clergyman with a choice between apostasy or death. It neatly divided church leaders into two incompatible groups: dead heroes, and living hypocrites. Many clergymen felt it was stupid to resist such deadly force, and submitted with a mixture of fear and hope. Often it was bands of lay people who defied the rulers no matter what the cost.

Reportedly, in the town of Abitina, a bishop called Caecilian submitted to demands, and told his congregation to disband. But 47 lay people disobeyed him. They stubbornly gathered for worship, and were all thrown in jail. As the unproven story goes, these prisoners received rations so meager that they starved to death within several months. And as they sat starving, their bitterness grew. It seems their anger was focused more on their traitor bishop than their pagan persecutors. According to their rumor, Caecilian had collaborated with the government, first to save his own skin, and then to eliminate any fellow Christians who would denounce him for it. As the parishioners starved, their friends' fury mounted against all clergymen who "obeyed Caesar."[36] By some accounts, the persecutions in North Africa were worse than anywhere else. By the time they ended in 311, there were many friends of martyrs whose hatred for compromised clergymen knew no bounds.

When these righteous rebels emerged from hiding, many began demanding that the surviving clergy be sacked from office. The clerics found themselves on trial in a court of popular opinion. What could they say in their own defense? To forgive others might seem virtuous, but for clergymen to ask forgiveness for their own weakness seemed yet another act of self-serving hypocrisy. Peter and all the male disciples ran away the night soldiers came for Jesus, and they were forgiven. But if Peter had lived in North Africa during the persecution of 303–11, he might have been branded a traitor for life. It was almost as bad as the case of Rabbi Zolli, leader of the Jewish community in Rome, who escaped to the Vatican as the German army rounded up all Jews in 1943. Accused of betraying his people, Zolli tried to argue, "Dead, what good would I have been to my people?" But the surviving Jews completely rejected him.[37] At least they were allowed to do that.

Soon after the Roman government proclaimed acceptance for Christians, a new archbishop of Carthage was appointed, whose name was Caecilian. Many people claimed he was the same Caecilian who betrayed the congregation in Abitina. A furious priest named Donatus condemned the appointment, accusing that Caecilian was nothing but a lackey of the occupation. He had done what the rulers wanted, and was rewarded with greater authority over those he betrayed. Donatus urged everybody to boycott Caecilian's services. He even threatened the laypeople, that if they took communion from Caecilian they would "eat the bread of pollution," and go with him to hell.[38] The rebellious "Donatist" clergy called their own conference and elected their own man, Majorinus, as the "true" archbishop of Carthage.

These protesters had now split the church in anger, and done it on the basis of accusations which others denied. Caecilian issued a call for unity and forgiveness, which sounded somewhat spiritual. But his accusers' outrage could not just be wished away. For some sense of their feelings, we can refer to a modern protest letter drafted by a group of Catholic women in Chile. In 1989, soon after Chile's period of tyranny under General Augusto Pinochet, the Chilean Church met to elect a new archbishop of Santiago. One of the candidates, Bishop Jorge Medina, was well known as a supporter of Pinochet. And lest this man gain leadership of their church, the protesting women wrote: "Have pity on the thousands of disappeared, tortured, exiled, unemployed [whose] voices are raised demanding justice . . . For us, it would be a great affliction and a scandal for our people if the naming of the new Archbishop fell on someone who . . . had remained silent or, worse, had worked in complicity with the military government that has assaulted the dignity of mankind and the values of the Gospel."[39]

Obviously, many Christians in North Africa didn't see Caecilian as their spiritual guide of choice. To them, Donatus' righteous anger seemed more spiritual than Caecilian's compromising diplomacy. But why was this a problem? Why couldn't people who admired Donatus follow him, while those who didn't follow Caecilian? What was to stop people from following whatever spiritual leaders they most respected?

At first the Donatist crisis seemed just a nasty local dispute over who should be archbishop. But behind the battle over who was spiritual enough to be archbishop, lay a deeper dispute over *what* was spiritual. The Donatists generally felt that real Christians should help their neighbors, not serve their people's oppressors. It was a matter of which lord they served. In reply, Caecilian and other loyalist clergy claimed the charges against them were false. But they also argued there was nothing wrong with loyalty to Rome. God acted through the emperor, not against him. Loyalty to the government was itself a spiritual quality, especially now that the emperor was a Christian.

At this point, Constantine issued a proclamation granting financial support for loyalist churches. The edict specifically said that the government would fund only clergymen who supported Caecilian. So the occupying power was offering the clergy cash incentives for loyalty. And perhaps this was the point where things passed out of control. So long as all Christians faced oppression together, they were basically united. But once the emperor supported one sect of Christians against others, the ground of reality seemed to shift. In standing up for their understanding of Christian principles, the protesters found themselves treated as traitors, both by the empire and their own church. "What," Donatus demanded to know, "has the emperor to do with the church?" Later, the rebel theologian Tyconius accused loyalist Christians of worshipping "no other king but Caesar."[40]

When many Donatists contemptuously rejected imperial pay as a bribe, the emperor turned to regional synods for wider support. He wanted his state church united, and he wanted it loyal. No band of rustic fools from the hills of Africa was going to block Rome's destiny. In 313, a synod of 37 bishops ruled it an excommunicable sin for parishioners or lower clergy to reject their duly appointed bishops. They had made it illegal for churches to choose their own leaders. This seemed to leave the rebels two options — either accept whoever was appointed over them, or else abandon their church to those same leaders. But many North African

Christians preferred a third option, of driving the loyalist clergy out of their country.

The next year (314), Constantine convened a larger council at Arles. These bishops, who were serving on Constantine's payroll, delivered a series of rulings to eliminate interference from subordinates. Their canon number 20 said a bishop could be appointed or removed only by a committee of seven already established bishops. Each appointed bishop had unlimited power to ordain, baptize, or excommunicate any Christians under him. Canon 17 said that people excommunicated by any local bishop could not be readmitted to any other church by any other bishop. Canon 21 barred any cleric who left his own see (perhaps due to conflict with his bishop) from serving as a priest anywhere else.[41] All the ways Rome had previously tied common workers to their tasks, lands, and masters, were now applied to priests and their flocks. For those who still brought accusations of immorality against their bishops, the council ruled no evidence was admissible unless it came from a loyal state official. Anyone who accused a bishop of wrongdoing and failed to convince a court of other bishops, would be thrown out of the church.[42]

Since this seemed to close every legal path of protest, the Donatists embarked on a path of defiance. And by 315, perhaps most native Christians in North Africa felt that no empire loyalist deserved to pose as their leader. Gangs of Donatist or Orthodox partisans began seizing each other's church buildings. In 316, Constantine ordered all Donatist churches and properties confiscated. The troops he sent to enforce this order met mobs of howling, stone-hurling protesters. Some soldiers lost their heads, charged the crowds, and started hacking people apart.

North Africa now became the breeding ground for a new "church of martyrs." For Donatists, refusal of loyalty to Rome and its state church became an article of Christian faith. The most fanatical rebels proclaimed that death in defiance of that authority was a guarantee of salvation in the next world. Emperor Constantine warned, "with the favor of the divine piety I shall come to Africa and shall most fully demonstrate with an unequivocal verdict as much to [bishop] Caecilian as to those who seem to be against him just how the supreme deity ought to be worshipped."[43] But at this display of unity between the government and its "universal" church, a Donatist preacher replied,

> *Yet the insatiable plunderer, i.e., the devil, takes it ill that he cannot gain possession of all by this artifice; the enemy of salvation has found a more subtle argument to violate the purity of the faith, Christ, says he, is a lover of unity, therefore let there be unity . . . He sends money either to seduce faith or to give an occasion for avarice by pretense of holding to the (Christian) law. But when in the face of all these enticements justice kept her course rigidly and inflexibly, judges are ordered to intervene, they are driven to put the secular power in motion, buildings are surrounded by troops, the rich are threatened with proscription, the sacraments are defiled, a mob of heathen are brought in upon us.*[44]

So obviously counterproductive was the use of force, that within four years, by 321, Constantine called it off. With no resolution in sight he pulled the troops out, basically granting the Donatists toleration as a separate church. To compensate the loyal clergy for buildings lost to the rebels, he gave more building funds to orthodox churches only. This cease-fire could have brought peace and some sort of reconciliation. But with each sect labeling the other as a servant of Satan, their mutual hate only escalated into low-grade civil war, with alarming acts of terrorism for Jesus. To cope with the Donatist fanatic fringe, the Roman government exiled all known Donatists from their home regions. That reduced the incidence of violent confrontation. But the exiled rebels only stewed in rage like modern Palestinians, plotting revenge in their refugee camps.

How could the authorities ever trust such people with freedom?

Watching the unfolding madness in North Africa, and surviving his own street battles for church office in Rome, Pope Damasus (366–84) felt something must be done to ventilate protest in the church. He warned his clergy, "We dare not keep silence when scandal arises, for the Prophet says, 'Lift up your voice like a trumpet.' . . . Therefore let the offenders put the matter right in synod, and remove those on whom the [clerical] status has unfittingly been conferred; else let us be informed of their names that we may know from whom we must withhold communion."[45] So, grievances against the state clergy should be aired, like the Donatist protests were from 313 to 315. But if protesters appealed to the courts again, the union of orthodox bishops would still be their judges. The bishops would still pass rulings defending their own positions. They'd still enforce their decisions by any means necessary.

The Decision to Terminate Religious Diversity

All this conflict tended to discredit freedom in the eyes of most church leaders. And as clergymen became government employees, they increasingly treated all critics as rivals for their jobs. Like politicians they tried to discredit their critics, morally and personally. The same problem divided the church in Egypt. Loyalist Greco-Roman clerics gained the top spots, and anti-colonial native Christians accused them of corruption. As Egypt's Archbishop Alexander warned fellow bishops across the empire,

> *Impelled by avarice and ambition, knaves are constantly plotting to gain possession of the dioceses that seem greatest. Under various pretexts they trample on the religion of the church. For they are driven mad by the devil who works in them, and abandon all reverence and despise the fear of God's judgment. As I suffer from them myself, I had to explain to your Reverence, that you should be on your guard against such individuals, lest any of them*

dare enter your dioceses also.[46]

Alexander's problems with dissident opinions led directly to the first empire-wide church council at Nicaea in 325. And I've already mentioned that council's decisions to standardize beliefs. But here I want to highlight the restrictions on freedom that council approved.

In addition to making the Nicean Creed, the bishops at Nicea approved a series of canon laws, which endorsed all the restrictions on subordinates from the Arles council in 314. Also, Constantine had already named his price for church patronage in 321, namely the right to approve all new bishops in the empire. "My will," he said, "must be considered binding."[47] So the emperor already held the power to hire or fire all the bishops in attendance at Nicea. This is probably why, in deciding the formula for a standardized creed, the emperor's will prevailed. Only five bishops dared object (to saying Jesus and God were of one substance), and of these protesters, only two, Theonas of Marmarica and Secundus of Ptolemais, refused all calls to submit. The council therefore stripped them of their jobs and exiled them to Illyria.[48] In this we can see the functional definition of heresy. A heretic was a Christian who sided with the minority in a church council decision, and even afterward refused to abandon his own beliefs to embrace those of the prevailing side.

The Nicean creed then became a new official pledge of loyalty to the state religion. For anyone unwilling to recite it, Constantine warned: "The privileges which have been granted in consideration of religion must benefit only the adherents of the Catholic faith. It is our will, moreover, that heretics and schismatics shall not only be excluded from these privileges but shall also be bound and subjected to the various compulsory public services."[49] Constantine also threatened non-conformists with loss of their homes: "Let none of you presume, from this time forward, to meet in congregations. To prevent this, we command that you be deprived of all the houses in which you have been accustomed to meet . . . and that these should be handed over immediately to the Catholic Church."[50]

With all this agreement on standard requirements, Constantine felt confident the problems of disunity were solved. With pride and enthusiasm, he wrote to officials across the empire: "Beloved brethren, hail. We have received from divine providence the blessing of being freed from all error, and united in the acknowledgement of one and the same faith. The devil will no longer have any power over us."[51]

But giving superiors more power over subordinates didn't ensure harmony, either in the church or state. Instead, the structure of "one see, one bishop" ensured a winner-take-all rivalry among candidates for church office. In Egypt, a Greco-Roman empire-loyalist named Athanasius secured appointment as archbishop, against the protests of native Coptic leaders. Each side accused the other of corruption, intimidation, and heresy. Even Constantine suspected the rebels' claims had justice. But to support mutiny against office holders would undermine the whole structure of authority. And Athanasius claimed the survival of Christian orthodoxy depended on his victory over heretical insubordinates. As St. Jerome ridiculed Athanasius' critics:

> We read in Isaiah, A fool will speak folly [Isaiah 9:17]. I hear that a certain person has broken out into so great madness as to place deacons before presbyters, that is, bishops. [In that case,] . . . what happens to the server of tables and widows that he sets himself up so arrogantly over those whose prayers the body and blood of Christ are made? Do you ask for authority? Listen to the proof . . . That afterwards one was chosen to preside over the rest; this was done as a remedy for schism, and to prevent one individual from rending the Church of Christ by drawing it to himself.[52]

This was a powerful argument and hard to discredit. But by 366, street battles over who should be greatest as archbishop of Rome left hundreds of people dead. Ammianus Marcellinus explained that the Roman see had grown so wealthy, that contenders would use any means to seize it.[53] Such Christians seemed to take Jesus' words about masters lording it over their subjects as a statement of God's will.

These power-struggle issues were not inevitable, as shown by the host of Christians who took no part in them. Many of the greatest saints stood outside the state church, and tried to uphold independent religion. Saint Antony remained in the Egyptian desert all his life, partly to avoid pressure from partisans for power over others. When he spoke to visitors, he did it as one person to another, without the slightest ambition for authority over anyone. Pachomius, who founded the first monastic community in Egypt, feared that with a rise of church overlords: "good men will no longer feel able to speak out for the benefit of the community, but will remain silent and still." For Pachomius, ambition for control was an immaturity to be overcome. He openly confessed and ridiculed his own craving for superiority, admitting that he sometimes imagined himself preceded by a voice calling "Make way for the man of God!"[54]

But for most clergymen, the agenda of building the organization led inexorably forward. Where churches gained legal power over communities, the highest management positions commonly went to those with the greatest ambition for godly authority. Some church officers were still appointed by popular demand, but increasingly it was clerical superiors who had the final say in hiring or firing. Priests were now hired to represent the organization, and rose in rank by approval of superiors within it. As officers of the state church they controlled access to the sacraments and to church membership. They controlled building funds, government grants, and aid to the poor. All this gave them power to either patronize or withhold aid from whomever they chose. Where Jesus and Paul said only God could judge each soul, these bureaucrats of the state church claimed authority to admit or exclude others from salvation.

Of course there was another kind of religious power, namely the power of personal spirituality. And this was something no institution could ever control. Personal power appeared or didn't appear, seemingly at random. Local holy people like Antony or the early female church leaders had no power to restrict, punish, or exclude others. They had only the positive power to attract and inspire. Leaders like that rose or fell according to their personal qualities in a natural democracy of the spiritual marketplace. In the realm of independent religion, no sex, class, or profession could hold a monopoly on leadership. Despite all efforts by the state clergy, it proved impossible to control who people admired.

The Official War on Religious Freedom

Over the course of the 300s, Rome took a series of additional measures to eliminate diversity and establish harmony. Since the Arian, Donatist, and classical pagan sects continued arguing with orthodox Christians, Constantine moved (in 333) to ban all books written by the Egyptian heretic Arius, and the anti-Christian philosopher Porphyry. Feeling Jesus must approve, he imposed the death penalty for possessing such books. This was part of an ongoing debate in which bishops called for rulings on which books should be read in church. An official decision came in 365, when the Council of Laodicea determined which books should be in the Christian Bible. The council included the controversial book of Revelation, but omitted other popular books like the "Letter of Barnabas" or the "Shepherd of Hermas." In all, the council specifically named 41 books as no longer welcome at church.

This listing of bishop-approved books could have been simply an endorsement of "the best" Christian books to date. But Egypt's archbishop Athanasius interpreted it as a ban on all other books. In 367 he issued a letter threatening to "cleanse the church of every defilement," and ordered police action against anyone possessing religious books that weren't on the Council of Laodicea's list. Rather than letting books of merit be chosen by popular acclaim, Athanasius claimed that authority for the bishops. He implied the lay public should have no role in choosing which books should inspire them. This was probably the point when the monks of Nag Hammadi collected their volumes of now-forbidden thoughts, placed them in clay jars, and buried them behind a rock in the desert.

A few years later in 380, Emperor Theodosius decided to further eliminate competing loyalties by declaring Christianity the only official religion. First he urged all residents of the empire to convert, and then issued a series of rulings to make them do so. In 381 he made it a crime to convert from Christianity to any other religion. Anyone who did so lost the right to will property to their families. Since conversion from Christianity to Judaism was worse, that got the death penalty. Apparently, some Christians were finding Theodosius' state church constrictive, and continued leaving to join other religions. To stop it, Emperor Theodosius declared, "Let Christians . . . who go over to pagan rite and cult . . . be outside Roman law."[55] An outlaw, of course, lost all protection under the law and could be murdered with impunity.

In 382, the government cut its support for imperial cults. It closed the altar of Victory in Rome, and turned the Vestal Virgins out in the streets. The next year, all divination at pagan temples became a crime. Theodosius even banned the Olympic Games. Then in 391 the government simply outlawed all non-Christian religions. At this, parties of Christian fanatics rallied to plunder, vandalize, or demolish classical temples across Italy, Greece, or Asia Minor. As the book of Deuteronomy said, "You must destroy all sites at which the nations you are to dispossess worshipped their gods . . . Tear down their altars, smash their pillars, put their sacred posts to the fire, and cut down the images of their gods, obliterating their name from the site." (12:2)

With this, our story of Christian freedom returns to North Africa. In 399, a government mission arrived in Carthage to enforce the closure of all pagan temples. We know of at least 60 people killed in the riots surrounding this official end of paganism there. It seems most orthodox Christians applauded the suppression of other peoples' religions. If they supported freedom for anyone other than themselves, it was now a crime to say so.

Supposedly, all Rome was now united with one faith/one administration. But there was one great division remaining. The Donatist and Orthodox sects still regarded each other as traitors against God, and still maintained their organizational divorce. Finally in 392, Theodosius moved to terminate the problem, ruling that any clergy dissenting against the state church must be fined 10 pounds of gold, plus lose all their immovable property.[56] Until 401, this was just a threat. But then several orthodox bishops including Augustine of Hippo, brought a lawsuit demanding enforcement. For the crime of maintaining an alternative church, they wanted the Donatists stripped of property and financially ruined. The case was delayed in appeals till 411, when the final ruling fell to a new church council of 565 African bishops — 279 Donatist, and 286 Orthodox.[57]

Theologically Invalidating Freedom

Like the Council of Nicea, this Carthage conference operated like a verbal wrestling match. Rather than discussing mutually helpful steps to the future, the contending parties took turns trying to totally discredit each other. By the contests' rules, the winning side had its arguments enshrined as official doctrine, while those voting for the minority position lost their jobs, homes, and wealth. With the stakes jacked up so high, the Donatist bishops appeared grimly steeled for martyrdom. When the presiding judge Count Marcellinus asked them to take their seats, they refused, answering that Jesus had stood for his trial.

For the prosecution, Augustine claimed that the real issue was respect for the sacraments. The Donatists, he said, taught that God cannot deliver his grace through sacraments administered by a sinful cleric. But actually the sacraments were sacred in themselves, regardless of which cleric handled them. The sacraments were beyond corruption; to think otherwise was to doubt their divinity. The parishioners should therefore realize it made no difference whether their priest was spiritual or not. If the church appointed him, God would work through him by virtue of the office.

By this logic, Augustine could have argued that female priests would be as good as male, since the sacraments would be from God anyway. But Augustine and the Donatists both believed a female priest would defile the sacraments, so that argument couldn't arise. Augustine's claim also suggested that the Eucharist would be equally valid if offered by a Donatist or a Catholic priest, but neither side recognized that either. While the Donatists said that their priests must be holy individuals, Augustine said they need only belong to a holy organization. And only one organization was holy, namely the state-backed church. To qualify for the priesthood, men needed only be male and appointed by the right superiors. If the parishioners didn't respect the priests picked to lead them, they should realize their feelings didn't matter. If they rejected their appointed leaders, they would be damned as Donatists.

So Augustine disposed of the Donatist notion that sin was like a disease, to be caught from a sinning priest. But if this was the issue, what happened to the question of people's right to choose their leaders? The whole Donatist heresy started when the hierarchy appointed a bishop, but his parishioners rejected him. Their reasons for denouncing Bishop Caecilian may seem spiteful, and the priests they preferred may strike us as vindictive. But those were the leaders many native North Africans respected. How could they be stopped from choosing their own heroes?

In India, most people felt it inevitable that students chose their religious teachers, and no guru could force himself on an unwilling student.

But for Augustine, this was just the problem to be solved. To him the challenge was obvious: If the church couldn't control who the people followed, then it wouldn't control the people period. The church would be just one voice among others, and anyone could feel free to ignore it. Such a position of abject weakness would be unacceptable for the official church of imperial Rome. Was not his church mandated by God to rule the world? Augustine felt it was an inescapable choice: either the church must govern, or else be governed. And if lower orders of Christians continued presuming a right to overrule their superiors, then either the insubordination or the subordinates had to go.

In the midst of this debate, Augustine felt he had to justify his argument theologically. He had to overcome the popular assumption that freedom was a Christian value. If ordinary Christians mustn't choose their own leaders, what actually disqualified them from doing so? Why was it best for the parishioners themselves to give up choosing their leaders? The answer was they were creatures trapped in a state of inborn sin, which rendered them blind to God's truth. To choose their own leaders in that case, could only mean the blind leading the blind. Where Jesus challenged people to think for themselves, Augustine seemed to prove they had no such capacity: "If man were good, he would be other than he is. Now, however, since he is as he is, he is not good, and does not have it in his power to be good — either because he does not see what he ought to be, or because he does see, but does not have it in his power to be what he sees he ought to be. Who would doubt that this is a punishment?"[58]

Augustine characterized the state of original sin as an instinctive disobedience to ultimate authority, inherited since the first disobedient acts of Adam and Eve. As evidence, he mentioned his own desire for sex. Despite his vow of chastity, he still dreamed of sex and woke with his penis erect. Obviously the body was tainted with inborn disobedience and couldn't be trusted. Augustine actually used the word *libido*, meaning a lower drive which should be subject to a higher good.[59] And in the face of this problem, he saw basically two options: Either give free rein to the chaos of disobedient desires, or else subject human weakness to a superhuman authority. Augustine implored the council to support option two. And this commonly passed as the Christian response to life down to modern times. For example, when a pastor at Cornerstone Church in San Antonio asked a study group, "How many of you have subverted your natures for Christ?" several people raised their hands. The pastor nodded and said, "That's good. We all have natures and we all have to forcibly subdue them."[60]

Other philosophers often spoke of life as a game of meeting human needs well, as in the saying "Eating must come before philosophy, and wealth before art." But Augustine assumed that spiritual growth happened by suppressing sin. He identified the tension of higher and lower drives in each person with the struggle between rulers and subjects. In that case, spiritual growth was primarily growth in submission to authority. And if people found this insufficiently appealing, then sinners were better off if forced to it: "For the effectiveness of God's mercy cannot be in the power of men to frustrate if he will have none of it."[61] For Augustine it was not important "whether anyone is compelled or not, but what he is compelled to, be this good or evil."[62] As he explained to the Donatists, "error has no rights; to disbelieve in forced conversions is to disbelieve the power of God."[63] Though it wasn't normal for people to think obedience was the highest virtue for adults, Augustine claimed it was.

Like many leaders of Roman society, Augustine cherished a hope that all people should find the grace to accept their God-given roles. As his vision of harmony later appeared in the *City of God*,

. . . there shall be this great blessing, that no inferior shall envy any superior, as now the archangels are not to be envied by the angels, because no one will wish to be what he has not received, though bound in strictest concord with him who has received; as in the body the finger does not seek to be the eye, though both members are harmoniously included in the complete structure of the body. And thus, along with his gift, greater or less, each shall receive this further gift of contentment to desire no more than he has.[64]

For such peace to prevail against the Donatist revolt, Christians needed to accept that their inborn nature made them unfit for self-determination. They needed to realize that free will was a delusion, and obedience the path of virtue: ". . . obedience . . . is, so to speak, the mother and guardian of all the virtues of a rational creature. The fact is that a rational creature is so constituted that submission is good for it, while yielding to its own rather than its Creator's will is, on the contrary, disastrous."[65]

Where Jesus asked, "Why can't you decide for yourselves what is right?" Augustine answered that his people could not because they were imperfect sinners. Since they were obviously imperfect and none could prove otherwise, they were disqualified from freedom. Of course later Catholic priests like Richard Rohr showed how this missed to whole point of Jesus' teaching: "We can't always be correct, but we can be connected."[66] But as Augustine saw it, faith required people to cease trusting their own minds, and turn for guidance to a higher authority.[67] And which authority was that? Of course they should submit to God and Jesus Christ; the only problem was discerning who spoke for the Lord. And fortunately, Augustine felt, it was obvious: God spoke through the appointed heads of the Roman church and state. Didn't Christ himself initiate the succession of true bishops? And if God was sovereign over all, how could Rome's rulers have authority unless God willed it? In other situations, Augustine honestly condemned the corruption of all earthly institutions. But in this argument with rebel subordinates, he claimed a heavenly source of worldly power. God acted in history through his chosen agents, who were the ones He had already placed in authority. In God's war against evil, only a powerful alliance of church and state could overcome the fallen population's propensity for sin.[68]

This argument was appealing mainly to the empire's rulers and church heads. Those in high office generally assumed they were less prone to sin than their subordinates. And the advantage of Augustine's argument for bishops was obvious. If the parishioners placed their trust in higher minds, then the bishops might lead without opposition. If everyone believed they were naturally damned from birth, and could escape eternal pain only by supporting the Orthodox Church, then that organization might gain a universal market for its services.

At the end of the 411 council, Marcellinus ruled that Augustine's party was the real church, and the Donatist church an illegal sect. He ordered Donatist churches closed, their property confiscated, and the death penalty for further participation in Donatist meetings. The order had to be enforced by the Roman army. It was somewhat like the story in Numbers 16 and 17, where a rebellious tribesman named Korah challenged Moses and Aaron's power, saying "You have gone too far! For all the community are holy, all of them, and the Lord is in their midst! Why then do you raise yourselves above the Lord's congregation?" But when Korah's followers gathered, Moses called for a test of divine favor, and the rebels suffered God's ultimate rebuke: "The earth closed over them and they vanished from the midst of the congregation." (Numbers 16:33)

177

Questioning the Mother of All Virtues

While Augustine lived, a number of European churchmen challenged his emerging doctrine against freedom. These critics such as Pelagius or Julian of Eclanum debated Augustine, and basically they lost. This seemed to prove that Augustine was right, but the defeated opponents may have won in the long term. Most modern Christians would probably agree that Augustine's opponents were far closer to Jesus' views on freedom.

When Pelagius heard Augustine's doctrine of original sin, he said, "It makes it seem as though the Devil was the maker of men."[69] Far from believing that people were born in sin, Pelagius said each newborn child was innocent and good as Adam and Eve on the morning of creation. When Adam and Eve fell into separation from God, it was their own failing, which harmed only themselves. Pelagius wanted to reverse Augustine's argument. Instead of assuming that people were naturally damned unless saved by the church, he claimed they were naturally good unless they damned themselves. The choice of following Jesus lay with each individual, and the church's job was to encourage free people to make that choice.[70] Somewhat predictably, the controversy-hardened bishops of North Africa brought charges of heresy against Pelagius.

In 415, two church councils reviewed the accusations against Pelagius, and both affirmed his views as orthodox. The mainly Eastern churchmen at these councils still held a basically Jewish understanding of sin. For them, sin was an error people *did*, not the essence of what they were. Many of them taught that Jesus affirmed the ultimate goodness of every soul, as in the letters of St. Antony: "A wise man has first to know himself, so that he may know what is of God, and all his grace which he has always bestowed upon us, and then to know that every sin and every accusation is alien to the nature of our spiritual essence."[71]

But Augustine knew another excuse for anarchy when he saw it. He petitioned Pope Zosimus to overrule the recent councils and condemn

Pelagius. Zosimus said he could see nothing wrong with Pelagius's teaching. Augustine had to explain that Pelagius would destroy Christianity, by denying any need for God and his church. If people believed they were naturally saved, they'd think they didn't need the church to save them. They would think their fallen lives were already good, and would follow their own sinful natures rather than God's representatives. Under furious lobbying by North African bishops, Zosimus reversed himself, and in 417 he declared Pelagius a heretic.[72] At this, Pelagius "took refuge in silence," possibly in a mixture of horror and sheer amazement.

The next challenger was Italian bishop Julian of Eclanum. Julian demanded a series of public debates with Augustine, hoping to unseat this theological horseman against freedom. The resulting series of verbal jousts was colorful and mutually insulting. Before an international audience Augustine found his claims to represent ultimate authority were unconvincing. Julian scored points, ridiculing the idea that sexual love was a sinful result of the Fall, rather than part of God's good creation. He famously objected that a merciful God would never condemn innocent babies to hell just because they died before baptism. By Julian's implication, love and marriage were good things. Babies were born good before the church made them good. God loved his children like the Prodigal Father. Natural goodness merited freedom.

Augustine's patience wore thin. His very participation in this debate started to seem like a concession to doubt over God's omnipotence. As he wrote in *The City of God*,

> *If we always felt obliged to reply to counterarguments, when would there be an end to the argument or a limit to the discussion? For those who cannot grasp what is said, or, if they understand the truth, are too obdurate to accept it, keep on replying and, according to the Holy Writ, "speak iniquity," and never weary of empty words. You can easily see what an endless, wearisome,*

179

and fruitless task it would be, if I were to refute all the unconsidered objections of people who pig-headedly contradict everything I say.[73]

Augustine probably assumed that Julian was just the latest tool of the Devil, trying to lead all Rome into an expanded Donatist rebellion. To deal with this negativity, he petitioned the Pope to throw Julian out of the church. The expulsion order finally arrived, with a requirement that all other Italian clerics renounce Julian's views or be fired as well. Eighteen bishops refused and lost their jobs.[74]

In his later years, Augustine began insisting that God's omnipotent power precluded the very existence of human freedom — because every thought and deed was actually predestined by God's will. But after Augustine died, the Catholic Church rejected this extreme view. Most bishops believed that people had choices in life, and were personally responsible for them. In this at least, the church upheld the orthodoxy of freedom. But for 1,500 years it retained the principle that original sin disqualified people from choosing their own leaders, laws, or beliefs.

The Future of Original Sin

In the centuries to come, the doctrine that original sin precludes freedom had a long career. Many Christians emphasized it so much, they seemed to make it the core of Jesus' "good news." By a modified version of this doctrine, the Roman church held itself above criticism from the sinful laity down to the twentieth century. For most of that period, any person who opposed a clerical superior was liable to criminal prosecution. And the penalties for this presumption slowly increased — from penances of fasting, to prison, to torture, burning at the stake, and finally military assault on whole communities which tried to choose their own values or leaders. For many people, this was "the" Christian response to liberty. But what happened to people who stubbornly believed that Jesus stood for freedom?

John Cassian (ca. 365–433), who founded Western Europe's monastic tradition, didn't directly contradict Augustine. But he did point out that the book of Genesis described Adam as capable of choosing between good and evil, both before and after the Fall.[75] In Deuteronomy also, the Hebrews were obviously free to choose their destiny: "See, I have set before you this day life and good, death and evil . . . choose life, that you and your descendents might live." (30:15, 19) Cassian felt it was obvious that the Bible called people to use their freedom wisely, not give it up completely.

In Greek Orthodox tradition, leaders like Basil the Great (329–379) usually treated their parishioners as good people who were trying to get better. Leadership in this church remained semi-democratic, somewhat as in the first centuries. Local people recommended candidates for parish priest to their bishop, and the priests elected their bishops.[76] Perhaps in the East people retained a more direct folk memory of how Jesus treated other people. The Armenian Church also kept a tradition of choosing its leaders by some form of local consensus. This was the biggest reason why the Armenians reclaimed independence from the Roman Church. They couldn't accept Rome's constant demands for obedience, or its attempts to appoint superiors over the locally elected leaders.[77] In a similar defense against central control, the Egyptian Coptic, Syrian Jacobite, and Nestorian churches all declared independence from the Church of Rome. Later the Greek and Latin churches slowly drifted apart, mainly over issues of who should obey who. So the call for unity through blind obedience to one supreme authority was just what broke the international Christian movement apart. As Nicetas, the Greek Archbishop of Nicomedia explained to a western bishop (Anselm of Halvberg) in the 1100s:

If the Roman Pontiff, seated on the lofty throne of his glory, wishes to

181

thunder at us and our churches, not by taking counsel with us but at his own pleasure, what kind of brotherhood, or even what kind of parenthood can this be? We should be slaves, not the sons of such a Church . . . In such case what could have been the use of the Scriptures? The writings and teachings of the Fathers would be useless. The authority of the Roman Pontiff would nullify the value of all because he would be the only bishop, the sole teacher and master.[78]

Of course this point was inadmissible in the supreme pontiff's court. If faith meant submission, then it grew logical to make blind obedience a requirement for salvation. When a host of movements for lay initiative appeared, including the Waldensians, Fraticelli, Beguines, Beghards, or other "Brethren of the Free Spirit," the Church warned them to do nothing without permission of the clergy. Where permission was denied but the revivalists went ahead anyway, the Church outdid pagan Rome in killing unauthorized preachers. Though the Christian martyrs of early centuries would rather die than pledge an oath of blind obedience, Pope Innocent III (1198–1216) felt he must explain, "Every cleric must obey the Pope, even if he commands what is evil; for no one may judge the Pope." Even on hearing that King John of England had signed the Magna Carta (1215), Innocent said, "By St. Peter, we cannot pass over this insult without punishing it."[79] For Innocent, the Magna Carta violated God's moral order by making a King submit to demands from those below him.

We might assume the Protestant Reformation rose to affirm religious freedom. But most Protestant leaders actually championed a full return to Augustine's doctrine against free will. John Wyclif (1320–84) contradicted his Church by teaching that only Adam and Eve ever possessed freedom — which they lost both for themselves and all posterity, as their punishment for disobedience. From that time forward no one alive had any real freedom, but all were slaves to inborn sin. Instead of teaching that God loves all souls, Wyclif and others insisted people must realize they could never be acceptable to the Father. No matter what they did, they would remain hopelessly unworthy of salvation, and deserve only eternal punishment. The good news of Christ was simply that God had overlooked the faults of some people, choosing them for predestined salvation through no merit or choice of their own.

Martin Luther agreed, claiming that God's omnipotence rendered each human "unfree as a block of wood, a rock, a lump of clay or a pillar of salt." Therefore, Luther supported slavery, feudal dues, and forced labor as seen in the Bible: "Sheep, cattle, men-servants, and maid-servants were all possessions to be sold as it pleased their masters. It were a good thing it were still so. For else no man may compel nor tame the servile folk."[80] As if to outdo Augustine's denial of freedom, the Lutheran Augsburg Confession of 1530 stressed:

> *Since the fall of Adam all men who are born according to the course of nature are conceived and born in sin. That is, all men are full of evil lust and inclinations from their mother's wombs and are unable by nature to have true fear of God and true faith in God. Moreover, this inborn sickness and hereditary sin is truly sin, and condemns to the eternal wrath of God all those who are not born again through Baptism [into the Lutheran church] and the Holy Spirit.*[81]

We should mention that the Catholic Council of Trent in the 1540s opposed Protestantism partly because it seemed to deny the existence of freedom. Most Catholics denied predestination, and affirmed that people are responsible for their own choices. Still the Catholic clergy found some common ground with the Protestants on original sin. In 1648, after the Treaty of Westphalia ended 30 years of religious war over the souls and tithes of Europe's people, both Protestant and Catholic rulers agreed that the populations of each state must follow the religion of their king. If the parishioners had recently demonstrated their power to choose between rival churches, then it was all the more important they be punished for doing so.

Upholding the Divine Right of Dictators

Naturally, Christian dictators claimed that monarchical rule was established by the Bible. There were "pro-monarchist" passages to be found there. In I Samuel, God reportedly called Saul to take sole power as a king. (9:1–10:16) But other verses such as I Samuel 8:4–22 had God warning that giving supreme power to one man must bring disaster. As usual, people in authority picked the verses they liked. And for Emperor Constantine this was a no brainer. Obviously, peace and order depended on the victory of one man's will over all others, so that strife could cease. This was the dream of all military empires in history, and now it became the church's dream as well. As an answer to the problem of suffering, it was basically the same as Ogyu Sorai gave in Imperial Japan:

> As soon as men are born, desires spring up. When we cannot realize our desires, which are unlimited, struggle arises; when struggle arises, confusion follows. As the ancient kings hated confusion, they founded propriety and righteousness, and with these governed the desires of the people. ... Morality is nothing but the necessary means for controlling the subjects of the Empire. It did not originate with nature, nor with the impulses of man's heart, but it was devised by the superior intelligence of certain sages, and authority was given it by the state.[82]

For Constantine and later Christian autocrats, the cross was not a symbol of suffering under tyranny; it was a token of lordly power.[83] And since the rulers stood at the peak of power, they felt there was no one higher in relation to God. So a gold medal from the 300s showed an angelic hand descending from above to lay a crown of dominion on Constantine's head. Later, a mosaic in S. Apollinare church at Ravenna portrayed Emperor Constantius IV standing Moses-like, handing down a scroll to his high priest. As in a cartoon, the emperor's figure was clearly labeled "Imperator," while the scroll was marked "Privilegia."[84] For Constantine and his descendants, "grace" meant "patronage."[85] As court historian Eusebius explained, Constantine was God's viceroy on earth, who would "frame his earthly government according to the pattern of the divine original, finding strength in its conformity with the monarchy of God."[86] As it was below in Constantine's Rome, so it would be in heaven.

The later Christian emperors appreciated Augustine's arguments that obedience was the "mother and guardian of all the virtues." Because in this version of Christianity, a helpful inversion of moral logic followed. Since ordinary Christians were too sinful by nature to decide things for themselves, the moral thing for them was obey whatever their superiors told them. Rather than trying to judge proposed actions by their own moral sense, people would judge each proposal by the status of its proposer. In that case, the Christian belief in God's kingdom no longer challenged the power of earthly rulers; it only confirmed their status as God's spokesmen on earth.

This view of power was of course contrary to the tale of Jesus' temptation in the desert. But it still usually passed for orthodoxy for well over a thousand years. During the Middle Ages, any who opposed their autocrats in church or state were officially recorded as diabolical heretics, or terrorists against God. As Canon Jean le Bel explained, the motives for the great French peasant revolt of 1358 were "uncontrolled diabolical madness" and "senseless beastly rage."[87] That was what official scribes were supposed to say about the many revolts they recorded. With the clergy and rulers so closely allied in controlling their subjects, all protest against unjust superiors seemed anti-religious. And the protesters often came to believe it themselves. In popular revolts across central Italy from the 1350s to 1370s, people commonly attacked both local lords and clergymen. It was a capital crime to rebel, so protests which would nowadays be peaceful strikes often turned into killing contests. In Viterbo in 1367, the locals massacred a group of Cardinals and their retainers. But such incidents only convinced most clerics that the Inquisition must work harder.

Next, in the 1370s a revolt against papal rule reportedly involved 1,577 towns or major villages. The chronicler of Milan said, "all the cities and villages of Romagna, the Marche, the Duchy of Spoleto, the Papal States, and the Campania of Rome, then under dominion of the priests, threw off the church's yoke, went under the flag of liberty, and made themselves free."[88] It's a matter of political perspective if these were godless people, or just demanding mutual respect between human beings. A record from Rouen, France in 1382 says the "rabble" marched into the Abby of Saint-Ouën, forced the abbot to tear up his charter of privileges over the villagers, and made the monks write up a new charter, "of the rights and liberties of Normandy . . . which restored the ancient rights to the commune at Rouen."[89] Was this something Jesus would condemn? The lords of Hungry certainly felt so. After slaughtering a host of rebellious villagers in 1514, they wrote, ". . . the recent rebellion . . . has for all time to come put the stain of faithlessness upon the peasants, and they have thereby forfeited their liberty, and have become subject to their landlords in unconditional and perpetual servitude . . . Every species of property belongs to the landlords, and the peasant has no right to invoke justice and the law against a noble."[90]

By the 20th century, basic freedoms for ordinary people would not seem contrary to Christianity. But down to the 1800s, most people felt it obvious where the church stood. Most orthodox Christians accepted that civilization depended on people submitting their wills to higher authority. Without that, life would be dog-eat-dog barbarism, with every organ in the social body rebelling against the head. So with due realism, King Louis XIV advised his son: "A measure of severity was the greatest kindness I could do to my people . . . For as soon as a king weakens in that which he has commanded, authority perishes, and with it the public peace . . . Everything falls upon the lowest ranks, oppressed by thousands of petty tyrants, instead of by a legitimate king."[91]

In nations or churches of divided authority, the usual results were civil war, or subjugation by external enemies. For the simple sake of survival it seemed obvious: each society must have one king, one faith, and one law. This, it seemed, was Christian civilization's primary message to the world. So when Jesuit missionaries came to China in the 1500s, they presented their faith as a doctrine of submission to the three sovereign lords — the ultimate Lord in heaven, the emperor on earth, and the sovereign father of each family.[92] If this doctrine of proper order achieved its ultimate expression, all humanity would be united under one emperor, with one world religion. And perhaps someday, a great expansion of empire would bring that dream to pass. But if no king or church could yet control more than a portion of the earth, then the best religion could do was uphold one chain of command for each kingdom. As the rulers of Reformation Europe managed to agree in 1648, "in a prince's country, a prince's religion."

In Reformation-age Europe, conformity with the ruler's religion remained the usual requirement for all residents of each state. If a subject supported the church of a different ruler, it was both treason and heresy. It was no more acceptable than if an ancient Jew worshiped Marduk and gave his allegiance to Babylon. Naturally, the ruler's choice of religion could be a fragile basis for unity. As Sebastian Franck remarked, "if one prince dies and his successor is of another creed, then this at once becomes God's word."[93] Even so, it seemed dangerously destabilizing to suggest that two or more ruling heads might be better than one.

Still the Reformation took one step toward affirming freedom. It established that national rulers were free to choose their priesthoods. And naturally the question arose: if princes should have religious freedom, was it godly for any others to have it as well? After a revolt of puritanical Christian rebels overthrew the English King in the 1640s, a restoration of divine-right kings seemed to show the answer. And to defend God's chain of command for the future, Sir Robert Filmer wrote a book called *Patriarchia*, or *The Natural Power of Kings Asserted* (1680). In this classic, he affirmed that all power came from God: first it passed down to Adam, then to the kings of Israel, and hence to the absolute monarchs of Christendom. Therefore the faith's primary charge to males was to obey their higher lords while ruling as sovereigns over their inferiors.[94] As in ancient Rome, this faith seemed to involve trust that a superior could do no wrong. William Blackstone put it clearly in the 1760s: "The King of England is not only the chief, but properly the sole magistrate of the nation. He . . . is not only incapable of doing wrong, but even incapable of thinking wrong."[95]

Of course such well-established faith would scarcely need defending if the world still found it convincing. And Sir Filmer wrote his *Patriarchia* to refute doubters like Thomas Hobbes, who had recently claimed, "In all times kings and persons of sovereign authority, because of their independency, are in continual jealousies, and in the state and posture of gladiators; having their weapons pointed, and their eyes fixed on one another — that is their forts, garrisons, and guns on the frontiers of their kingdoms — and continual spies upon their neighbors; which is a posture of war . . . Force and fraud are in war the cardinal virtues."[96]

Meanwhile in Eastern Europe, the notion that all power came from God met the test of Muslim Turkish rule. Under a Turkish Sultan, the Greek Orthodox Patriarch Gregory V felt constrained, by both his Muslim rulers and his own religious tradition, to condemn the rising movement for Greek freedom. In his "Paternal Exhortation" of 1790, Gregory called Greek Christians to stop bombing and killing Turks. They should remember that God had placed them under the Ottoman Sultan, and their cry for freedom was "an enticement of the Devil and a murderous poison destined to push the people into disorder and destruction." Later, Patriarch Gregory threatened to excommunicate any local priests who aided or sheltered Greek freedom-fighters.[97] No doubt the patriarch knew his own life depended on giving such orders, and on his church obeying them. The Ottoman rulers had already killed, enslaved, or exiled seven Orthodox patriarchs for failing to control their subordinates. And when Gregory failed to halt the movement for Greek independence, they killed him too.

Is Christianity Anti-Democratic?

Throughout the Reformation, it seemed clear, as Voltaire would put it, that nations with one ruler and religion had peaceful tyranny, while those with two religions or political parties had civil war. Surely in that case, God willed unity whatever the cost. When the Protestant movement washed through Denmark in 1536, King Frederick I at first refused to ban either Catholic or Lutheran clergymen, declaring he had no lordship over souls. Denmark's lords then tolerated the chaos of competing churches for all of four years. Finally the king called an official debate, ruled the Protestant sect victorious, and established that as the only church of his land. In Poland, the national Diet approved religious freedom for Catholic, Protestant, and Eastern Orthodox believers in 1555. But within a decade the fear of internal division and external enemies generated a new alliance of rulers, landlords, and the Catholic Inquisition.[98] In France the outcome of religious competition was even more tragic. In general, if a kingdom's population grew divided in religion, there was usually open conflict till one church prevailed. And if all religious competition was a struggle for monopoly control, then simple self-defense required England's Puritan, Anglican, and Catholic churches to deny each other's rights to exist.[99]

The first colonists to the Americas carried all these assumptions about God's chain of command with them. Though many were refugees from conflicts over state religion, most settlers assumed that their colonies must also have official churches, with membership and tithing required by law. The Puritans of New England felt it was a religious necessity to expel "interloping" Anglican missionaries, and hang several Quaker ones for heresy. Meanwhile in officially Anglican North Carolina, Rev. Charles Woodman condemned an invasion of Baptist "enthusiasts," whose "Love Feasts and Kiss of Charity . . . Lasciviousness, Wantonness, Adultery . . . brought into Contempt" the Christian faith. Woodman predicted that if these self-appointed evangelists were not chased away, it would mean "the End of Religion: Confusion, Anarchy, and every Evil Work."[100] As in Massachusetts, most clerics thought it obvious that anyone differing from their state's religion of must either conform, or go elsewhere.

Perhaps this sense of an "elsewhere" for dissidents was the first serious breach in the walls of religious jurisdictions since the primitive Jesus movement. In Europe, Catholics under a Protestant prince could flee to a Catholic land, and English Puritans under a Catholic queen could sail for Holland. But in the New World, religious dissidents felt they could encroach on Native land, and set up their own official churches. So the shores of North America grew dotted with colonies of different state religions — Congregationalists in New England, Anglicans in Virginia and Carolina, Catholics in Quebec, Maryland, and Florida. Though England had only one national church, its American colonies had several. And in the spaces *between* these colonies, the dissidents and pioneers of different churches mixed together. Especially around the Delaware Valley, the land began filling with a mixture of Quaker, Baptist, Presbyterian,

Congregationalist, and Lutheran neighbors. None of these groups had a majority, but they needed to cooperate in carving roads or building town halls. Probably most settlers believed that their own church was the only true one and their neighbors were going to hell. Some didn't want their children to play with families from other churches, but they still ended up building schools for the whole community. In general, the locals managed to get along. According to Mark A. Noll, "The result was a degree of interdenominational tolerance probably unknown anywhere else in the world at that time."[101] That overlooks the religious diversity of India or China, but for the Christian world it applies.

Some colonists saw the chaotic mixture of religions as a problem to be solved, hopefully by imposing their own church as the official one. Others felt that religious diversity was a hardship of the primitive frontier. But some settlers decided this mixing of misfits was a breakthrough, to a kind of community beyond force-backed conformity. So Roger Williams (1603–1683) and other deviants from Massachusetts set up their alternative colony of Rhode Island, and wrote the first official charter of religious freedom since Constantine's declaration of 313. According to this charter:

1. Individuals who did not voluntarily join a church were not accountable to the social covenant of that church.
2. State or church authorities had no right to enforce church attendance, since only God moves the heart from within.
3. Churches should make no attempt to rule the general public, nor should the government try to rule religion.[102]

This colony became a haven for all manner of people who didn't fit in other colonies. Back in Massachusetts, Cotton Mather was disgusted. Rhode Island, he accused, had become a sink, a cesspool, a latrine for the religious refuse of the whole world: "Antinomians, Anabaptists, Anti-Sabbatarians, Arminians, Socinians, Quakers, Ranters — everything except Roman Catholics and Real Christians."[103]

But while Rhode Island's principles seemed anarchical and "anti-clerical," they were not anti-religious. To the surprise of most educated people, free competition of churches tended to increase rather than destroy the public demand for religion. Instead of plunging society into chaos, the babble of religious disagreement generated some constructive ideas. Soon it was similar in Pennsylvania, where William Penn argued that people should decide religious matters by their own conscience, not have sheriffs, armies, rulers, or appointed clerics do it for them. And most people in his colony thought Penn was being pro- rather than anti-religious. This out-of-control society must be where Voltaire got his insight that nations with one church have oppression, those with two have civil wars, but those with a hundred religions have peace.

Like Donatists, the American revolutionaries resented "spiritual lords" of the Anglican Church being appointed from England to guide them. They felt it ungodly that non-Anglicans in Carolina were forced to pay taxes to the state-backed Anglican Church. And these attitudes also applied to their actual rulers. As preacher Jonathan Mayhew argued,

> *Rulers have no authority from God to mischief . . . It is blasphemy to call tyrants and oppressors God's ministers. They are more properly "the messengers of Satan to buffet us." No rulers are properly God's ministers but such are just, ruling in the fear of God. When once magistrates act contrary to their office . . . when they rob and ruin the public instead of being guardians of its peace and welfare — they immediately cease to be the ordinance of God and no more deserve that glorious character than common pirates and highway men . . .* [104]

192

Growing numbers of people wondered how submission to dictators ever became a Christian virtue. Wasn't mutual accountability and mutual respect more like Jesus' point? Wherever religious competition was not silenced by force, the Christians who thought freedom was godly tended to win this argument.

For the American Revolution to succeed, the assumption that Christianity stood for freedom had to be widely accepted. And thanks to numerous earlier writers or preachers across the Western world, this view was growing popular. For example the French Catholic Étienne de la Boétie, published his views on tyranny around the year 1549: "To free oneself it is not necessary to use force against a tyrant. He falls as soon as the country is tired of him. The people who are being degraded and enslaved need but deny him any right . . . Be firmly resolved no longer to be slaves — and you are free! Deny the tyrant your help, and like a colossus whose pedestal is pulled away, he will collapse and break to pieces." [105]

When such ideas gained support in the American Revolution, it was popular Christianity rather than "secularism" which undermined both divine-right kings and divine-right churches.[106] Some rebels like Patrick Henry still insisted an independent America must continue upholding an official religion. But a majority of Constitution writers felt they were being good Christians in rejecting that. They mostly agreed with James Madison that state backing for churches had always brought "pride and indolence for the clergy, ignorance and servility in the laity, superstition, bigotry, and persecution." Thomas Paine added that he had always believed "My own mind is my own church."[107] It might not have been the greatest insight, but at least Paine wasn't killed for it.

Of course the old state-backed churches didn't tolerate this sort of godless anarchy. So in the early 1800s, the Pope condemned a whole series of Latin American independence movements, as if submission to the King of Spain was a fundamental article of Jesus' faith. To uphold the seemingly godly principle of top-down command, the Roman Church continued upgrading its rules and restrictions, building on its foundation of church council decrees. In 1917, the revised Code of Canon Law, number 1386.1 clarified that no priest could write, edit, or contribute to any publication without permission from his local bishop. To meet this requirement, every diocese needed a censor to process requests for the right to speak.[108] The restriction that inferiors could not appeal complaints over the heads of their own supervisors remained a key principle of church government. Even in the 1990s, when nuns of the Missionary Sisters of Our Lady of Africa protested of sexual abuse by priests, the church hierarchy ruled their case must be judged by the bishop whose staff they accused.[109]

6. And How About Equality?

During the French Revolution, a kind of religious war broke out between rejecters and defenders of Christianity as they knew it. Both sides seemed to accept that a vision of liberty, equality, and fraternity was diametrically opposed to everything that religion ever stood for. As revolutionary mobs plundered churches and killed priests, the scenes resembled Christian vandalism on pagan temples in the 390s when Emperor Theodosius stripped cults of state protection. If the state patronized a religion and then disowned it, it was like a green light for pent up resentment. To most clerics, the revolution was an attack of rabble from hell to destroy God's order. And sure enough, the ancient dream of communist equality reared its head. The fanatics in the streets shouted for church wealth, maybe all wealth, to be seized and shared by the people.

According to Acts, "The company of those who believed was of one heart and soul, and no one said that any of the things he possessed was his own, but they had everything in common." (4:32) And when the founders of monastic orders tried to follow this rather unrealistic dream, most Christians saw it as a holy thing. Saint Antony was only one of many who literally took Jesus' advice, "Go and sell all you have, and give it to the poor." But when the rabble of Paris demanded all things be shared, it seemed a triumph of all evils the Inquisition held at bay. And naturally, the rabble and their spokesmen soon found the difficulties of communal bliss insurmountable. After furious debate in the people's Assembly, the government turned its army loose on looters. Then it also began massacring protesters who wanted to re-establish traditional religion. For many traditionalists, it seemed the most anti-Christian act of all to kill the King and Queen. But eliminating rival leaders was also a long-standing religious practice.

When the traditionally Christian states united to crush the revolution, they suffered shocking defeats by the patriot armies of godless liberty. The lords of Christendom soon found themselves stripped of authority and fleeing their kingdoms. Marching into Rome, the revolutionary armies seized the Pope and threw him in jail. Imposing freedom of religion by force, the French removed all legal restrictions on religious minorities. As in revolutionary America, the French declared legal equality of all religions. The Jews were released from their ghettos, even in Rome. Out they came, mixing with the Christian population, and praising the virtues of Judaism's equality with Christianity.

The Godless Rabble for Equality

Later, the forces of Christian law and order regrouped to prevail once more. Even before that, Napoleon returned to tradition by crowning himself emperor and restoring the old role of religion in his chain of command. After a Concordat with the Catholic Church in 1802, he authorized a catechism for the schoolchildren of France. It taught boys and girls that "to honor the Emperor is to honor God himself . . . if they should fail in their duties to the Emperor . . . they would be resisting the order established by God . . . and would make themselves deserving of eternal damnation."[1] The war then became a traditional battle for supreme power, as the old autocrats united to throw off their French liberators. After that, for several decades more the rule of royal families and loyal state churches prevailed as God's will. It seemed the alternative dreams of equality and freedom were no more viable for Christendom than Lord Cromer, the later English Viceroy of Egypt, thought they were for the Middle East: "What Egypt required most of all was order and good government. Perhaps . . . liberty would follow afterwards. No one but a dreamy theorist could imagine that the natural order of things could be reversed and that liberty could first be accorded to the poor ignorant representatives of the Egyptian people, and the latter would then be able to evolve order out of chaos."[2]

The young United States also passed through an anti-clerical phase, where many people scorned both Anglicanism as a pro-royal religion, and Catholicism as another foreign-backed conspiracy. But once the European armies of France, Spain, and Britain had left the continent, no foreign powers backed these churches. All churches in America found themselves equally lacking in state patrons. And with no such political advantage to fight over, there was basically peace among religions, at least within the American state's borders. Until the run-up to the Civil War, crusades to the death for religious causes ceased. It was mostly on the expanding state's frontiers that issues of control still seemed to be literal battles between good and evil.

Among Bible-reading Americans, an old debate still simmered as to if the book taught submission to God-chosen authorities, or if it supported equality for each soul. But probably most Americans approved arguments like Catharine Beecher's, that the "principles of Democracy, then, are identical to the principles of Christianity."[3] This would be a surprise to most Europeans. Even many Americans felt it was half-baked idealism. Democracy in religion seemed to lead toward growing differences instead of consensus. As churches went their separate ways, even family members increasingly disagreed about standards for relations between men and women, parents and children, different races, or economic classes. Over time, America became an enormous country with many alternative Christian cultures, talking at each other mostly in a single common language. The discussion of values escaped all clerical control, and became a public ongoing American argument. As Marcus Borg put it, America's "culture wars" were to a large extent "Jesus wars," because people on various sides of each issue claimed to represent Jesus' values.

Concerning people's common rights, founding fathers like John Adams tried to curb any slide toward communistic equality. Adams urged a property requirement for the right to vote, and warned that if this was overcome by pressure from commoners, "New claims will arise; women will demand the vote; lads [under 21] will think their rights not enough attended to; and every man who has not a farthing, will demand an equal voice with any other, in all acts of state. It tends to confound and destroy all distinctions, and prostrate all ranks to one common level."[4]

This worry also applied to Black people. On one hand, Presbyterian minister James H. Thornwell defended enslavement of Blacks, claiming it was a heresy of atheists, communists, Red Republicans and Jacobins that "the duties of all men are specifically the same." Real Christians, Thornwell insisted, accepted that God assigned different lots in life to different people, and only the requirement "of true obedience is universally the same."[5] On the other hand, other Presbyterian ministers in a General Assembly of 1818 announced an opposite doctrine from the Bible: "We consider the voluntary enslaving of one part of the human race by another as a gross violation of the most precious and sacred rights of human nature; as utterly inconsistent with the law of God . . . and as totally irreconcilable with the spirit and principles of the Gospel of Christ."[6] With this degree of difference between its ministers, the Presbyterian Church broke into separate Northern and Southern denominations.

Clearly, both anti-slavery abolitionists and defenders of private human property were convinced beyond doubt they were defending the Christian way of life. And vast numbers of these people proved willing to kill or die before allowing equality to the Blacks in their midst. As a poor Southern White farmer said in the 1850's, he wished "there warn't no niggers here. They are a great cuss to the country . . . But it wouldn't never do to free 'em and leave 'em here. I don't know anybody, hardly, in favor of that. Make 'em free and leave 'em here and they'd steal everything we made. Nobody couldn't live here then."[7]

Like conservative Europeans facing the revolutionary rabble, Southern society closed ranks against the ideology of abolitionist fanatics. A Richmond, Virginia newspaper called for an end to sending southern boys for education in the North. They should stay where "their training would be moral, religious, and conservative, and they would never learn, or read a word in school or out of school, inconsistent with orthodox Christianity, pure morality, the right of property, the sacredness of marriage." A South Carolina leader said his state was "the breakwater . . . to stay that furious tide of social and political heresies" such as socialism, abolitionism, feminism, utopianism, or universalism.[8] Clearly these people were starting to yearn for traditional Christianity as it had been in Europe.

The Backlash against Rule by the Rabble

Down to the reigns of Mussolini or Franco in the 1930s, possibly most people in Europe still assumed that absolute monarchies or military dictatorships were Christian, while rule by consent of the sinners was against God's will. In the orthodox medieval view, the church was an institution set down by God to rule his earthly creatures. But after the French Revolution had scorched all Europe from Madrid to Moscow, traditional values were never quite the same. The Pope returned to his Papal States and ordered Jews back into their ghettos. But several other nations left the Jews free. Wherever people had tasted freedom of religion, or freedom from religion, the power of churches to punish dissent and enforce tithing ebbed away. As Augustine feared, the churches were losing control of their flocks — because they lost control over who the people followed. Growing numbers were flocking to new ideologies or organizations like the Socialist Workers Union. They took their tithes from the churches and helped other causes instead. If they stopped coming to church at all, the clerics could do nothing but utter threats of hell.

Since most of us have forgotten medieval realities, we may be impressed to see what the loss of state backing meant for churches. As

Will Durant explains concerning medieval Sweden, "The Church required a tenth, annually, of all nonecclesiastical produce or income; it exacted a small fee for every building raised, every child born, every couple married, every corpse interred; it claimed a day of gratis labor from every peasant yearly; and no one could inherit property without making a contribution to the Church as the probate court of wills."[9]

In defending this monopoly on legally required sacrifices, the old churches counted it heresy for radical followers of St. Francis or other lay movements to treat religion as a freely given service. And the popular response of rejecting state churches was a kind of taxpayer revolt. Like governments commonly do, these churches tried to deny all right of their taxpayers to rebel. They treated the rise of democracy as an anti-clerical plot, which would strip the churches of all authority, all wealth, and force God's messengers to live like beggars in a secular humanist world. This was what "disestablishment" of the churches meant for them.

To battle this trend, in 1832 Pope Gregory XVI warned believers that the freedoms of conscience, worship, the press, assembly, and education, led to nothing but "a filthy sewer of heretical vomit."[10] The Papal State defended its medieval standards as God's own, and was soon widely seen as the most repressive regime in Europe. In 1864, as the secular Republic of Italy moved to "liberate" regions around Rome, Pope Pius IX replied: "In these times the haters of truth and justice and the most bitter enemies of our religion deceive the people and lie maliciously." He rejected any notion that "the Roman Pontiff can, and ought to reconcile himself, and come to terms with progress, liberalism, and modern civilization."[11] As forces of the Republic advanced to the Vatican's gates, a great emergency council of bishops counter-attacked by adopting a new doctrine of papal infallibility — "through the divine assistance promised him in Blessed Peter, the infallibility with which the divine Redeemer willed to equip his Church when it defines a doctrine of faith or morals."[12] Instead of defining what values Christianity stood for, these bishops designated which human authority spoke for God. Instead of saying, "Why do you call me good? No one is good but God alone," these officers claimed to be the ultimate authority. The new ruling claimed that Jesus' religion taught unconditional obedience to the chief priest.

When the governments of the Western world heard about the proclamation of papal infallibility, their reaction was immediate. The USA cut off diplomatic relations with the Vatican. Germany, Austria, Italy, and Belgium removed education from church management and put it under state control. Several nations banned religious orders, seized church property, or legalized secular marriage.[13] Bismarck's German government launched a real persecution of Catholics, known as the *Kulturkampf.* As in ancient Rome, many people felt there was an unbridgeable conflict between patriotism and religion, unless it was religion patronized by the state. Worst of all, Catharine Booth, who helped found the Salvation Army with her husband William Booth, said "The Pope can claim infallibility only because he is a bachelor."[14]

By this time, most official churches in Europe had lost all government aid for enforcing their decrees. And this was a vast loss of the churches' powers to make "their" people pay or obey. Back in the 1700s in Anglican England, it was still a law that "if any person . . . shall by writing . . . deny the Christian religion to be true, he shall . . . for the second offense . . . suffer three years imprisonment without bail."[15] Without such powers, how was the church supposed to enforce anything? How could a church handicap its competitors for popular support? How could it fight those who enticed parishioners to support other organizations? Were not the advocates for divorce of state from church worse enemies of God than common criminals? Many church leaders blamed the Freemasons for their woes. They said the Freemasons were a secret society of atheists and Jews, who engineered the French Revolution and remained dedicated

201

to more anti-clerical revolutions. As Pope Pius IX accused, "It is from them that the synagogue of Satan, which gathers its troops against the Church of Christ, takes its strength."[16] For Pius and other conservative leaders, the rising communist and socialist movements were all part of this Freemason-Jewish conspiracy to destroy Western civilization.

By enormous contrast, large numbers of lower-ranking Christians welcomed the modern world's movements for greater social equality. The anti-slavery movement was almost entirely driven by idealistic lay Christians. While Black protesters claimed that Moses and Jesus stood for equality, their White supporters helped build the first global movement of protest for other people's rights.[17] In Europe, the decline of godly autocratic governments opened a door for lay Christians to take leadership roles — not so much within their churches, but in public affairs. In 1837, for example, an assembly of German Catholics gathered in Mainz, whose president, Franz Josef Buss, proposed an agenda for the nation that he hoped all Christians would support. The main points were:

1. Legal limitations on the hours of work, to protect families,
2. A ban on night labor for children,
3. Protection of Sunday as a day of rest, and
4. Health care and accident insurance for all workers, to be funded through employee and employer contributions.[18]

Basically, Buss was acting as any good father might. The remarkable thing was he wished to treat the whole of Germany as he would have his own family treated. Many Christians objected that this agenda violated "biblical values" such as economic freedom, personal accountability, or the separation of earthly politics from heavenly religion. But by the 1880's, even a "man of blood and iron" like Chancellor Bismarck would feel it necessary to steal thunder from his "Christian democratic" critics, by enacting reforms such as disability insurance and old-age pensions.

Such agitation from laypeople led to something unthinkable in the previous age — Christian political parties. And these were composed mainly of activist rather than passively pious Christians. In the fledgling democracies of Europe, Italy had its Christian "Partito Populare," and Germany its Catholic "Center Party." These political parties commanded substantial blocks of support, and could make or break ruling coalitions. Poland would see something similar in the 1970s with its Solidarity party. But in the early twentieth century, these parties of activist Christians faced an autocratic backlash from both their churches and states. Neither the heads of Europe's churches nor rising politicians like Mussolini and Hitler wanted uncontrolled popular movements of lay Christians. From his side, Pope Pius XII denounced "laicism" as a threat to clerical authority.

The prophets of fascism, most prominently Franco, Mussolini, and Hitler, considered themselves men repressed, and idealists in revolt. In the wake of WWI, as most Europeans turned their backs against militarism and some countries slashed military spending, these military men felt themselves stifled beyond endurance. For them, the new democratic establishment was a denial of all that was heroic in Europe's past. As far as they could see, it had always been the striving for superiority that made men great. And nothing could be more destructive of greatness than the abolition of superiority itself. Their post-war society actually seemed ready to reject the whole struggle for survival of the fittest. Democrats and socialists spoke of "equality," as if eliminating superiority was the goal of life. Should the inheritors of a noble warrior tradition surrender to this? Or should they make themselves central to European civilization once more by any means necessary? It was still plausible that the old autocrats could make a comeback. In most of Europe the traditions of democracy were still paper-thin.

During the 1920s and 30s, the Vatican negotiated agreements with the dictators of both Italy and Germany. In both agreements the church received state protection and support, in exchange for renouncing any role in politics. The 1929 pact with Mussolini's government gave land and money to the church, state sovereignty to Vatican City, plus recognizing church canon law to govern family and religious matters among Catholics. The price was an agreement to disband the Partito Populare, and exile its leader Don Luigi Sturzo. The Pope (Pius XI) urged Christians to support the Fascist party against godless socialism, calling Mussolini "a man sent by Providence."[19] In Germany, Adolf Hitler observed, "The fact that the Curia is now making peace with Fascism shows that the Vatican trusts the new political realities far more than it did the former liberal democracy with which it could not come to terms."[20] As Hitler explained his own treaty with Germany's churches in 1933, "In consideration of the guarantees afforded by the conditions of this treaty, and of legislation protecting the rights and freedom of the Catholic Church in the Reich . . . the Holy See will ensure a ban on all clergy and members of religious congregations from political party activity."[21]

We might think this was a modern policy for separating church and state. But this separation of powers actually worked in an opposite way to the separation of church and state in North America. In North America the government pledged not to patronize any particular religion, while leaving citizens free to voice their beliefs. But the German and Italian agreements offered state patronage to recognized churches, while denying church members any right to speak of their values in public. Basically, the old order was restored. Subordinates should initiate nothing without authorization from above. All right of subordinates to criticize their superiors was denied. Morality was defined as obedience to superiors in both the church and state. In such a moral universe there was no such thing as inferiors holding their superiors accountable to a "moral principle."

The church members soon learned the price of this purely nonpolitical role for religion. When some of them dared break their silence to oppose shocking abuse of ethnic and political minorities, Hitler shot back, "When they attempt by any other means — writings, encyclical, etc. — to assume rights which belong only to the state, we will push them back into their own proper spiritual activity."[22] As under tyrants of the past, many Christian leaders counseled a pious but convenient separation between ethics for the sacred and mundane realms.

Under the Nazi regime, most Catholics proved disturbingly submissive. But Hitler was right to worry about traditional Christian values. Some dangerously large demonstrations of Catholics demanded an end to euthanasia for handicapped people, or to killing Christians of Jewish ancestry. Far fewer Christians risked their lives to protest mass murder of Jews and Communists. The most morally principled religious group was the Jehovah's Witnesses. Ninety percent of members in this church went to prison or died for refusing to obey unjust orders. But the mainstream Protestants were the most obedient group. As historian A.J.P. Taylor tried to explain it, "Lutheranism, at first a movement of Reform, became, and remained, the most conservative of religions; though it preached the absolute supremacy of the individual conscience within, it preached an equally absolute supremacy for the territorial power without."[23] According to Gerald Strauss, traditional Lutheran educators sought to instill faithful abdication of moral responsibility: "their model Christian was an essentially passive being prepared to acquiesce rather than struggle, distrustful of his own inclinations and reluctant to act on them . . . hesitant to proceed when no one guided him, certain only of his own weakness as a creature and of the mortal peril of his condition as a sinner."[24]

Many Christians in Fascist Europe saw Franco, Mussolini, and Hitler as restorers of a properly Christian continent. In this return to tradition, the heretical slogans of "Liberty, Fraternity, Equality" would be finally erased. Instead, both church and state would instill duty to "Fatherland, Family, Work." In supporting Franco's crusade to overthrow the secular humanist Spanish Republic, Hitler called upon the Lord: "Let us thank God, the Almighty, that he has blessed our generation and us, and granted us to be part of this time and this hour."[25] Later, many Christians saw the Nazi attack on Russia as a great crusade to destroy the faith's Communist-Jew enemies. The Vatican saw an opportunity for eastward expansion and set up a Congregation for the Eastern Churches under Cardinal Eugène Tisserant. Where fascist powers conquered traditionally Eastern Orthodox regions like Serbia or Ukraine, there was talk of a new unified Christendom. In many churches, all this passed for something Jesus would approve. But Hitler at times showed greater awareness of the real relationship between Christian values and those of his enemies: "Christianity is the hardest blow that ever hit humanity. Bolshevism is the bastard son of Christianity; both are the monstrous issue of the Jews."[26]

At Christmas 1944, as an overwhelming coalition of democratic and communist allies moved to liberate Europe, Pope Pius XII gave belated acceptance for rule by consent of the rabble. He was willing to recognize "any of the various forms of government, provided they are in themselves adapted to secure the welfare of the citizens." But since the masses could lose their way, he said democracy alone would prove unworkable unless the people accepted guidance by the clergy. A proper role for the clergy, he said, "communicates that supernatural strength of grace which is needed to implement the absolute order established by God, that order which is the ultimate foundation and guiding norm for every democracy."[27]

Even in the USA, many Christians warned that popular will must be checked by an ultimate authority. As the Fundamentalist textbook *America's Providential History* pointed out, "Even if Christians manage to outnumber others on an issue and we sway our Congressmen by sheer numbers, we end up in a dangerous promotion of democracy. We really do not want representatives who are swayed by majorities, but rather by correct principles."[28] What principles were those? Were they principles of obeying higher authorities, or about treating other people as equals? Immanuel Kant had described the greatest principle as trying to live as he would want everyone else to live. But Kant was commonly seen as a semi-Christian, who didn't really accept the Bible's final authority.

The Rabble of Democratic Churches

The rocky rise of democracy in society ran roughly in tandem with the fate of democracy within churches. There were always some Christians who spoke of a "priesthood of all believers," and claimed that an equal potential for all souls was the original Christian vision. But whether church members believed this or not, if modern states backed no religion, faith was "reduced" to a matter of personal initiative. In that "secular humanist" situation, a church's powers of "Godly discipline" were no greater than its strength of peer pressure. Jesus became "merely" a personal inspiration for each believer, not a ruler giving orders for the world to obey. Of course each church could still decide its "orthodoxy" and expel members for "heresy," but the deviants were free to worship elsewhere, or set up their own churches. Many preachers still tried to discredit their rivals as false Christians or to intimidate listeners with threats of hell. But where preachers and listeners were relatively equal members of society, attempts to shame or intimidate people commonly backfired. In the deregulated environment, various brands of religion had to compete for business in a positive way. They could only try to *attract* supporters. The style of preaching slowly shifted in tone, from frankly authoritarian, to more or less inspirational.

Theoretically, Protestants rejected the notion that any particular religious experts were God's appointed mediators between heaven and humanity. They hoped to recover the sort of community they saw in the

New Testament. At first, Baptist churches chose pastors from among their lay members — just as Augustine said the sin-prone laity must never do. And these Baptist pastors were usually local farmers or businessmen, selected more for personal piety than for certification or selection by higher administration. Of course the original founders of every church stood for their own freedom, but the Baptists were especially zealous about it. As Gordon James wrote of this "fundamentalist" tradition in 1987,

> Baptists believe that every individual has the right to construct his own statement of belief, likewise do churches, associations, and conventions. This being an absolute of Baptist belief, it is also an absolute that an individual is only bound by personal beliefs. No church can be bound except to its own beliefs . . . It is the foundational position Southern Baptists have called soul competency, and the related doctrine called the priesthood of all believers and liberty.[29]

If this wasn't clear enough, W. R. White explained that Baptists believe "the individual is primary . . . No building, work of art, human or religious institution is to be placed above him."[30] Other denominations made roughly the same claim, as when the Quakers made the "still, small voice" of personal conscience come first. These people would really overturn the ancient superiority of group over individual. Where medieval tradition stressed an infinite chasm between human and divine authority, numerous new enthusiasts claimed each soul was a spark of divinity. And this was the increasingly prevailing view in North America. Even before 1900, probably most North Americans felt that: "religious authority lies in the believer — not in the church, not in the Bible, despite occasional claims of infallibility and inerrancy."[31]

While most reformers wanted freedom to re-decide almost everything about Christianity, they also wanted stricter accountability to the Bible.

They commonly insisted the Bible was infallible, and the main aim of the Protestant Reformation was not freedom, but to enshrine the Bible (rather than the church) as an unquestionable authority. Of course this required they discuss the book, and agree what it said about slavery, women, parenting, property, nationalism, war, etc. To some degree, each Sunday School class re-entered the whole history of debate over what was primary, outdated, right, or wrong in the Bible. And as seen in times of the anti-slavery, civil rights, or feminist movements, those debates could divide churches as dramatically as when Jesus had it out with the scribes and Pharisees. Like Marcion, many modern Christians wanted to spurn the Old Testament's sagas of holy war. Others felt that Revelation was a hate-monger's hallucination which didn't belong in the book. "Conservatives" felt the Sermon on the Mount was a secondary thing, and the Bible's real point was the substitutionary sacrifice. Martin Luther had tried to judge each part of the Bible by whether he felt it agreed with Jesus. He concluded, "Whatever does not preach Christ is not Apostolic, even though it be written by St. Peter or St. Paul." The book of James he spurned as "an epistle of straw," since it argued for salvation through deeds of love, not faith alone. As for the Old Testament, "The Second Book of Esdras, I throw in the Elbe." Rejecting any notion that the whole Bible was dictated by an infallible hand, he wrote, "The discourses of the prophets were none of them regularly committed to writing at the time; their disciples and hearers collected them subsequently . . . Solomon's Proverbs were not the work of Solomon."[32] Actually, modern scholarship supports most of these bombastic statements.

If growing numbers of believers presumed to both judge the church, and reach their own conclusions about scripture, then the very principle of ultimate religious authority might soon be extinct. In the relativistic future, Christians would simply gather as equals to discuss the Bible's meaning, and none would have a right to overrule another. Since American Catholics were often surrounded by Protestants doing this, they increasingly did it too. In 1829 the American Catholic Church declared itself in favor of lay Bible reading. In place of the medieval ban on lay access to the scripture, the clergy merely expressed a pious wish that parishioners would read it "with due care, and a humble and docile spirit."[33] After that, Catholic churches faced the Protestant "curse" of a critical, scripturally literate laity, willing to debate the Bible's meaning with a priest. Many parishioners also demanded lay control of church finances, property, and the hiring or firing of clergy.

As Augustine feared, re-deciding the content of religion by debate could be divisive. Those trying to renew the church wanted to have their say, but at some point they also wanted a new closure on debate. By some "consensus" or vote, they hoped to reach a new and hopefully final decision. In that case their debates tended to have winners and losers. The winners tended to take their views as a new orthodoxy, and the losers often felt their church had betrayed God. As David Klinghoffer fumed, "Now, say the liberal denominations, let the people decide! In place of these hallowed traditions, kitsch religion substitutes the prevailing opinions of the secular world . . . The Protestant mainline churches increasingly reject the authority of their own traditions, allowing men and women to believe what they wish about virtue, sin and salvation."[34]

As in democratic politics the parishioners of a democratic church could split over any issue, be it the requirements of membership, budget priorities, women's rights, or visions of the new world order. As any democracy could veer "right," "left," forward or back, so discussion in church might lead the community in any direction. Where religion was an expression of community feeling, the risks of hypocrisy or blandness ran high. A congregation might try to be nice, avoid real struggle over consensus, and live in what M. Scott Peck called "pseudo-community." On the other hand it might abandon compassion in a drive to abolish sin.

The very proliferation of churches might seem inherently democratic, but democracy within each church could produce legalism, anarchy, or even a triumph of ethno-religious hate. Some churches welcomed leadership roles for women; others ejected any pastor who let a woman speak in church. Some re-emphasized ancient traditions like polygamy or casting out devils. As A. J. Jacobs demonstrated in *The Year of Living Biblically*, it was physically and morally impossible to actually honor all passages in the Bible as equally true and equally binding. Many Protestant pastors made bold attempts to become more legalistic and literalistic than any Orthodox Jew. But the Second Vatican Council of 1962-65 actually urged Bible readers to sift the wheat from the chaff: "These books, even though they contain material which is imperfect and obsolete, nevertheless bear witness to truly divine teachings."[35]

Of course some believers ridiculed the notion that "God is a democrat." "Strong Christians" like Spain's fascists or the Ku Klux Klan's members counted themselves enforcers of a higher law on the wayward population. Likewise, many church leaders in Guatemala believed it their sacred duty to silence dissent from the heathen Indian majority by any means necessary. In America, it was still common in recent decades for patriotic supporters of their democracy to also support a theocratic idea of rule by holy law. As a Brazilian politician put the same idea, "if everyone were a Christian, we should have no need of a Constitution, since we already have one: the Bible. Everything that is praised in the Bible should be prescribed and everything that is condemned there should be proscribed."[36] In a more subtle attempt to defend its own higher principles from shifting human sentiments, the Vatican moved in 1983 to correct North America's Catholic bishops for their sympathetic support of women's rights. The bishop's "Pastoral Letter on Women" was revised to explain, "To identify sexism as the principal evil at work in the distortion of relations between men and women would be to analyze the underlying problem too superficially."

The letter went on to criticize women's successful efforts to gain greater equality in pay, jobs, benefits, and rights, because these "owe more to the tradition of the Enlightenment than to Catholic tradition."[37]

Such believers gave credence to the notion that real Christianity was inherently anti-democratic. But for those who felt their religion involved equal regard for others as for themselves, Christianity might totally change its spots. It might switch from insisting "error has no rights," to full-blown support for universal human rights.

The Post WWII Wave for Human Rights

In the decades following WWII, churches around the world grew more evenly split over the issues of freedom and equality. In Spain, Franco's militants slowly lost their reputation as the party of God, despite the fervent support of Opus Dei. The defenders of British, French, or Dutch colonial empires appeared increasingly less spiritual than the rebels for independence. In the USA or South Africa, law-breakers for racial equality eventually gained recognition as heroes rather than enemies of Christian civilization. But during the same decades, Western churches and governments came together to defend Christian civilization from a new enemy, namely the Communist movement for "sharing all things." And as with many efforts to fight foreign evils, there was a lot of confusion over who was or wasn't working for the enemy. Rather than opposing particular corruptions and hypocrisies of Soviet-style communism, there was a tendency to oppose all movements for greater social and economic equality as communist-inspired. In that case, defending the rights of private property became a fundamental tenet of Jesus' religion, which trumped concern for dispossessed people. The various movements against privilege and injustice in Africa, Asia, or Latin America then appeared to be anti-Christian threats against the West. This view helped to justify not only the Cold War's massive weapons spending, but a whole series of military "counter-insurgency" or "contra" operations across the Southern world. In supporting these wars, vast numbers of Western Christians seemed to accept that the foreign interests of international corporations, their countries' security, and their God's will, were basically one and the same. But all this was subject to a mushrooming debate.

In 1963, Pope John XXIII signaled a reversal of official doctrine concerning freedom and equality. He urged a universal charter of fundamental human rights, not as something to be earned, but as an unconditional recognition of every human being's "equal natural dignity." John explained this was crucial to world survival, because peace was only possible if both individuals and nations respected each other's basic humanity. The Vatican II conference he sponsored then issued a "Declaration on Religious Liberty," saying "the exercise of religion, of its very nature, consists before all else in those internal, voluntary and free acts whereby man sets the course of his life . . . No merely human power can either command or prohibit acts of this kind." The declaration even admitted that the church had at times opposed freedom and acted in a way "hardly in accord with the spirit of the Gospel or even opposed to it."[38] With this, the Roman Church officially rejected Augustine's doctrine that "error has no rights." After many centuries of debate over what Jesus taught on freedom for the rabble of humanity, the Church handed victory to Augustine's debate opponents, Pelagius and Julian of Eclanum.

Over the next few decades, many church heads tried to recover an authoritarian-style clergy, but local Christians around the world increasingly pushed the other way. In Poland's Solidarity movement of the 1970s, numerous priests and workers joined as co-leaders in a national renewal movement, with tactics similar to those Gandhi or Martin Luther King claimed to learn from Jesus. As the Solidarity Workers' Defense Committee put it, ". . . live as if we had democracy in Poland. Don't burn down party headquarters, build your own. Don't worry about the Party or the state. Forget about the government labor unions, found your own . . ."[39] When Pope John Paul II came to Poland in 1979, he stressed a version of Christianity which had been eclipsed for centuries by Pharisee-style control-freak leaders. He told the rebellious crowds, "The future of Poland will depend on how many people are mature enough to be non-conformists."[40]

At times, John Paul II seemed to stand in the lead of history's greatest wave of democratic revolutions, as churches of various stripes played major roles in basically peaceful revolts in Haiti, the Philippines, Paraguay, South Korea, Chile, Argentina, Brazil, South Africa, or Ukraine. With a passion worthy of St. Paul, the Pope wrote, "The question of morality, to which Christ provides the answer, cannot prescind from the issue of freedom. Indeed, it considers that issue central, for there can be no morality without freedom."[41] In Russia, the Orthodox theologian Aleksei Khomiakov had agreed, "it would be unfair to suppose that the Church requires unity or enforced obedience. On the contrary, it rejects either. In matters of faith, enforced unity is a falsehood, while enforced obedience is death."[42] It seemed a majority of Christians had switched loyalties on the issues of freedom and equality. Instead of believing their religion supported autocratic rule to control sinners, they claimed Jesus stood for mutual respect between fellow-sinners.

The Retreat to an Authoritarian Jesus

Within their churches, however, many priests and pastors felt the democratization of God had gone too far. As in the days of Gnostic movements, professional clerics wanted to prevent a bastardization of their religion. In the Catholic Church, the post-Vatican II experiments with lay participation in leadership gave way to cautious protection of the priesthood's role. Where the lay community grew increasingly vocal about problems and solutions in church, the great defender of equal rights

Pope John Paul II took a different line toward his own community. Using language straight out of early medieval times, he warned the flock, "Satan, the liar and the father of lies" had clouded "man's" capacity to think for himself, so that "giving himself over to relativism and skepticism he goes off in search of an illusory freedom apart from the truth itself."[43] Among American Protestants as well, some pastors of formerly democratic churches like Jerry Falwell began calling for a more traditional priestly leadership: "God never intended for a committee nor a board of deacons nor any other group to dominate a church or control a pastor. The pastor is God's man, God's servant, God's leader. When you tie the hands of God's man, when you keep him from acting as the Holy Spirit leads him, you have murdered his initiative, you have killed his spirit."[44]

In Russia after the dissolution of the U.S.S.R., many clergymen of the Orthodox Church hoped to recover their influence as custodians of Russia's national faith. Responding to a surge of lay interest in reviving the church, Patriarch Pimen urged caution, and even seemed to discredit all religious initiative from outside the clergy's ranks: "Often what lies at the root of all this arrogance, [is] temptation through vanity when one makes an idol of oneself and attempts to set oneself inappropriate spiritual tasks. As a consequence, one becomes divorced from the Church and its shepherds, and even sets oneself up as a shepherd, speaking on behalf of all believers and criticizing the Church leadership."[45]

Apparently, many church leaders wanted equal rights in human society, but felt the community Jesus created should stand above human standards. Where many fresh thinkers hoped to "improve" the church, John Paul's chief enforcer of orthodoxy, Joseph Ratzinger (later Pope Benedict XVI) drew another line on change. He fired or silenced a host of Catholic thinkers including Hans Küng, Edward Schillebeeckx, Charles Curran, Leonardo Boff, Matthew Fox, or Uta Ranke-Heinemann. Concerning many of the scholars who made the Vatican II reforms possible, Episcopal

Bishop John Spong said, "A whole generation of scholars was muted . . . with the result that today Roman Catholic scholarship has all but disappeared from its priestly ranks."[46]

In the stressful post-WWII "free world," growing numbers of Christians turned to an old-fashioned religion, in which submission to higher authority was still the main point.[47] Their preachers stressed Bible verses in which God seemed to favor submissive sheep over free adults. Of course, for normal people to accept such constraint, they first had to find "self-denial" attractive. And that was why so many preachers stressed the theme of guilt. They helped modern people recover the old medieval sense that, not only were they guilty of many wrongs, but they couldn't help doing wrong, because their souls were defective and their minds couldn't be trusted.[48] Only after accepting that would they truly submit to an external guide.

These defenders of tradition took religion much as the Romans did. Instead of asking questions like "What is true?", "How good can our relations get?", or "What works to heal suffering?", they asked "Which master will I serve?" Of course most Protestants sought their guidance from a book rather than an institution. As Carl F. H. Henry explained, "The Bible alone and the Bible in its entirety, is the word of God written, and therefore inerrant in the autographs."[49] So, where Jesus had repeatedly shocked the scriptural literalists of Israel with his criticism of biblical traditions, these new Pharisees insisted once more that the Book was unquestionable. And this kind of religion sold well, because it offered infallible guidance by a superhuman authority. Without that, many pastors warned that all would be chaos. And many people felt it was spiritual to desire an escape from the stressful uncertainty of trying to decide for themselves what was right. There were even many Pharisaical Christians who felt America's experiment with freedom was a proven failure. This was how it looked at the Creation Museum in Petersburg, Kentucky where a biblically literalist story of the human race, ended with a display of the modern American family. This family showed every sign of godless living, contempt for authority, drug use, and dysfunctional chaos. The sign asked, "What happens when absolute authority is eliminated and man's opinion is the only measure of good and evil?"[50]

All this retrenchment to tradition could go so far as reversion to full-blown tribalism. And in the 1990s, after many Europeans were convinced that no Holocaust against ethnic minorities could ever again gain Christian support, another attempt at genocide targeted Muslim populations in the Balkans. Soon after this in 2000, the Vatican's spokesman Cardinal Camillo Ruini announced a correction to Pope John XXIII's declarations on human rights. Ruini said the Church opposed the European Union's Charter of Fundamental Human Rights, because "it failed to take account of the historical and cultural roots of Europe, in particular Christianity, which represents Europe's soul and which still today can inspire Europe's mission and identity."[51] And even at this, the Catholic Church was far more inclusive than many others. Some modern churches remained frankly opposed to social, ethnic, or religious equality among the world's people. They seemed to view their churches as fortresses of the elect against armies of the damned. As Pat Robertson claimed, people who "want a larger community of nations living at peace in our world, are in reality unknowingly and unwittingly carrying out the mission and mouthing the phrases of a tightly knit cabal whose goal is nothing less than a new order for the human race under the dominion of Lucifer and his followers."[52]

As in the past, preachers who claimed that belief in an almighty God precludes freedom were often powerful, assertive individuals. People like Augustine, John Calvin, or Jerry Falwell had a tremendous sense of personal vocation. Falwell, for example, could believe in democracy, the equality of rights under the American Constitution, and the value of personal initiative in a system of free enterprise. He could powerfully demonstrate all these values in his own life, and still preach a kind of Christianity described as passive submission to an external authority: "A child has to depend on someone else for its needs and that is just what attitude a man must have toward Christ . . . Only as we reach a point of total helplessness . . . will we know peace and victory in the Christian life."[53]

In this sort of preaching, many pastors seemed to wobble between insisting we are incapable of guiding ourselves, and declaring that we alone are responsible for the state of our souls. The difference between self-transcendence and self-repression seemed deliberately obscure. It was unclear if submission towards higher minds and penance for sin were eternal requirements, or steps on a journey toward greater maturity. As in centuries past, the preaching of self-renunciation often conveyed different messages for leaders than for followers. And these messages often seemed addressed from power-holders to subordinates. If such an interpretation of Jesus' teaching continued to thrive without coercion in a basically free society, it suggested that many Christians really wished to choose that way of living for themselves, their children, and their neighbors.

7. Correcting Non-Violence

I heard in Sunday School that Jesus was a gentle pacifist. And the Bible made this sound very noble: "When they hurled their insults at him, he did not retaliate; when he suffered he made no threats. Instead he entrusted himself to the one who judges justly." (1 Peter 2:23) But actually, I don't think there was anybody in my church who thought pacifism was respectable. It seemed to be virtuous for Jesus, but it would be weak and cowardly for us. Except the time Martin Luther King urged forgiveness on Whites after they bombed his home.

Clearly, most Texan Christians thought pacifism was for spineless fools, and there was close to zero tolerance for conscientious objectors refusing to fight for their country. It was a traditional Bible-belt opinion of God's feelings, which was adequately stated by the New Orleans *Sunday Delta* back in 1856: "The coward does not know himself, but God knows him, and even if he buried his head in the sand, ostrich-like, the great eye would perceive and despise his meanness."[1]

In the Cold War world, non-violence seemed about as functional as Gandhi's advice to the British in 1940:

I would like you to lay down the arms you have as being useless for saving you or humanity. You will invite Herr Hitler and Signor Mussolini to take what they want of the countries you call your possessions . . . If these gentlemen choose to occupy your homes you will vacate them. If they do not give you free passage out, you will allow yourselves, man, woman, and child, to be slaughtered, but you will refuse to owe allegiance to them.[2]

Did this represent Jesus? Did he reject all use of force for self-defense or law enforcement? Did later Christians reinterpret his life so completely that we couldn't even tell?

Gentle Jesus Meek and What?

With any written text, we can't help but imagine a tone of voice for the words. And most Bible readers I've heard in church make Jesus sound like a high-minded philosopher. But in reading the Gospels aloud as if they were plays, I find them extremely argumentative. For long passages Jesus reads like a confrontation junkie, ready to debate anyone at almost any time. He invalidated people's behavior and insulted them in public. I've discussed his abuse of legalist Pharisees, but he also ridiculed other power holders. Where landlords demanded their tenants pay debts by yielding the coats off their backs, Jesus advised the debtors to hand over their under cloaks as well, which meant they would be standing there naked.[3] His lines like "Why don't you strike my other cheek as well?" may have been stunning humor, delivered to crowds of underlings who were used to being slapped down by overlords. He aimed to shame greedy abusers in shocking ways. Then of course, he also vandalized the Temple of Jerusalem, which was roughly as alarming as an attack on the Vatican during the Middle Ages.

In these stories, Jesus wasn't avoiding conflict. It seems his question was not whether to fight, but how to fight. We call him "pacifistic" because, rather than threatening to beat, imprison, or kill his enemies, he just threatened to humiliate them in public debate. His critics, however, grew to fear this game. They wanted his arguments ended, hopefully forever. Like other authorities of the ancient world, they wanted their critics discredited, demonized, terrorized into silence, or simply eliminated. In other words, his enemies were afraid of conflict, but Jesus wasn't. Riane Eisler thinks it was his enemies' fear of open encounter which made them violent.[4] They would rather have people killed or banished than have to deal with them face to face.

Concerning holy violence, we don't see Jesus calling, like the Zealots or Essenes did, for a crusade to purge foreigners and their influence from

Israel. He didn't seem to accept demonization of enemies as a mark of spirituality. Of course Matthew quotes him saying "I have not come to bring peace, but a sword," and some Christians take that more literally than "He who lives by the sword, dies by the sword." But how would his criticisms of Israel's leaders sound in modern Israel? There's a Jewish prayer from the *Gates of Redemption* which is read aloud in synagogue worship services. It reflects the lines of the Old Testament Jesus preferred, and the sort of arguments he made to his country:

> *When will redemption come?*
> *When we master the violence that fills our world.*
> *When we look upon others as we would have them look upon us.*
> *When we grant to every person the rights we claim for ourselves.*[5]

Of course later the living memory of Jesus faded, and the old poetry of religious war resurfaced in Christian preaching. The New Testament's pastoral letters suggested that Christians were now God's chosen people and those of other religions weren't. They said Jesus would return with a terrible sword to destroy his enemies. No doubt, this dualistic language of good versus evil had greater popular appeal than words of compassion for enemies. This sort of talk didn't necessarily imply controlling other people through violence. But once Jesus' followers started seeing evil as an external problem in other people, they were already thinking like belligerents on a cultural battlefield.

The Means of Moral Conflict with Rome

At first, most Roman officials judged Christianity as a kind of atheism, because Christians didn't seem to believe what Romans believed. A second-century Christian named Tatian boasted, "I do not wish to rule, I do not wish to be rich, I despise military honors . . ."[6] Another named Octavius accused, "All that the Romans hold, occupy and possess is the spoil of outrage; their temples are full of loot, drawn from the ruin of cities, the plunder of gods and the slaughter of priests."[7] The Jewish-Christian *Recognitions of Clement* insulted the army, claiming military action was cowardly rather than brave.[8]

Since such talk seemed to cast contempt on every virtue that made Rome great, a Roman patriot like Celsus tried to expose its stupidity. Sounding much like later Christian defenders of order, he argued "If everyone were to adopt the Christians' attitude, moreover, there would be no rule of law: the legitimate authority would be abandoned; earthly things would return to chaos and come into the hands of the lawless and savage barbarians; and nothing further would be heard of Christian worship or of wisdom, anywhere in the world."[9]

Of course the emperor-warlords also claimed to stand for world peace. They even said that Augustus Caesar had achieved it, which is why they called him the world savior. These rulers assumed that peace could only happen if one strong hero defeated all his rivals, and then ruled uncontested. It was a solution to the world's strife which remained popular till recently, even among Christian clergy. But for the first several centuries, most Christians rejected the whole game as an abomination.

Clearly, the motley assemblies of early Christians were not seeking military power. The whole of Israel was simply eliminated for resisting Rome, and Christians knew the same could happen to them. If they had moral objections to the Romans' orders, they could argue or refuse to obey, but fighting it out with the Roman army wasn't a serious option.

Basically, they did what we call civil disobedience. And while we are used to people being jailed for that, an automatic death penalty was more usual back then. At least the Romans' clampdowns on treason-prone groups were usually short-lived and spotty. Rome's leaders generally hoped a few horrible examples of torture in the arena would keep everybody in line.

Obviously the Romans took their loyalties seriously. But Christian refuseniks could be deadly serious as well. Many of them believed that the power to intimidate must give way to the power of care. They felt it was consistent with their message to renounce threats of violence from their side. When accused of disloyalty to superiors, some of them offered justifications, and some begged for mercy. But almost none of them gave violence for violence. At least in non-violence, the early church displayed an almost perfect unity.

The way I heard it as a child, the Roman army was the early church's worst enemy. While the first Christians were pacifist apostles of love, the legions worshipped naked force. Of course this simplified things. But it does seem that most ancient Christians did deplore the army, and refused to join it. Until at least 200, a large majority of Christians believed it was an abomination to serve in the army of "Babylon" and its emperor, "the beast." To take that employment, men had to swear blind obedience, kill on command, offer sacrifices, venerate the legion standards, and maybe worse.[10] Many church leaders tried to forbid this work for even the most desperate Christian job seekers. According to the *Apostolic Tradition* of Hippolytus (ca, 215), "A soldier who is in a position of authority is not to be allowed to put anyone to death; if he is ordered to, he is not to do it."[11] Clearly that was a stumbling block. Not only were most Christians opposed to killing; they also gave higher authority to their religious leaders than to military commanders. Hippolytus upheld these sentiments, but he was speaking of Christians enlisted in the army. Apparently, they were starting to appear there.

223

It took another 100 years or so, but by 312 the army actually played a major role in Christianizing the empire. After all, Rome became a Christian state through a military coup. For that to happen, there had to be a growing alliance between the army and the churches. From seeing their ideals as close to opposite, these organizations had to shift towards a basic alignment. And it seems clear that the church changed the most.

The Rise of Christian Soldiers

From at least the conversion of centurion Cornelius in Acts 10, some of the soldiers stationed near Christian communities joined the movement. It raised a problem for churches, somewhat like the problem of preaching to slaves. What could a preacher safely say to people who were legally bound to obey other masters? Rather than urge soldiers to desert (which would be a major crime) the preachers generally advised army converts to serve out their enlistment honorably, and tell other soldiers about Jesus. Luke's gospel included a word for soldiers attributed to John the Baptist. Instead of telling the troops to lay down their swords, John simply urged "Rob no one by violence or by false accusation, and be content with your wages." (3:14)

If the early church and the army had anything in common, it was the sense of being a special force with a mission. And in preaching to Gentiles who respected the army, it seemed helpful to urge military-style virtues in church. So 2 Timothy advised, "Take your share of the hardship, like a good soldier of Christ Jesus. A soldier on active service will not let himself be involved in civilian affairs; he must be wholly at his commanding officer's disposal." (2:3–4) This was an image irrelevant to the movement's female majority, but for male members it could be morale-boosting.

During periods of persecution for Christians, converts in the army were naturally torn between protecting their church, and proving themselves loyal Romans. The accounts of martyrs include soldiers who refused orders to kill fellow believers. But probably most Christian soldiers tried to discredit the persecution by showing patriotism against other enemies. During persecutions under Marcus Aurelius in the 170s, Christian troops near the Danube claimed their prayers brought down lightning to defeat the Germans. Bishop Appollinarius of Hierapolis claimed such cases proved that support from the Christian God was vital for national security.[12]

While the army oppressed the churches, many preachers counterattacked by trying to convert soldiers. And their arguments often sounded oddly militaristic. Instead of trying to discredit the army's cult of Victory, Athenagoras (ca. 177) tried to show its compatibility with Christianity. Pagan gods, he said, were actually human heroes, revered for their glorious deeds. Christianity would simply uplift reverence for these heroes to a higher worship, for the Creator above them all. Later, Aurelius P. Clemens argued that belief in the Christian God served the army better than trust in the goddess of winged victory. "Why soldier," he asked, "if you lack faith in your own powers, arm yourself with the feeble solace of a woman's shape? Never yet has an armored legion seen a winged girl guiding the weapons of the fighting men . . ."[13] Naturally, the troops tended to accept those aspects of a religion that complemented their view of the world. Military men who accepted Christianity tended to see it as the cult of a heavenly ruler, a war of good against evil, and an elite force of faithful warriors. In that case it could be a suitably manly religion, which might inspire the troops on Rome's threatened frontiers.

Another image that Christians and army officers shared concerned the rising world order. Christians spoke of a day when strife would cease, and one Lord would unite the world. The Old Testament had predicted a "fifth empire," (after Babylonia, Medea, Persia, and Greece) in which God's own people would rule the earth. Many Christians felt this empire would come to their church rather than Israel. But Roman historians such as Aemilius

Sura claimed the same sequence of empires must lead to a universal dominion of Rome.[14] It might seem these dreams were different. While Christians believed God's elect must prevail in the end, Roman patriots believed that those who prevailed *were* God's elect. These ideas could fit. If both Christian bishops and Roman army commanders envisioned one world order, one law, and themselves as victorious over evil, then they might be comrades in arms. The book of Revelation proclaimed a Christianized cult of victory: "He who conquers will have this heritage, and I will be his God and he shall be my son." (21:7)

If it was Christian to view life as a war against evil, then the church was Jesus' army. And in that case it was appropriate that Cyprian of Carthage said the rite of baptism was equivalent to the army oath of obedience. After enrolling in God's army, Cyprian explained, the Christian soldier must serve "in accordance with the regulations." Tertullian added that for those deserting their Christian duty, "The pay of delinquency is death."[15] Around the early 200s Christians started using the term *pagani* for their detractors. This word was a term of abuse for ignorant villagers, but in the army it also meant cowards who tried to evade military duty. The Christians used *pagani* to mean people who shirked the call to fight for Christ.[16]

Rome's Need for a Trans-Tribal Religion

Especially after 175, the empire's security came under growing threats. The emperors' desperation to enforce loyalty increased, and the persecutions of suspect groups grew worse. But part of the problem was with Rome's official religion. The old "cult of Victory" involved belief that the king of gods (Jupiter) granted victory in battle to the most worthy. This made it seem that whoever prevailed on the battlefield was chosen for power by the gods. For a time after Augustus Caesar, this belief seemed to unify the empire under a central command. But as military power accumulated with the growing frontier armies, this cult increasingly fostered a ruthless scramble for power, as emperor after emperor died at the hands of military usurpers.[17] By the early 200s it seemed each general wanted victory for himself, and reverence for the emperor made the generals covet his position all the more. Naturally, some generals hoped to foster a deeper sense of loyalty. But what belief could unite the polyglot troops from many conquered nations? It couldn't just be a regional cult from one ethnic group such as the Latins. The army needed a religious basis for trans-tribal unity. And its generals needed to become patrons of that cult.

On the Near Eastern frontiers a possible solution appeared. Rome's armies in that region were immersed in a world where monotheistic religions were the obvious cultural bulwarks of monarchy. Across the Near East, from Persia to the would-be kingdom of Israel, religious leaders and rulers commonly believed their nations must have one God, one king, and one law. Soon this was also true of the first Christian kingdom in Armenia. Of course ordinary believers saw these religions in terms of personal salvation. But the idea before the Roman commanders' noses was that a Near-Eastern monotheistic religion could be a ruler's best bet to inspire loyalty. Perhaps the fickle cult of Victory was not the best religion for a world empire.

Rome's main enemy in the East was Persia, and especially with the rise of its Sassanid Empire in the early 200s, this was a formidable foe. The Persians repeatedly drove the Romans back toward the Mediterranean Sea. On this front, Rome's commanders faced an enemy of superior religious fervor — a mainly Zoroastrian army, fighting for one world under one God. The Persian generals invited their troops to see themselves, not just as conscripts or mercenaries, but as warriors of the Almighty. State priests called the troops to a holy battle for the salvation of all. For the Romans to fight this vision, they needed an equally compelling counter-vision.

The Christian general Constantine was born and raised in army camps on the Eastern frontiers. As he rose through the ranks, he was careful to show respect for the diverse religions of his mainly Eastern men. Constantine wanted no god or any ethnic portion of the army against him. He saw that the Christians had converts from all ethnic groups, and along with several other generals, he moved to end religious persecution against them. In supporting freedom for Christians, he gained more respect from almost every quarter. At first, being pro-Christian was a badge of toleration for all.

Still, Constantine was a traditional military man of his age. For him, religion was a means of gaining supernatural help for his desires. His desire was supreme power, and he sought it from a deity of ultimate power. As he won battle after battle with rival generals, he claimed support from the Christian God. And feeling his devotion was rewarded, he blessed the churches with his patronage. Though all other religions remained legal during his reign, his domain was increasingly called a Christian empire. But Joseph Campbell feels the emperor's religion was something different — "something that has since been called Christianity — though it is difficult to construe its relationship to the lesson of Christ's temptation in the desert."[18] Basically, Constantine represented Christianity as the army could understand it. For him, it was Rome's new official cult of Victory.

From Prince of Peace to Champion of Holy War

Of course having a Christian emperor made army service more acceptable to Christians. But for several centuries more, the church still saw violence as a necessary evil, rather than a virtuous thing. Down to the 1100s, most Christians thought violence was a lamentable way of the world. They felt that Jesus would never approve of settling differences through contests of beating or killing. The priests of early medieval times spoke endlessly of Jesus' torture on the cross, and the bloody deaths of holy martyrs. And though these stories seem sadistic, they assumed sympathy for victims of violence. They praised those who observed the commandment, "Thou shalt not kill." Before the church could endorse holy wars, inquisitions, and witch hunts, this whole attitude had to change. The whole sense of the church's mission had to shift — from pastoral care for the less faithful, to war against the treason of unfaith.

The first official compromise came in the early 300s, as Constantine practiced killing in defense of a now-Christian state. Many church leaders cautiously accepted it, partly because the emperor patronized their church. The priests now told their people to obey the rulers, even if those rulers told them to kill. And between the years 300 to 500, the government shifted from trying to ban Christians in the army, to requiring that *only* Christians could join the army. In Byzantine Rome, the army chaplains led their troops in prayer to Mother Mary, asking her to lead their legions to victory.[19] But the church still considered violence a sin. The clergy claimed to stand above killing, and expected the emperor to recognize their exemption from it. After doing their duty in battle, soldiers were not allowed to enter a church without confession and penance for the sin of killing.[20] For example, in Anglo-Saxon England, the Penitential of Archbishop Theodore instructed, "If anyone kills a man in vengeance for a kinsman, let him do penance as a homicide seven or ten years."[21] For centuries this remained the clergy's usual attitude toward violence.

Another important moral compromise arose in the 800s, as Europe faced new invasions of Viking, Magyar, or Saracen raiders. When the emerging Papal State faced Islamic invaders, Pope John VIII (872–82) made a fateful announcement. To attract defenders he offered a promise, that those who killed in defense of the church would "by no means be denied entry to heaven."[22] Here, John was dealing with an ongoing perception that Christianity stood for non-violence. He stopped a bit short of claiming it was meritorious to kill the enemy, and merely argued it would bring no guilt on a soldier's soul. The change may strike us as a meaningless technicality. But instead of viewing warfare as a tragic if sometimes unavoidable evil, the Pope now taught that killing, if done for a church-approved cause, was not a sin at all.

From this level of acceptance for killing, it took about two more steps to reach a full endorsement for holy war. First, when Pope Leo IX (1048–54) faced *Christian* rivals to the Papal States, namely the Normans of South Italy, he escalated his appeal by claiming it was actually meritorious to kill the church's enemies. According to Leo, God would reward the deed. And then in 1095, Pope Urban II took the step beyond killing in self-defense, to proclaim a Christ-sanctioned attack on foreign nations.

When Urban announced the great crusade to the East, he hoped to unite all Christians in a common cause. He wanted to banish endemic local warfare between Christian rulers, and extend a "peace of God" over all Christian lands. Instead of fighting each other, Urban wished all men of the faith to unite against a common external enemy: "Let those who for long have been robbers now be soldiers of Christ. Let those who formerly used to do battle with brothers and relatives now fight lawfully against barbarians. Let those who for long were hirelings for a few pieces of silver now earn eternal rewards."[23]

This was a vision of huge popular appeal. Most Christians felt it was a giant step towards unity across Europe. In one bold move, Europe's many bands of brigands and mercenaries were largely diverted to more glorious combat in the Middle East. Few objected that the strategy involved a fundamental change in values, which basically reversed Jesus' strategy. Instead of extending compassion from insiders to outsiders, the church now sought to unite insiders through shared hostility to outsiders. This logic involved drawing a line down the middle of the world, dividing the loved from the unloved portions of humanity. On one side of this line, the law of mutual compassion and brotherly love supposedly applied. On the other side, God willed an opposite principle, roughly as described in

Deuteronomy: "In the cities of these nations whose land the Lord your God is giving you as a patrimony, you shall not leave any creature alive." (20:16) We should note that the "infidels" killed by the First Crusade included the Orthodox priests in Jerusalem's shrine of the Holy Sepulcher. And once the church announced such a moral division of the planet to be God's will, the controversies only grew over where to draw the dividing line.

With this campaign, the style of popular preaching shifted in tone. St. Bernard, for example, was famous as a man of compassion. But when his lord the Pope proclaimed holy war he changed the message: "The Christian glories in the death of the pagan, because Christ is thereby glorified."[24] And while speaking of moral change, we may notice that Urban II's war was one of the church's first major initiatives following the great divorce between clerics and women in 1074. Could the elimination of women from clerical families have cleared the way for a more violent religion?

If Christianity was now bent on destroying rather than changing its enemies abroad, the new mindset also appeared on the home front. Already by the early 1100s we hear of Christian warlords claiming the context of holy war for their own feuds. As Count Helias of Maine was proud to say,

I wanted to fight the heathens in the Lord's name, but behold, now I discover a battle nearer at hand against Christ's enemies. For everybody who resists truth and justice reveals himself as an enemy of God . . . I shall not discard our Savior's cross, which I was signed with in the pilgrim's manner; instead I shall inscribe it on my shield and helmet and all my arms . . . Protected by this sign, I shall proceed against the enemies of peace and justice, defending the interior of Christendom by fighting. For my horse and arms will be marked with the holy sign, and all my adversaries who rise up against me

231

[such as Helias' rival William Rufus] will be fighting against a knight of Christ.[25]

This kind of vigilante reintroduced warfare between Europeans, as a godly instead of a criminal activity. And as local wars rekindled after the crusade's first wave, many traditional Christians tried to protest. During the 1100s in southern France, a popular "Peace of God" movement arose. The monks of St. Martial helped launch the movement by urging the whole lay population to pray with them, in a great appeal to God, to end local warfare in Aquitaine. But now it seemed, the church hierarchy felt that anti-war protest was anti-religious. Bishop Gerard of Arras ruled that the Peace of God movement was a heresy. Besides, he said it violated God's proper division of labor, in which the lay people must work, the clerics should do the praying, and the rulers must rule, be they warlords or not.[26]

Probably most ordinary people still supposed that warfare was against God's will. And their methods of protest were often fine examples of non-violent civil disobedience. In 1233 an "Alleluia" movement spread across Italy, where laymen and women of all classes marched and sang for peace. In 1291, the four trade unions of Parma united in persuading all magistrates to swear an oath renouncing violence in civil disputes. They formed a power-sharing agreement with the which "suddenly ended all rioting and bickering" in the city. Another tactic of peaceful protest was mass evacuation. The people of Paris did this in 1252, almost vacating the town till the corrupt provost mended his abuse. Another popular protest in 1394 almost emptied Languedoc, and compelled Charles VI to promise "ending all violence and oppression."[27]

But despite any popular protest against violence, a more holy context for fighting proved useful to mercenaries and security service providers. With the blessing of local clerics, numerous militia groups formed to enforce "the peace of God" within Christendom. In thirteenth-century Bologna, the Militia of the Blessed Virgin Mary devoted itself to vigilante battle against crime and heresy.

From Pastoral Care to Holy Violence
Inside the Church

Before the crusader wars began, it was highly unusual for the church to kill "unorthodox" parishioners. As the very idea of "religious" killing shocks us today, so it would shock most clergymen before the 1100s. Until then, almost all priests were content to call the local sinners to repent and believe. Unbelief and general ignorance were normal, not criminal. The priests were supposed to instruct the people, not punish their ignorance. In the light of later church violence against its own parishioners, this may sound like a whitewash. But when King Robert of France burned thirteen heretics at Orleans in 1022, it was the first recorded case of capital punishment for heresy since 385.[28] As late as the mid-eleventh century, Peter Damian could boast that while Christian saints laid down their lives for the faith, they refused to kill unbelievers in turn.

Inside the realm of Christendom, heresy was an issue mainly for the clergy. Basically, priests or bishops could be fired for contradicting their superiors. When early church councils "condemned" Arius, Donatus, or Nestorious, this meant the men lost their jobs and parishes. For laypeople, the maximum penalty for "unorthodoxy" was excommunication, which meant exclusion from worship services pending an apology. The clergy could prescribe "penances" for sin, like fasts of bread and water, as a price of readmission to church. But until the 1100s, excommunication almost never involved additional punishments like prison or death. The clergy sometimes investigated cases of lay heresy, but this was usually just a matter of settling disputes among parishioners. If certain locals accused others of apostasy, the bishop could be called to judge the case. And if the dispute seemed dangerous, he might actually come. But on reaching the village, the bishop would typically find a common shouting match, as one group denounced its enemies as vile sinners, and the other said their detractors were even worse. If nobody listened to reason, the bishop might turn the case over to God. And in that age, this meant having the accused undergo a trial by fire or water. The usual logic was that God would protect the innocent, with survivors proved blameless. This was about the extent of any campaign to punish heresy among the laypeople.

For decades after the crusades began, the climate of pastoral care on the home front was little changed. But in 1185, we hear Pope Lucius III accusing his bishops of tolerating every kind of heresy among the people. And Lucius was right — they did tolerate it, as they always had. But now Lucius insisted that heresy was a growing danger, and he demanded stronger means to correct it. Since Christendom was waging a holy war against outside unbelievers, shouldn't it do more to fight the unbelievers within as well?

The shift toward greater coercion inside the church happened as the crusades against Islam faltered. As the war bogged down with disturbing waste of lives and wealth, a new cynicism appeared toward the church's infallible wisdom.[29] Soon a popular religious protest movement spread through Italy, France, and Spain. Like the old Donatists, these Cathar (or Albigensian) dissidents demanded rejection of corrupt church officials, and their replacement by supposedly more spiritual priests. The Catholic bishops tried to discredit them verbally, but failing that, the conflict escalated to threats and killing. Quite suddenly, the church found itself at a crossroads. If it authorized warfare against unbelieving outsiders, should it use deadly force against disobedient parishioners as well? Basically, the official answer was "yes." As Pope Innocent III reasoned, "The civil law punishes traitors with confiscation of their property, and death . . . All the more, then, should we excommunicate, and confiscate the property of, those who are traitors to the faith of Jesus Christ; for it is an infinitely greater sin to offend the divine majesty than to attack the majesty of a sovereign."[30]

When Innocent III sent crusading armies to destroy the Cathars, most observers were amazed. Residents of Milan tried to protect their Cathar neighbors (in 1212), and found their Holy Father in Rome actually threatening to kill them all: ". . . no multitude can resist the Lord of armies; leaving aside Old Testament examples, just as He recently subdued the heretics of Provence . . . through the army of the faithful, so He has the power to reduce your city to nothing."[31] It now seemed contrary to church doctrine when Bishop Wazo of Liège rescued a crowd of Cathars from orthodox attackers, arguing "God their Creator and Redeemer showed them mercy."[32] Unlike the Pope, Wazo said it was Jesus' way to let the wheat and the tares grow together till God would judge his harvest.

Somehow this resorting to force generated more enemies than it destroyed. And in 1227, Pope Gregory XI was shocked to find that even his Bishop Filippo Paternon of Pisa was a Cathar sympathist, secretly plotting to overthrow the Roman Church. With alarm, Gregory decided he couldn't fully trust his clergy. He appointed a special clerical committee, whose full-time task was investigating disbelievers, without the distraction of pastoral care. From this internal security team, the Inquisition grew. And to strike more fear into church critics, in 1231, Gregory adopted the death penalty for heresy into canon law.[33] Later, in 1252, Pope Innocent IV approved the use of torture, "with restraint," for extracting the truth in heresy trials. If we can imagine it, many leading clergymen were now prepared to use torture on their own parishioners. The church was now equipped for a purge of unbelievers from Europe. As Pope Nicholas III warned in 1280, "Whoever knows of heretics, or of those who hold secret meetings, or of those who do not conform in all respects to the orthodox faith, shall make it known to his confessor, or to someone else who will bring it to the knowledge of the bishop or the inquisitor. If he does not do so, he shall be excommunicated."[34]

Of course we should admit that lay people often led in attacks on non-conformists, and many clergymen urged restraint. As the mood of war on unbelievers turned to massacres of Jews or doubters, many church leaders tried to stop the violence. Pope Innocent III corrected the over-zealous saying, "No Christian shall do the Jews any personal injury . . . or deprive them of possessions . . . or disturb them during the celebration of their festivals . . . or extort money from them by threatening to exhume their dead."[35] But such words had little impact at the scenes of crusade-like atrocities. For a typical incident, in 1114 an angry crowd in Soissons denounced certain of their neighbors as enemies of Christ. The bishop placed the accused in prison pending trial, partly to protect them from the mob. But the townspeople, "fearing that the clergy might be too lenient," broke into the jail, dragged the suspects out, and burned them alive. Several crusader wars later, around the year 1200, a priest in northern France reported, "In this country, the piety of the people is so great that they are always ready to send to the stake not only avowed heretics, but those merely suspected of heresy."[36]

As commonly happens, use of deadly force tended to generate a more deadly response. For a chilling example, in 1376 anti-clerical fanatics in Florence seized all church property, leveled the Inquisition's offices, and hanged any priests who dared to resist.[37] This, apparently, was what the church would get if it failed to suppress its critics. The options seemed no better than those Jesus faced. But unlike Jesus or the early martyrs, the church administration now demanded pre-emptive extermination of its enemies.

By this point the idea of deadly war between "true believers" and "false believers" had become "popular." Probably most priests were innocent of inciting mob justice or "religious" murder. But as people in war fear the enemy, so ordinary people in Western Europe showed a rising terror of unbelievers. They feared infidels as agents of evil, and believed God would punish communities that tolerated apostasy. In times of crisis, these beliefs could trigger panic attacks on non-conformists. During the bubonic plagues of the 1340s, rumors spread that anti-Christians were poisoning the wells. And in over 500 German towns, terrified mobs rushed through the streets, massacring all the "Jews and poisoners" they could find. All this was lamentable popular superstition, and the clergy often deplored it. But the church was partly responsible for teaching people to blame their troubles on unbelievers. Its statements suggested that God would reward the totally faithful, and punish those who tolerated unbelievers in their midst. Either way, safety lay in rooting out non-conformists.

Holy Civil War within Christendom

By the late 1200s, the context of holy war had raised tensions between cultural groups from the Balkans to Spain. The Teutonic Knights launched their northern crusades to conquer and convert the Slavs. France exterminated the Cathar heretics, suppressed the order of Templars, and repeatedly expelled all Jews. In the Fourth Lateran Council of 1215, the church ruled that people of different religions must wear specific clothes, to mark them as heretics in enemy uniform. Church policy increasingly enforced social apartheid between Christians, Jews, and Muslims. To block friendship and love between these groups, the customs of Tortosa, Spain warned, "If Jewish or Muslim males are found lying with a Christian woman, the Jew or Muslim should be drawn and quartered and the Christian woman should be burned, in such a manner that they should die. And this accusation can be brought by any inhabitant of the town without penalty."[38] Later, Spain completed its crusade to destroy Moorish Grenada, then required all Jews and Muslims to either convert or get out of the country. Even after that, the Spanish government still imprisoned or killed any converts who retained vestiges of Jewish or Moorish culture. Finally, in 1492, it expelled both "races" en masse.

Supposedly, all these purges of impure sinners would purify Christendom and win God's favor. But apparently the purges were insufficient, because Christendom kept suffering massive setbacks. After the Near East crusades collapsed, armies of pagan Mongols swept through Eastern Europe, routing the Holy Roman Emperor's forces in Germany. Later the Black Death swept through the continent like an apocalypse of divine vengeance. And next the Ottoman Turks began reversing the tide of crusade, pushing deep into Europe, and putting the Eastern churches under Muslim rule.

On top of all these external defeats, the church decreed a string of crusader wars between Christian states. For example in 1239, Pope Gregory XI called for a holy alliance against Emperor Frederick II. And over the next three centuries, at one point or another, almost every region of Western Europe stood under mass excommunication while at war with rulers backed by the church. In 1324, Marsilius of Padua complained that the church was systematically destroying Europe with repeated invocations of holy violence against all critics.[39] The rulers in turn declared holy wars of their own, as when Edward III forced England's priests to serve as fundraisers for his attack on France. It was still a shock when Pope Julius II (1503–13) actually mounted a war horse and led Papal State troops into battle against other kingdoms.

The Killing Time's Decline

Christendom's holy civil wars reached a crescendo with the Protestant-Catholic Thirty Years' War of the early 1600s. Here, competing churches tried to eliminate each other in a battle for institutional monopoly on religion. Leading up to this conflagration, Martin Luther had reasoned, "If we strike thieves with the gallows, robbers with the sword, heretics with fire, why do we not much more attack in arms these masters of perdition, these cardinals, these popes, and all this sink of the Roman Sodom, which has without end corrupted the Church of God, and wash our hands in their blood?"[40] Likewise, John Knox claimed the book of Deuteronomy gave an eternal command — that God's people must attack and completely massacre any community of rivals: "To the carnal man this may appear a rigorous and severe judgment; yea, it may seem to be pronounced in rage [rather] than in wisdom. For what city was ever yet in which . . . were not found many innocent persons . . . ? But in such cases God wills that all creatures stoop, cover their faces, and desist from reasoning when the commandment is given to execute his judgments."[41]

By this point, most clergymen believed that the notion of loving enemies was sheer insanity. The Reformation-age wars, combined with the witch hunts, turned Central Europe into a vast religious killing ground. But as these wars ground their way down to international exhaustion, the fanatics for holy war slowly lost their credibility.[42] Ordinary people across Europe turned from their churches in horror and disgust. The population of Germany didn't recover from the fratricide for a century or more, and the reputation of Christianity never recovered. Finally by 1648, it grew obvious that no church could win or hold a monopoly on religious authority by force. And from that point on, the well-worn power of churches to threaten and punish people started to become a weakness. The most domineering churches simply drove their supporters away.

The Roman Church found it difficult to criticize its own role in the holy wars and witch hunts. Repenting of that violence seemed to imply an infallible church had been wrong to kill so many. But ever-more clerics wanted to claim a different direction. In China, Jesuit missionary Matteo Ricci (1552–1610) tried to represent his faith, not it as it really was in history, but as he felt it should have been: ". . . on the whole and so far as one can see — for I should not dare to exaggerate — ever since 1,600 years ago, when our countries became Christian, in more than thirty kingdoms which adjoin one another, over more than 10,000 square *li*, there has not been a single change of dynasty, not a war, not the slightest dispute."[43]

Exporting Christianity by the Sword

Turning from the age of Christian civil war, the people and nations of nominally Christian Europe went in several different directions. First, large numbers of lay people wrote off religion as snake pit of murderous fanaticism, unfit to be discussed in public. Second, a dedicated minority tried to return their churches to a focus on compassion and service. The leaders here were mainly women, as was most famously seen in the emerging female service orders of the Catholic "Counter-Reformation." The third major response was to turn Christian violence outward again toward the non-European world, as had happened with the Crusades.

For some centuries, Europeans had described the non-Christian regions of the world as *in partibus infidelium*, with an assumption that God meant Christian kingdoms to take dominion. And since Europe had been the world's most war-torn continent for several centuries, it now had a substantial edge in the arts of war, with which to export Christianity by the sword. In discussing the conquests to follow, I don't mean to highlight the violence of Christians while ignoring that of anybody else. It's just a matter of focus on the topic being discussed, which is basically a comparison of the methods used by colonial-age Christians with those of the first Christians.

Before Europe's "age of exploration," both Christianity and Islam had often spread peacefully, by word of mouth and popular appeal. That's what happened in much of the Roman Empire, in Armenia, or Ireland. But in the colonial-age missions to Africa, the Americas, and Asia, such appeal was often dampened by indiscriminate violence against the potential converts. Also, a number of the colonial powers tried to impose their religion as the only legal faith, which was an unusual idea outside of Christendom. In China or India there was no official control of religious life. People followed whatever schools they wished of Hinduism, Taoism, etc. In Islamic regions there were large minorities or majorities of non-Muslims, like the Christian Copts in Egypt, Eastern Orthodox Christians in the Balkans, or Hindus in India and Indonesia. The idea that all people of a kingdom must conform to the king's religion seemed foreign and unworkable. But for most European colonizers this was the Christian way. They imagined Jesus tolerating no diversity.

The Portuguese assumed that claiming the Indian Ocean for Christianity meant claiming all property there for Christians. Declaring a Christ-given monopoly on ocean trade, they attacked and killed any Arab or Indian merchants found on the seas. Basically, they made trading while non-Christian a capital crime.

In the Americas, the Spanish read out official proclamations of annexation to the uncomprehending Natives. Then they considered these people legally bound to obey Spain's kings and bishops. The practice of local religions was suddenly subject to the Inquisition, with "heresy" and "treason" treated as relatively indistinguishable capital offenses. The Spanish conquistadors seemed to presume they were continuing their re-conquest of Spain from the Moors, but further afield. They even named the town on the mouth of the Rio Grande "Matamoros," which was the old battle cry of "Slaughter the Moors!" But a good number of Spanish priests or monks felt these means of empire building were counterproductive to the faith. As one Franciscan friar in New Mexico complained, the country could have been won "in a Christian manner, without outraging and killing these poor Indians, who think that we are all evil and the King who sent us out here is ineffective and a tyrant."[44]

In China, the Jesuits at first took an open-minded approach. They emphasized that Jesus' teaching was complementary to Confucian wisdom,

241

which won the emperor's authorization to teach Christianity there. But the Vatican demanded a more all-or-nothing monopoly on truth, and required its missionaries teach that native Chinese culture was an erroneous evil. Jesus, they were sure, would never recognize what was good in another culture. When the Jesuits tried to defend their compromising ways, the Vatican ordered them out of the country.

In Japan, the missionary effort suffered blowback. After a Spanish ship wrecked on the coast, its captain spilled the beans on how Christian states conquered other countries: "Our Kings," he reported, "begin by sending into the countries they wish to conquer, religieux, who induce the people to embrace our religion; and then when they have made considerable progress, troops are sent who combine with the new Christians; and then our kings have not much trouble in accomplishing the rest."[45] After that (in 1614) the Shogun Hideyoshi banned all preaching of Christianity, declaring it an ideology of treason.

In the young USA, many colonists felt their country presented a blank-slate opportunity for a fresh vision of Christianity. Here, faith might be based on freedom rather than rule by supposedly God-appointed overlords, and by brotherhood rather than conquest. At first in Maryland colony, Fr. Andrew White tried to urge mercy on the Natives: "It is more prudence and charity to civilize them and make them Christians than to kill, rob, and hunt them from place to place, as you would do a wolf."[46] But in the course of conquering their own empire, many Americans would firmly endorse Anna Ella Carroll's patriotic prediction: "the wings of the American eagle" must spread the "Protestant Bible and the American Constitution . . . over the countries of the world."[47] For Democratic Senator Henry S. Foote, Americans were the new children of Israel. Their blessed nation had, "under the direction of Jehovah himself, acquired what was deemed a good and valid title to all the territory included in the promised land, by force of arms alone."[48]

Clearly this approach to human relations could be found in the Bible, even if Jesus didn't share it. And though most Americans claimed to liberate those they conquered, both American and Spanish missions involved a certain ambiguity toward the prospective converts. As *De Bow's Review* explained in 1849, "The race must soon become extinct . . . The experience of the Polynesians and the American Indians has proved that the aboriginal races, under the present philanthropic system of Christianization, can no more change their habits of life than the leopard can change his spots."[49]

As when Arab raiders used the banner of Islam in attacking other countries, American raiders claimed a patriotic duty to raid and seize new lands. Moving into Mexican Texas, they staged an immigrant revolution, overthrew their host government, and changed the law so only Anglo-American immigrants could own land. And as the clamor for further conquests grew in 1846, the Philadelphia *Daily Sun* claimed the annexation of all Mexico was a duty of religious compassion: "In poor, degraded Mexico, even the first elements of civilization are wanting — and these are, respect for property, and the right to worship God according to their own conscience. To extend our free system into such a country would be the brightest stretch of mercy."[50]

Unsatisfied by the seizure of all northern Mexico to the California coast, a series of enterprising raiders, called "filibusters," launched attacks on other Mexican states like Sonora, plus Canada, Cuba, Central America, and Ecuador. In describing their exploits in the 1850s, the *Democratic Review* was moved to boast, "in no part of the world nor in any age, are the traits of a conquering and a dominant people to be found in greater perfection than among ourselves."[51] The fundraisers for filibustering expeditions appealed to nationalism and religion, presuming the two to be identical. But as the *New Englander* and *Yale Review* pointed out "the outside world is unable to recognize any difference between a filibuster expedition sailing from Mobile or New Orleans for the lofty purpose of giving some more tropical country the full benefit and glory of American institutions, and an expedition for piratical purposes."[52] Somehow, those who doubted the glory of these raids seemed less faithful than the mercenaries.

Meanwhile in India, Britain's Governor of Madras affirmed that the colonial project's goal was "nothing short of the conversion of the natives to Christianity." There followed foreign funding for evangelical schools, systematic discrimination in job promotion for Christian converts, and direct pressure on Hindu and Muslim soldiers to convert.[53] The resulting 1857 Mutiny drew a British response of indiscriminate killing in cities like Allahabad, and that was about it for the moral appeal of Christianity during the coming century.

As the basically Christian empires of England, France, or Russia moved into Eastern Europe and the Middle East, their bankers, missionaries, and armies worked together as natural allies. They made deals for finance, trade, and "protection" with Christian communities within the Ottoman Empire. The Christian Serbs, Greeks, Armenians, or Lebanese Maronites made special agreements for support from foreign Christian powers. Then, as resentment rose against unequal advantages for Christian sects, the Western powers intervened in the interests of their spiritual relatives.[54] Things unfolded roughly as the shipwrecked Spanish captain warned the Japanese.

Of course many missionary groups like the Sisters of Charity thought only of serving sick, hungry, or uneducated people. And many missionaries offered service that was of lifelong help to non-Christians, without requiring their conversion. For them and their supporters, colonial violence in Jesus' name was deeply offensive. Perhaps over time the march of Christian soldiers grew more civilized. English church leaders managed to shame their government into renouncing the slave trade. They wanted their faith spread by teachers who practiced what they preached. In a similar spirit, the American Board of Missionaries (in the 1880s) called exclusively for married couples to serve in the Hawaiian Islands. Their aim was "nothing short of covering these islands with fruitful fields and pleasant dwellings, and schools and churches; of raising up the whole people to the elevated state of Christian civilization."[55] It was a gentler approach to establishing cultural supremacy. And where the land was too vast to populate with missionaries, the people could be brought to the missions. Canada's churches lobbied the government to require that Native families place their children in Christian boarding schools. Then they proceeded to process over 100,000 Native children over the next hundred years.[56] They tried to eliminate the cultures of other people, but at least they preferred brainwashing children to killing them.

In reaction to all abuses of the colonial age, a growing minority of idealists called for an end to racism, nationalism, and militarism. How, they wondered, did these things ever get to be Christian? Some protesters called on the British government to take the high road in granting colonies the same freedom Britain wanted for itself. And these moralists often received a polite hearing, though men of realism considered them soft-headed. As Lord John Russell patiently explained (in 1849), "the loss of any great portion of our colonies would diminish our importance in the world, and the vultures would soon gather to despoil us of other parts of our Empire, or offer insults to us which we could not bear."[57] Basically, mainstream Christians upheld imperialism. Though they wouldn't put it crudely, they accepted claims equating their own nation's self interest with God's will. In Germany, most people wanted freedom and benevolent government at home, but only a few Germans opposed military expansion to control foreign neighbors. Even fewer warned that domination of outsiders could easily lead to domination for insiders as well.[58]

By 1880, a great race was on to claim all remaining uncolonized portions of the world. France pushed beyond Algeria into the Sahara. Germany and Britain filled the maps' gaps in Southern Africa, using their new machine guns to handle troublesome locals. With pious pride Russia expanded into the Balkans and Central Asia. And with similar pride the USA took Cuba and the Philippines. After praying over the Philippine situation, President McKinley felt his nation had a duty "to uplift and civilize and Christianize" the mainly Catholic Filipinos, "and by God's grace, do the very best we could by them, as our fellow men for whom Christ also died."[59] After this, all the industrialized nations joined in attacking China to impose military-enforced "open doors" for foreign products and missionaries.

As the twentieth century began, it seemed an unstoppable destiny that all people of the planet must soon come under Christian tutelage. This was Western civilization's high noon, which seemed to fulfill the great mandate: "Go ye therefore unto all the world." As the USA joined Britain in the colonial mission, Rudyard Kipling was moved to write "The White Man's Burden." And as prejudiced as all this seems now, there was a real feeling of earnest responsibility for helping the world — perhaps a lot more than later generations of Peace Corps volunteers or Live Aid concert goers displayed. The missionaries and colonizers could be generous, as when American Protestant churches sent over $750,000 dollars in one year (1922) to support Chinese kindergartens, schools, colleges, hospitals, leper colonies or orphanages.[60] But so greatly were these foreigners identified with the arm-twisting imperial powers, that by the 1940s almost every missionary in China was evicted.

God's Hand in Social Darwinism

Of course the ideology of empire-building came from Rome, not Jesus, and the notion that Jesus could pass for a patriotic empire booster would have been stunning in the first century. But churches had adjusted to ruling ideologies before. In the early 1900s, however, the ideologies of Western powers took an even darker turn. Because after claiming support from religion, the colonizing superpowers next claimed additional support from evolutionary science.

For many ordinary church people, Darwin's theory of evolution at first seemed a satanic insult against the dignity of humankind. If that theory was true and people were descended from animals, didn't that mean they *were* animals? And if this was believed, how could anyone be expected to treat fellow humans any better than they treated their animals? But Herbert Spencer soon reinterpreted Darwin's theory in a way flattering to human ambitions. If evolution progressed by the survival of the fittest, then mankind was the winner of that struggle. Humans had won dominion over all creatures of the Earth, not by passively receiving it from God, but through dint of hard struggle and sheer superiority.[61]

When Darwin's theory was presented in this way, it grew popular. The Christians of industrial-age Europe began incorporating social progress through competition into their basic beliefs. Perhaps evolution was God's way of separating the wheat from the chaff, and the saved from the losers. If life on Earth was a race for survival of the fittest, then it would be fitting for God's plan if Christian civilization was victorious over all others. Maybe this sort of competition was simply the way God's hand worked in history. In that case, military victory and economic success were empirical signs of God's favor. Perhaps it was not that the holiest would inherit the earth, but that the strongest *were* the most holy.

By 1900, it was widely accepted as common sense that all creatures (and communities) were inescapably rivals in life's battle for supremacy.

It was the law of life that only victors had a future. And by this logic, which led straight to World Wars I and II, Jesus was simply irrelevant to reality. According to Scott Bader-Saye, "If one attempts to situate Jesus' ethic in the context of the modern myth of a primal war of all against all, in which violent struggle becomes a necessary part of the created order, then one can only say . . . that Jesus' ethic is not directly relevant and stands 'outside history.' "[62] In this context, the old imperative of Christian jihad against infidels was confirmed by scientific realism, because somebody had to come out on top.

Still, among sentimental fools and women, the peace movement was growing. As women grew more vocal in church, they commonly hailed Jesus as the Prince of Peace and denounced the arms race. The only political parties openly opposed to militarism were socialists, but purely Christian sentiment against militarism was also on the rise. As Europe slid toward general war before 1914, ordinary people across Europe pledged themselves to an international strike. These workers of Germany, France or England would simply refuse to fight and kill each other. It was a fine sentiment. But since the great powers also claimed to represent Christ's will, it seemed unpatriotic and womanish to oppose their ambitions for world supremacy. When the imperative of real war kicked in, several strike organizers were shot as the call of God and country swept all else aside.

During WWI, the general populations of Europe proved horrifyingly obedient to their masters. Where they had supported their nations' race for colonies, now they suffered unbelievable casualties in a war between colonizers. In response, most priests and pastors called for even greater sacrifice while selling war bonds. The few German mothers who demanded an end to the slaughter were simply shot as traitors. But Kaiser Wilhelm remained worried. If the demands for human sacrifice grew greater than his people could bear, would they turn with vengeance to a party of peace? Couldn't the churches somehow help resolve the fratricide in a way compatible with traditional order? After meeting the Vatican's representative in 1917, Wilhelm reported asking, "What must a Catholic think . . . when he hears always of efforts by the socialists only, never of an effort by the Pope, to free him from the horrors of war. If the Pope did nothing . . . there was danger of peace being forced on the world by socialists, which would mean the end of the power of the Pope and the Roman Church."[63]

As the war dragged on to disaster, Kaiser Wilhelm's fears came true in Russia. Next, socialist revolts almost gained control of Poland, Hungary, and Germany. In the wake of the war, many Christians turned to pacifism. Greater numbers of educated idealists rejected religion, blaming it as the main cause of war. But for most people, peace movements still seemed to be against Jesus. To many traditional Christians, it seemed clear that socialist revolutionaries "for peace" had nearly plunged all Europe into an abyss of godless chaos.

This is where an ideological brand of Darwinism and godly nationalism joined hands for an alliance of remarkable force. Among Germans who remained loyal to church and state, a fascist interpretation of WWI grew popular. Their nation had not lost due to any moral or military inferiority; godless traitors had betrayed it from within. And once those traitors to God and country were dealt with, the contest for national supremacy must resume with renewed urgency. For the Nazis, Darwin's theory of evolution was a natural imperative to rule or be ruled, and kill or be killed. Basically, they interpreted life as an inevitable war to the finish between races. The challenge was inescapable. The only question was which people would win creation's great battle for survival.

As WWII began, possibly most Christians in Europe saw nothing particularly incompatible between their faith, and an ideology which made all life a killing contest. In a side-show of that titanic war, militant

Catholic Croats embarked on their own ethnic cleansing of Serbian Orthodox Christians and Muslims, to make way for a Catholic "Greater Croatia." Later of course, that led to Serbian nationalists trying to do likewise to the Muslims of greater Serbia. The problem was that "kill or be killed" Christians generally made so many enemies that the world united against their utter barbarity. And this was a form of scientific evidence that evolution actually worked in other ways. Darwin had written another book called *The Ascent of Man*, in which he explored mutual support, group cooperation, and social morality as forces for the evolution of society.[64] This part of Darwin's research had been neglected by the super-patriots for world conquest. Later, scientists like Lynn Margulis and Dorion Sagan demonstrated how co-operation between one-celled organisms had enabled multi-cellular life to evolve. And from there, evolution continued mainly through mutual support and symbiosis between multi-celled creatures. According to these researchers, "The brutal destroyers always end up destroying themselves — automatically leaving those who get along better with others to inherit the world."[65] Did Jesus say that?

Defending Christian Civilization Worldwide

As the post-war Western powers faced growing demands for independence from their colonies, Western churches were again split over what Jesus would do. Some colonial revolutionaries were Muslims, and some were socialists, who believed that freedom and equality were anti-Christian. In general, the colonial powers in India, Algeria, Indo-China or Angola, portrayed the rebels as enemies of Christian civilization. Despite bombing local communities to suppress the rebels, they claimed to have the best interests of the colonized people at heart.

At first, many people in the United States identified with the independence movements, and expressed disgust with European efforts to re-impose colonial rule. Not only was their own country founded in an anti-colonial revolt, but the founder of their religion was also a colonized man, killed by colonial rulers. Soon however, this kind of common sense gave way to self-interest, and American Christians grew more adamant for defending Western power. All those rebellions to throw out Western businesses and missionaries from China, Algeria, Vietnam, etc. seemed to be part of a global plot.

Over the next several decades, the USA basically tried to fill the political space left by departing European colonists in Asia and Africa, along with upholding its business interests in Latin America. In doing this between 1946 and 1967, the U.S. government spent, according to Senator William Fulbright's calculations, about $904 billion dollars on "military power," as compared to $96 billion on "social functions" like health, education, and welfare.[66] And as if this wasn't enough, even private and church funding for foreign missions sometimes turned to military intervention. In the 1980s, Christian leaders like Pat Robertson and Beverly LaHaye (of Concerned Women for America) raised funds for the Nicaraguan Contras and the death squads against peasant rebels in Guatemala or El Salvador. The notion seemed to remain that the landholding descendants of Spanish conquerors were Christian, while the marginalized native Indian peasants were against God. And with a similar concern for civilization as he knew it, Jerry Falwell called for lifting economic sanctions against South Africa, because it was a bulwark against communistic barbarism.[67]

All this showed a lot of ongoing violence in the name of Christian values, and a lot of modern people concluded that Christianity was just a violent religion. But the popular allure of Christian knights killing those they hated was actually fading fast. People watching news coverage of events in Selma, Alabama or My Lai, Vietnam increasingly viewed the violent Christians as total hypocrites. Many authoritarian preachers like Jerry Falwell still claimed it was simple cowardice to renounce violence against their people's enemies.[68] But many non-violent Christians in the

251

American South, Latin America, or South Africa, were clearly risking their lives more than Falwell. And their statements of principle sounded more like Jesus too. For example, in helping lead the non-violent movement that overthrew Brazil's military dictators, Bishop Dom Helder Camara explained his tactics as follows:

> *The main rule, of course, is to absolutely refuse to commit any violence on person's lives or dignity. But there is what we might call a strategy of nonviolent action. This strategy . . . is adaptable, depending on the nature of the conflict, and the forces against which the conflict is to be waged. Generally speaking, the strategy of nonviolent action aims to cause the foundations of unjust power to collapse. Oppressive, repressive power rests on resignation, collaboration, and obedience on the part of the people. Nonviolence tries to organize non-collaboration and disobedience by as many people as possible. No power can last long, even by force of arms, against a whole population that refuses to obey it and recognizes another power instead. The strategy also includes a tireless dialogue with half-hearted agents of the unjust power to try to get them to rally to the cause of justice.[69]*

Where the South African authorities claimed to defend Western civilization against barbarism, they found themselves confronting a growing coalition of church leaders, following a strategy of Martin Luther King-style civil disobedience. When the regime declared war on godless terrorism, they found themselves attacking non-violent Christians. As Peter Walsh reported in 1985, ". . . hundreds of clergy and church workers were detained; many were tortured. Others were banned and severely restricted . . . Death squads assassinated Christian activists . . . Vigilantes and *kitskonstabels* intimidated, terrorized and killed."[70] They continued this crusade against human equality until many of their own soldiers and police grew ashamed.

By the 1980s and 90s, popular Christianity played a major part in the wave of democratization across Eastern Europe, Latin America, Africa, the Philippines or South Korea. In these movements, the international links of church denominations often served as networks of support which dictators hesitated to attack. And while some churches still made a cult of ethnic loyalties and endorsed violence against their supposedly evil neighbors, the great democratic revolutions of the late 1900s were almost all non-violent. Or at least they won when they turned to non-violent strategies. In the Philippines, the churches trained over half a million people in tactics of peaceful resistance before the democratic victory of 1986.[71] Non-violence, it seemed was once again prominent as a Christian value. Peace movements seemed to be getting more respectable, especially if they appeared in other people's countries.

The Recurring Dream of Total Victory over Evil

In recent decades, probably most Christians felt their religion had left its days of holy wars and inquisitions far in the past. Many proudly claimed their faith was the purest message of peace among all religions of the world. But the Bible's themes of war for God and divine vengeance, which appeared in the text at various points from Genesis to Revelation, still seemed fundamental for vast numbers of believers. The recent enthusiasm for an almost exclusively Jewish "greater Israel" (as a precondition for Armageddon) and the incredible popularity of Apocalypse literature showed an ongoing appetite for holy violence. The rhetoric of holy war still had a certain righteous appeal. As in computer games, purely metaphorical violence could be fun in a moral cause. When Pastor Rod Parsley spoke out for a more biblical America in 2006, he rallied a Washington crowd in a moralistic but entertaining way:

Now this revolution is not for the temperate. This revolution — that's what it is — is not for the timid and the weak, but for the brave and the strong, who step over the line of their comfort zones and truly decide to be disciples of Christ . . . So my admonishment to you this morning is this. Sound the alarm. A spiritual invasion is taking place. The secular media never likes it when I say this, so let me say it twice. Man your battle station! They say this rhetoric is so inciting. I came to incite a riot. I came to effect a divine disturbance in the heart of the church. Man your battle stations. Ready your weapons. Lock and load![72]

At other times, the language seemed more ominous, as when Christian Reconstructionist Gary North advised, "Pluralism will be shot to pieces in an ideological (and perhaps literal) crossfire, as Christians and humanists sharpen and harden their positions in an escalating religious war."[73]

This sense of religion as a holy war remained a matter of verbal argument and metaphor in North America. But as the American superpower grew more involved with Middle Eastern affairs, a more literal sort of competition arose. As the pressure of ethnic and resource conflicts grew in the Middle East, Western powers intervened as partisans in the polarized conflicts of Jews against Arabs, or autocratic rulers versus religious rebels. The interventionists found themselves operating in a head space where 4,000 years of religious history formed the context of modern conflicts. In that setting, tribal loyalty, blood vengeance, holy law, and promised land, were still fundamental realities of life. In that region's history it had long seemed obvious that there could not be enough land, water, fish, and bread for all. The question was who there would be enough for. And that would be determined by the strength of loyalty binding groups of people to defend their own. Even in the oil age, those bonds between insiders and against outsiders remained, despite Moses, Jesus, or Muhammad. In the regions where those prophets called for a commonwealth of tribes, the religions they launched stood for holy tribalism, defended by blood vengeance. While intervening in this cultural world, Western diplomats, consultants, or troops often adjusted their views to the situation around them. It was a reality which seemed to come from the Bible, perhaps especially those aspects of biblical tradition that Jesus rejected.

To the surprise of many in Washington, Oklahoma Senator James Inhofe reported that the conflicts in the Middle East were not over territory, resources, or power; they were "a contest over whether or not the word of God is true."[74] Likewise Lt. General William Boykin famously explained that Islamists hated America, not because of its colonial-style interventions in their countries, but "because we're a Christian nation, because our foundation and roots are Judeo-Christian . . . and the enemy is a guy named Satan." [75] Views like this struck most Americans as a blast from an almost forgotten past. These were traditionally Middle Eastern attitudes, exerting influence over Western policy makers in the region. In that traditionally Black versus White world, America became the Great Satan, and its enemies the Axis of Evil. After Arab fanatics attacked America on 9/11, President Bush explained, "They have no justification for their actions. There's no religious justification, there's no political justification. The only motivation is evil."[76] Where many Christians had assumed that such things disappeared with the Dark Ages, once again the Western world heard its own leaders speaking the language of holy war.

The actual war "on terror" was a series of skirmishes between conventional armies and gangs of criminals. But since this police action was labeled a war against evil, the normal rules of criminal justice did not apply. Rather than trying to arrest criminals and bring them to trial, army units and air force strikes hit areas where suspects might be hiding. It began to seem normal to catch criminals by firing missiles into cities or villages, and accepting the collateral damage to neighbors as the normal cost of law enforcement. As a poster of U.S. Air Force jets dropping their bombs said, "Do unto others."

As with other police operations, the authorities offered rewards for turning in suspects. In Afghanistan, U.S. intelligence agents offered between $3,000 and $25,000 for anyone turning in Taliban or al Qaeda fighters. A flyer they distributed urged "Get wealth and power beyond your dreams. You can receive millions of dollars helping the anti-Taliban forces . . . This is enough money to take care of your family, your village, your tribe for the rest of your life." Almost immediately the prisons of Afghanistan and Guantanamo Bay were full of goat herders, cab drivers, cooks or shopkeepers, turned in by their neighbors or enemies for cash.[77] And since these suspects were accused of evil crime rather than ordinary crime, their right to a trial was denied.

In such a war, it could once again seem an act of Christian virtue to pre-emptively attack other nations, because they were suspected of being about to do wrong. Though Pope John Paul II urged President Bush to stop invoking God to justify war, Bush explained, "We are in a conflict of good and evil, and America will call evil by its name."[78] Since the enemy in Iraq was so named, the normal rules for treatment of prisoners did not apply. Instead, methods used in the old Inquisitions or witch hunts seemed appropriate. As Captain William Ponce advised interrogation officers in August 2003, "The gloves are coming off gentlemen regarding these detainees . . . we want these individuals broken." But the results of torture were no better than in previous centuries. As one tortured detainee, former district mayor Haj Ali explained, "Abu Ghraib is a breeding ground for insurgents . . . All the insults and torture make them ready to do just about anything."[79] Watching this war unfold, even lifelong opponents of dictatorial regimes in the Middle East like Syrian dissident leader Yassin Haj Saleh said, "However opposed Syrians are to our own regime, they now distrust the Americans more."[80]

The American demographic group most supportive of the Iraq invasion was White Evangelical Christians, of which around 80% (in

2005) thought it was the moral thing to do.[81] It actually must have seemed fairly normal to a nationalistic Christian when Vice-Presidential candidate Sarah Palin referred to the Iraq invasion as a mission from God. As her pastor Ed Kalnins had explained, "I really think it is a holy war. It's a war of gods . . . When someone fights in the name of God, that becomes a holy war."[82] If many worried that such talk could generate WWIII, there was no shortage of Christians claiming it was God's plan to bring on the Apocalypse. Instead of seeing evil as something we all struggle with, self-righteous Christians saw it as an external enemy. Rather than hoping to lead by example in changing the cruelty of everyday evil, they hoped to defeat it by military force. The moral lesson they seemed to offer went back to an age before Moses: If you hate and fear other people, attack and kill them.

For one example of the medieval-style religious hate which at least temporarily bloomed in the blogosphere, let me quote one rant by an American Christian who I won't name:

Why can't these supposed Muslims assimilate OR go back to Saudi Arabia? After all, that's where Ninja-land is! They should be glad to be near Mecca as possible. It would make them happier. What are they doing in "other lands"? Or they can happily party with Iran — fireworks and all, make it nuke! — woweeee! that would be a blast! Besides, there's nothing better than going to paradise right? Now, the way to go is partying! Now, they'd be happy in Saudi too because they can happily abuse their women, marry infants and all those really wacko things that they claim are okayed by Moe de Pedo — and it's perfectly legal in Saudi! That's where they can stay . . . this planet isn't the 7th century anymore . . . dang . . . or you know, they can kill themselves! That's a one way tour to paradise (visualize those virgins . . . oh la lah!).

Overall, Christianity after 2000 seemed to be polarizing over the issue of violence as never before. Peace movements were now global and growing beyond any previous popularity. But at the same time, possibly never since the first century when Revelation was written, was the idea of a holy Armageddon so popular with so many. For a taste of it, the Christian Youth rock band "Delirious" recently performed in Philadelphia, singing "We're an army of God and we're ready to die . . . Let's paint this big ol' town red . . . We see nothing but the blood of Jesus." The crowd was screaming back "We are warriors!"[83] We've already mentioned the visionary slaughter of infidels in the *Left Behind* books. But of such enthusiasm displayed in many arts, John Dominic Crossan had a theological complaint: "To turn the nonviolent resistance of the slaughtered Christ into the violent warfare of the slaughtering Jesus is, for me as a Christian, to libel the body of Jesus and to blaspheme the soul of Christ."[84]

258

8. Correcting Compassion

In a lot of Catholic churches you'll see pictures of Jesus with a big red heart on his chest. It's the Sacred Heart of Jesus, and I suspect this image is the source of the phrase "bleeding heart." A bleeding heart, of course, is someone who gets carried away with sympathy, and is a sucker for people's hard-luck stories. Seems to me, it's mostly Christian conservatives who use the term "bleeding heart" as an insult.

Of course sometimes Mother Mary is also shown with a red heart open on her breast. And I suppose it's more respectable for mothers to have a bleeding heart. Luke describes Mary as the soul of mercy, and says that before bearing Jesus she announced, ". . . the arrogant of heart and mind he has put to rout, he has brought down monarchs from their thrones, but the humble have been lifted high. The hungry he has satisfied with good things, the rich sent away empty." (Luke 1:51–53) It sounded like she might take mercy to a revolutionary extreme. Centuries later in the 1100s, Joachim of Fiore claimed that Mary's speech, called the "Magnificat of Mary," was a great prophecy that signaled a coming age of the Holy Spirit. And St. Francis with his first followers believed their lifestyle of bleeding-heart compassion was a sign that age had begun. But later, in the 1200s, the Franciscan scholar Bonaventure corrected this overzealous belief. He explained that Mary's vision concerned the next world — the world after death, not a reform of society.

This conflict of interpretation between Joachim of Fiore and Bonaventura was the topic of Josef Ratzinger's doctoral thesis. And Ratzinger (later Pope Benedict XVI) concluded that Bonaventure was right: the kingdom of real compassion would come in another world. The church should therefore focus on saving souls for a better afterlife, rather than trying to rearrange things on this temporal planet.[1] Ratzinger's opinion was consistent with a lot of church tradition. For example, during the huge debates over slavery, child labor, and other injustices before the American Civil War, a Catholic layman wrote in 1859, "The age attaches . . . too much importance to what is called progress of society or the progress of civilization, which, to the man whose eye is fixed on God and eternity, can appear of not great value."[2]

But Ratzinger was also contradicting many other Catholics, like Pope John XXIII, Mother Teresa, and American Catholics like James Cardinal Gibbons, John A. Ryan, and Dorothy Day. Gibbons helped form the Knights of Labor. Ryan led the Bishops Program of Social Reconstruction, which pushed to restrict child labor, require minimum wages, etc. And Dorothy Day helped organize even poorer people, explaining "We are trying to say with action 'Thy will be done on *earth* as it is in heaven.' "[3] Of course all these people were repeatedly told they should stick to the Bible, and to saving souls for the next world.

Bleeding Hearts and Righteous Believers

Jesus held a number of ancient West Asian beliefs, like belief in possession by evil spirits, faith healing, and a real Devil. He believed that after dying, each person would be judged for how they lived. But instead of just saying that their good and bad deeds would be weighed on a scale, he claimed the standard of judgment would be this: "Just as you did it to the least of these who are members of my family, you did it to me." (Matthew 25:40) Basically, Jesus thought compassion was more important than correct theological ideas, following rules, obeying superiors, or avoiding pollution from contact with disgusting people.[4] But later, many church leaders made a host of things more important than compassion. Medieval clerics commonly made obedience to superiors the most important requirement for admission to paradise. Reformation preachers often stressed doctrinal correctitude over everything else, which is what they generally meant by "faith alone." If correct beliefs were all that mattered for many Protestants, then their explosion of sectarian divisions over doctrines was hardly surprising. For example, I have a relative who is so religious she refuses to join any church she knows of. Since they all compromise the true doctrine, she's a denomination of one.

Legalistic Christians have made moral rules the most important thing, which has fuelled a rise of self-righteous exclusivity. As Frank Schaeffer reflected, "A church split builds self-righteousness into the very fabric of each new splinter group, whose only reason for existence is that they decide they are more moral and pure than their brethren."[5] Some churches grew so righteous they approached zero tolerance for sinners. But most were not so zealous as Rev. R.J. Rushdoony, who called for restoring all the Old Testament penalties Jesus opposed, including death for adultery, blasphemy, and possibly Sabbath breaking.

These shifts in priorities involved correcting or demoting compassion. But the most directly relevant change here has been the trend toward rejecting charity and claiming it to be a stupid idea. In recent decades, it increasingly passed as Christian to dismiss charity as counter-productive pandering to free-loaders. It wasn't just that many Christians weren't very charitable, or that they judged certain other people as undeserving. This was a shift toward seeing all needy people as unworthy of help.[6] This attitude appeared on the sociological map recently, when a 2002 survey of 44 nations showed that Americans were both the most religious national group surveyed, and the least compassionate. The USA had the highest number of people agreeing that the poor have only themselves to blame.[7] Christian Reconstructionist Gary North said it flat out: society should not aid the poor; "subsidizing sluggards is the same as subsidizing evil."[8]

This popular rejection of "bleeding heart liberal do-gooders" was especially strong in the American Bible belt. It seemed to imply a revised modern "Christianomic" policy for both private and public spending.

Judging by the economic and social policies supported by the Christian Right, perhaps the new Christian economics resembled Milton Friedman's market realism. As Friedman advised Chilean dictator Augusto Pinochet, "the major error [of past U.S. governments], in my opinion, was . . . to believe that it is possible to do good with other people's money."[9] Or maybe the ethics of many modern fundamentalists resembled those of General Pinochet himself. Like Francisco Franco, Pinochet pledged he would "extirpate the root of evil," bring a "moral cleansing," and establish a nation "purified of vices."[10]

Wealth as God's Reward, and Charity a Subsidy for Sin

Like all accounts of history, the Bible conveys great arguments over money. In Proverbs we find conventional advice for success: "In the house of the righteous there is much treasure, but trouble befalls the income of the wicked." (15:6) By this ancient common sense, rich and powerful people had the rewards of virtue, and others only got what they deserved. This logic was so obvious that Jesus' disciples were stunned by his denunciations of successful people. In Luke, Jesus says nothing good about the wealthy or powerful; instead he denounces greed (12:13–21), advises his followers to share everything (12:33, 18:22), and warns of punishment for selfishness. (16:19–31)

According to Luke's perhaps over-enthusiastic account in Acts, the primitive Christians were devoted to spiritual communism: "All who believed were together and had all things in common: they would sell their possessions and goods and distribute the proceeds to all, as any had need." (2:44–45) We even have a Stalinistic purge of wealth-hoarders, as both Ananias and Sapphira were reportedly struck dead for holding back private property from the commune. (51–11) This was a great inspiration for monastic orders in the Middle Ages, and also for idealistic cadres of modern Communists. Just as many early Christians insisted that sexual love was incompatible with spirituality, Jesus seemed to insist that money was incompatible: "You cannot serve God and money." (Matthew 6:24) In a spirit compatible with Mao Tse Tung, the book of James asked, "Is it not the rich who are exploiting you? Are they not the ones dragging you into court?" (James 2:6–7)

Naturally, all this anti-materialistic idealism was quite unworkable, as most anti-capitalists have found. But we have several accounts of primitive Christians trying to live by such values. From around the year 125, a philosopher called Aristides described the Jesus movement as a community violating every principle of economics:

> *They despise not the widow and grieve not the orphan. Anyone who has distributes liberally to those who have not. If they see any strangers, they bring them under their roof and rejoice over them as though they belonged to their own family: for they call themselves brothers and sisters, not after the flesh, but after the spirit of God . . . And if there is among them anyone who is poor or needy and they themselves do not have an abundance of necessities, then they will fast for two or three days so that they can provide the needy with the necessary food.*[11]

I personally wouldn't wish such a lifestyle on my enemies, but those were their ideals at the time. And this primitive Christian attitude was not so different from the common sense of ancient peasants. Those old time rustics defined friendship as willingness to share, and viewed their landlords or rulers as bloodsucking parasites. Through the Middle Ages, it was common for such peasants to picture the Devil as a fat, greedy, big man. This figure of evil would eat everything for himself, leave nothing for others, and grow fat while others starved. Only later, in the early modern period, did another image of evil gain prominence — of an ugly old hag who had nothing, but who coveted what others had, and would use her evil influence to get it. This was a switch in the face of evil, from that of the most advantaged, to that of the most destitute members of society. Where traditional peasants had seen greed as the chief evil, the later church seemed to accept that jealousy — the jealousy of wretched people towards their betters — was an evil of greater concern. As Rev. James Hutchinson explained in 1697, witchcraft was the means by which "others of the poorer sort could get their malice and envy satisfied."[12]

Back around 400, Bishop John Chrysostom used to boldly denounce greedy rich people from his pulpit, pointing them out and challenging them by name before the whole assembly. But by the land enclosures of recent centuries, in which growing numbers of peasants were evicted from their farms, most priests and pastors warned the dispossessed they should look to their own sins for the cause of their misfortunes.

Like cream rising to the top, the appeal of personal success supplanted community care as a primary religious value. For example, around 1500 the Catholic Church quietly stopped observing its own canon laws against charging interest on loans. It then became a major money lender across Europe. And what the early idealists called greed, Calvinist theologians made an essential virtue. As a typical Puritan minister in colonial New England stressed, "religion will teach you that industry is a SOLEMN DUTY you owe to God, whose command is 'BE DILIGENT IN BUSINESS.' "[13]

Even poverty had its purposes in God's plan. As many English pastors emphasized, poverty was God's punishment for sin, and a spur to virtue. As the Industrial Revolution gained strength, Arthur Young explained, "Everyone but an idiot knows that the lower classes must be kept poor, or they will never be industrious." The early economist J. Smith added, "It is a fact well-known to those who are conversant in this matter, that scarcity, to a certain degree, promotes industry, and that the manufacturer [i.e., the manual worker] who can subsist on three days' work, will be idle and drunk the remainder of the week."[14]

In the same way that priests of the Middle Ages felt it was un-Christian for peasants to oppose their landlords, so it seemed contrary to God for industrial-age people to oppose business owners. In 1799 the English Parliament made it a penal offense for any association of workers to "conspire" for better pay, limits on the hours of work, or on the quantity of work an employer could require. This law also rewarded informers for reporting such conspiracies.[15] And many preachers praised such laws for defending godly order. By a similar moral standard, the crown blocked the colonial legislatures of Virginia and South Carolina from restricting the importation of Black slaves. The colonists' concern that slaves would soon outnumber free people was overruled, lest demands from ordinary people limit the slaving corporations' right to do business.

In the revised morality of early modern times, the ethic of people taking care of each other gave way to praise for Christian self-reliance. Of course traditional charity was still honored in popular religion. When the Protestant revolution swept aside old structures of Catholic charity in Flanders, Juan Louis Vives could successfully appeal to the town council of Bruges: "As it is disgraceful for the father of a family in his comfortable home to permit anyone in it to suffer the disgrace of being unclothed or in rags, it is similarly unfitting that the magistrates of a city should tolerate a condition in which citizens are hard pressed by hunger and distress."[16] It was a judgment many Christians still upheld. But the cause of compassion was increasingly left to the church's women.

Is Compassion a Manly Virtue?

For most of church history, it seemed almost unarguable that Jesus and the Bible required different values and ideals from each sex. Women were to cultivate chastity, obedience, and loving support, while men cultivated strength, authority, and initiative.[17] The women's values applied mainly to private life, and men's values were for public affairs. In other words, men should be somewhat like Old Testament patriarchs, and women should act like loyal Middle Eastern wives. But once lay people began reading translations of the Bible, they saw for themselves how Jesus appears in the Gospels. Rather than hearing second-hand descriptions of Jesus' power and lordship, they read of a man who combined firm leadership with compassionate service. In him, the traditional values of men and women seemed strangely mixed.

Still, the gender gap in qualities and virtues remained vitally important for many church leaders down to the present. James Dobson, a founder of "Focus on the Family," recently wrote an article called "Gender Gap?" which listed "the countless physiological and emotional difference between the sexes." Perhaps most importantly, Dobson explained that love was a primary need and a "life-blood" for women, while men had less need for love. It was clear to Dobson that this made men more fit to serve as Christian leaders, and that men's less love-constrained priorities should receive women's loving support.[18] In this division of ideals, compassion seemed an effeminate virtue, which rendered women unfit for leadership in the real world. As Riane Eisler noted in *The Chalice & the Blade*:

> . . . women [commonly] define power, as the responsibility of mothers to help
> their children . . . develop their talents and abilities. It is here that what
> [Jessie] Bernard calls "the female ethos of love/duty" remains the primary
> model of thought and action — but only for women. And it is here that what
> [Carol] Gilligan calls the feminine morality of caring — a positive duty to

266

do unto others as we would want them to do unto us — also governs. But again, it is only as the model of thought and action for those who are not supposed to govern: women.[19]

Between the different virtues for men and for women, most male clerics had little doubt as to which was more godly. It seemed obvious that things should be managed by those best suited to rule, or everything would soon collapse in ruin. To prevent the weakening effect of women's values on church leaders, the medieval Western church banned women from preaching, singing, speaking, managing church finances, or even being married to a priest. And with somewhat similar logic for the family, an 1850s English manual for parents advised: "In the family it is usually weak mothers who follow the philanthropic principle, whereas the father demands unconditional obedience without wasting words. In return it is the mother who is most often tyrannized by her offspring and the father who enjoys their respect; for this reason he is the head of the whole household and determines its atmosphere."[20]

We have some record of how it was for children in this atmosphere. Back in the 1600s, John Aubrey wrote of his childhood, "in those days, fathers were not acquainted with their children." Roger North said, "We were taught to Reverence our father, whose care of us then consisted chiefly in the Gravity and decorum of his comportment, order, and sobriety of life . . ."[21] Most people, it seems, believed that aloofness, formality, and control were the primary virtues for fathers. The Russians upheld such family values even better. As General Pyotr Nikolayevich recalled of his father's generation in the 1800s, "harshness had become a moral principle. To show benevolence was to be weak, to be cruel was to be strong."[22] For such Christianity, the worst sin for a man was not selfishness, but weakness. If he was weak, the world of surrounding evil would be free to move in, and do whatever to his property, his women, and his self-respect.

Perhaps we can hardly imagine it today, but in medieval and early modern times, the death rate for men in duels was almost astounding. The prevailing culture of Christian gentlemen, far from encouraging forgiveness or compromise, demanded a Middle Eastern-style code of blood vengeance for any insult. Most men of any authority carried swords, and felt morally obliged to use them. As Philip Chesterfield observed, "In France, a man is dishonored by not resenting an affront, and utterly ruined by resenting it."[23] Somehow, all this still has appeal. We can still recall America's Wild West as an age of old fashioned virtue, where men boldly claimed other people's property, always carried loaded guns, and suffered no challenge to their superegos.

All this superiority (or defense of it) seemed to be Christianity's requirement for men, partly because the church attributed such behavior to God. Reflecting on it, Anthony Cooper (1671–1713) had to wonder at his own upbringing. The God of his fathers seemed to be one "whose character it is to be captious and of high resentment, furious and resentful . . . encouraging deceit and treachery amongst men, favorable to a few . . . and cruel to the rest."[24] If this was true of most fathers on earth, was it true of the ultimate father? Of course questions like that spurred many traditionalists to defend manly religion as they knew it.

For many centuries Christianity seemed to rely ever more on intimidation to control people. And these centuries coincided with the rise of exclusive male control in religion. But at some point the means of intimidation started to grow counter-productive. Those who felt called to enforce godly authority upon others often found they simply alienated their neighbors. So in the 1600s, Oliver Cromwell managed to divide England into military districts; each with a "Major-General," charged to enforce "godliness and virtue." Some historians compare these enforcers to the committees for public virtue in recent Revolutionary Iran. And so offensive was Cromwell's reign of virtue that some clergymen complained not one in twenty parishioners came to church any longer.[25] It was still illegal not to attend church, and illegal to withhold tithes. But which pastors felt ready to go after their neighbors, and try to enforce yet more externally imposed discipline? There had to be a better way to lead, and there was. As the new female religious orders inspired new standards of care, so male leaders increasingly explored other ways to care and lead.

Concerning relations between the sexes, the original Protestant dream was basically a throwback to the Old Testament. In a spirit of godly patriarchy, the celibate priesthood was replaced by pastors who were masters of families. The logic prevailed again, as in Judaism, Eastern Christianity and Islam, that a religious leader should be a family man among others. This even suggested that a pastor might be matured rather than corrupted by a woman's influence. But probably few pastoral couples felt it was Christian to show any real passion for each other.

Of course the pastor needed to be a role model for other married men. The question was, what vision of the Christian family would he offer? Many pastors tried to display exemplary control over their wives and children, taking this as the biblical way. And many laymen took such stern examples to heart. They too would be godly fathers, leading their families in prayer and Bible study. Some of them read the Bible so much they discovered biblical justifications for divorce or polygamy. Partly to curb their laymen's immature zeal for authority, some pastors tried to set a different example that would be more in line with the New Testament's passages about charity and kindness. And in churches which didn't forbid women to speak, there might be discussions of the Bible in mixed company, like a salon for civilized conversation. The participants might agree that Jesus' style of compassion was something relevant for both mothers and fathers. Soon it might actually seem spiritual (rather than anti-religious) when Mary Wollstonecraft said that moral progress depended on removing the barriers to dialogue between men and women. "In France," she claimed, "there is understandably a more general diffusion of knowledge than in any other part of the European world, and I attribute it, in part measure, to the social intercourse that has long subsisted between the sexes."[26] All this mixing of traditionally male and female values was endlessly controversial, and many Christians hoped to draw a line on it. Some felt sure that any further blurring of sexual roles was a corruption of God's design. Others wanted to preserve sex-specific roles, but also develop a deeper dialogue between "different but equal" partners.

By the nineteenth-century in England or America, the general population was increasingly divided over manly ideals. On one hand, there was growing respect among women for "restrained manhood." A restrained man was civilized, gentle, devoted to his family, successful in a hopefully intellectual profession, and religious in a morally restrained way. He might be a poor but kind man, like the petty clerk Bob Cratchit in *A Christmas Carol*. But preferably he was a man of some professional standing like Rev. Washington Gladden, who ran for city council in Columbus Ohio in hopes of curtailing municipal corruption.

On the other hand, the ideal of "martial manhood" retained great popular appeal. Such men took pride in physical strength, a forceful character, and the capacity to dominate others.[27] Back in the East, men like this might lead the gangs of New York, or go into politics. But many headed west to carve out empires on the frontiers, like James Bowie or William Walker. Such men could still claim to be the real men, and even the real Christians. People had a hard time deciding which kind of man was more respectable. For example, in the early 1800s, Robert Owen tried to convince powerful Englishmen it would yield profitable benefits to abolish child labor, and provide education for every child. And though some people thought he was heroic, probably most businessmen, politicians, and church leaders thought Owen was a soft-headed fool.[28]

At least with competition allowed between churches and political parties, people were freer to choose what sorts of men they preferred. And it was increasingly the same for families and mates: people could vote with their feet. But down to the present time, America has remained divided over which sort of men it wanted it its pulpits, in the office of president, or maybe the office of pastor-in-chief.

The Gospel of Wealth

Concerning changing Christian views on economic life, for centuries America set the pace. Because in America, economic reality seemed to be transformed. In coming to colonial North America, ordinary immigrants left behind a world where stifling constraints seemed God given, and entered one where God seemed to will no limits. For example, ordinary people in England had for centuries been forbidden to enter forests to hunt or gather wood. The forests belonged to nobles or big landlords, and trespassers could have their eyes cut out. Even to own a hunting-type dog was forbidden to ordinary folks. But on arriving in the New World, people from this background found themselves able to roam vast forests, and kill as many wild animals as skill allowed. We may think of settlers on the American frontiers as poor by our standards. But their rising wealth in seized land, farm produce, and cash income soon dwarfed whatever they left behind in England, Italy, Russia, or China. For close to the first time in world history, ordinary people's resentment of wealthy people gave way to simple envy. It was the emotion of people who bore some hope of becoming fabulously rich themselves.

For North American Christians, the Bible still portrayed an ancient world in which most people were dirt poor, and most wealthy or powerful people were oppressors who lived off the toil of others. In church, the Bible's tales of charity for the suffering still sounded spiritual. But from the perspective of America's workday world, such sentiments often seemed like relics from the past. Already by the mid-1800s, a popular consumer culture was on the rise. The excitement over getting what only an elite could ever have before could be almost irresistible. Many church leaders pondered how to respond. Some affirmed the whole development as a positive trend, which confirmed the success of godly virtue in America. Others challenged consumerism as a shallow response to life. As *Harper's Monthly* reflected in 1856, "Pestilence is a more appalling calamity than War, and requires a stouter heart to meet it . . . Still greater courage and firmness are required to remain poor, when there is a chance of becoming rich by means which most men do not scruple to employ . . . But the most decisive proof of independence and courage is to be truly religious . . . in a gay, and worldly, and proud society."[29]

Anti-materialism, which had seemed so holy in the Middle Ages, was rapidly giving way to affirmation of the quest for wealth. The sanctity of private property seemed ever more central to Christian morality. As Rev. Samuel B. How argued before the Civil War, both the Old and New Testaments "entirely agree" on the rights of property owners, even owners of slaves. And so, "the desire and the attempt to deprive others of property which the law of God and the law of the land have made it lawful for them to hold, is to strike a blow at the very existence of civilization and Christianity."[30]

Frankly, praying for wealth no longer seemed so selfish. In Victorian-age America, tracts of daily invocations for alignment with "the Spirit of Infinite Plenty" grew popular. One such affirmation read, "I think of myself as a child of God, heir to all the riches of the Kingdom. This is the truth about me. My prosperity is assured."[31] Where traditional figures like St. Francis, and probably Jesus, seemed to make a religious point of having nothing in this world, the image of holiness was updated. Congregationalist minister Bruce Barton wrote a popular new biography of Jesus as he would live in the bustling 1920s. In *The Man Nobody Knows*, this modern Jesus was an enthusiastic businessman and a motivational speaker. He was an avid outdoor sportsman and designer of effective advertizing campaigns. This Jesus outdid modern Americans at their own virtues. It had probably been true for decades when James D. Hunter observed in 1987, "the Protestant legacy of austerity and ascetic self-denial is virtually obsolete in the larger Evangelical culture. . ."[32]

In an increasingly popular "gospel of wealth," economic success was a primary sign of God's favor. And by the mid-twentieth-century, "ordinary" middle class North Americans stood among the richest and most powerful people in world history. Increasingly, these people simply stopped identifying with poor people. Poorer "disadvantaged" or "third world" people just seemed to be losers, suffering from their own lack of virtue. In that case, biblical injunctions to charity like "You shall not harden your heart or shut your hand against your poor brother" (Deuteronomy 15:7) seemed generally counterproductive. Charitable groups like the Salvation Army were well meaning, but tended to foster rather than control unvirtuous living.

To many self-made moralists for economic success, the whole notion of sharing things began to sound both socialistic and immoral. The "social gospel" of old-fashioned civic-minded churches started to seem like rank heresy. Back in the early 1900s, the National Catholic Welfare Conference could call for fairness and compassion toward poor families, and ordinary churchgoers felt it was a noble sentiment.[33] But by 1953, such views seemed tainted with socialist ideology. The chief investigator for the House of Representatives Committee on Un-American Activities, J.B. Matthews, accused that "the Communist Party has enlisted the support of at least seven thousand Protestant clergymen" as "fellow travelers, espionage agents, party-line adherents, and unwitting dupes." The doctrine of a "social gospel" had "infected the Protestant theological seminaries."

Matthews asked the nation, "Could it be that these pro-Communist clergymen have allowed their zeal for social justice to run away with their better judgment and patriotism?"[34] Of course similar charges could have been brought against Pope John XXIII a few years later, since he claimed the church must lead in meeting the global challenge of social injustice, and support measures "whereby imbalances among various classes of citizens may be reduced."[35]

As large numbers of poor people from rural areas migrated to the cities, many of the more affluent city dwellers moved out to more exclusive suburbs. Then the suburban communities seceded from their cities, kept their tax revenues for themselves, and often invested in security systems to zone out poor people from gated communities. To control the unvirtuous, many wealthy Christians felt it essential for their governments to spend vast sums of taxpayer dollars on the best military, police, and penal systems, even if this meant cutbacks to public education, health care, and famine relief. If real believers trusted in "faith alone," then "works" of organizing care for people seemed a bit faithless. Such efforts seemed to place hope in human deeds and the welfare state, instead of in God. If everybody looked to God for help rather than human-run programs of health, education, and welfare, there would be little justification for taxes to penalize virtue and reward unfaith.[36] Business would be free to maximize profits without the burden of "social obligations" to the public's less successful people.

Even in cases of disasters from disease, modern Christians could adopt the ancient attitude Jesus rejected, that the sick were suffering due to their own sins. Paul Cameron, a founder of the Traditional Values Coalition, felt it moral to urge that the National Institute of Health should end all programs for helping "victims" of HIV infection. Cameron felt it would be more in accord with God's judgments to quarantine infected people in AIDS "leper colonies."[37] In this version of Christian morality, perhaps the

274

main concern for incapacitated people was to make them pay their own way and stop them from stealing. Where global drug corporations held patent monopolies on expensive AIDS drugs, maybe the primary ethical issue was protecting the property rights of corporations from thieves who would compete to offer cheaper AIDS drugs to Africans.

In the past, orthodox religion generally stood for obedience to the powers that were. But the prevailing powers of the modern world were international corporations and their political clients. Where Christians tried to combine biblical morality with obedience to these authorities, the result was a new mixture of values. It was an attempt to combine corporate interests in economic de-regulation with Old Testament family law. It could then appear both Christian and patriotic to reduce regulation of global corporations, while advocating stronger controls and punishments for individual sinners.

At some point, the gospel of wealth became a kind of cult, whose primary ethical value was "greed is good." It basically held that profit made right, and the desires of rich people reflected God's will. Many Christian business leaders felt that religious freedom and the gospel of wealth both suggested God's endorsement for a virtually unregulated economy. It could then appear both faithful and "conservative" to support unlimited consumption of natural resources, including forests, fisheries, and finite water supplies. Some argued that maximized consumption was clearly God's will, since the faith of their fathers concerned taking dominion over the world while renouncing love for it. So the fundamentalist textbook *America's Providential History* explained that people concerned to sustain the environment "lack faith in God's providence . . . The Christian knows that the potential in God is unlimited and that there is no shortage of resources on God's earth. Christians know that God has made the earth sufficiently large with plenty of resources to accommodate all the people."[38] Some pastors denounced environmentalism because it questioned the American way of life and seemed hostile towards God's people. As Mathew Hagee put it, "These environmentalists, they're trying to tell you that somehow all of these terrible things are going to happen because of us. Something WE did. They want to tell you that it was America that did something bad, because they want to be able to tell us what we did wrong and send us the bill for it."[39] Of course this ignored the whole rise of religious concern for self-control in managing the planet, as seen in H. Paul Santmire's *Brother Earth*, John B. Cobb's *Is It Too Late? A Theology of Ecology*, Matthew Fox's *Creation Spirituality*, Sallie McFague's *Models of God: Theology for an Ecological, Nuclear Age*, etc.

On the world stage, major Western corporations wanted more access to foreign markets and resources, as they'd had in the days of colonial empires. And many advocates for such self-interest abroad claimed to be champions of freedom, democracy, and Western civilization. Their patriotic support for the supremacy of their own nations' interests, plus their respect for the sanctity of privatized property, made these people seem to be the strongest upholders of Christian values. And for several decades this was a winning political combination in the USA. In Republican Party election campaigns, religious self-righteousness applied for both the pro-family values and pro-big business wings of the platform. But growing numbers of evangelicals such as Pat Robertson recognized a contradiction between loyalty to global corporations and traditional community values. And many of these more authentically traditional people proposed to defend their social values, even at the expense of corporate freedom. In that case, the Republican Party alliance of conservative Christians with corporate interests could not really hold.

Instead of thinking it was Christian for people to take care of each other, the gospel of wealth upheld the maximization of personal benefit. "Compassionate conservatism" came to mean an agenda to cut public programs for helping people, and making charity a strictly private matter. For decades a "moral majority" of "values voters" supported "the common wisdom embraced by all serious economists"[40], such as John Williamson or Milton Friedman. In general, these experts proposed,

1. Removing government restrictions on business profit making, such as minimum wage requirements, price controls, trade barriers, or environmental safeguards.
2. Slashing spending on social and community welfare.
3. Privatizing public services including water, transport, health, education, or prisons, and running these programs for private profit. As economic advisor Grover Norquist put it, "I don't want to abolish government. I simply want to reduce it to the size where I can drag it into the bathroom and drown it in the bathtub."[41]
4. Equalizing the tax rate for rich and poor. As Clyde Wilcox and Carin Larson reported, "One activist in Virginia told us in no uncertain terms that a flat tax was biblical policy, and therefore there was no room for discussion."[42]
5. Spending more public money on security forces, which actually meant record deficit spending on military contractors.

Eventually, the pursuit of such values contributed to the U.S. "bankster" economic meltdown of 2008. But not before it spelled similar trouble with oligarchy corruption in other largely Christian nations like Chile, Argentina, Russia, or South Africa. As Russian minister Pyotr Aven explained of the team which privatized his nation, "Their identification of themselves with God, which flowed naturally from their belief in their all-round superiority, was unfortunately typical of our reformers."[43]

For economically struggling Christians, the gospel of wealth tended to make religion a prayer for wealth. It became, as Jonathan Walton explained it, a faith that God would "make a way" for poor people to get the finer things in life. Those who gambled on mortgage scams were often encouraged to believe that "God caused the bank to ignore my credit score and blessed me with my first house." Many people read books like Bruce Wilkinson's *The Secrets of the Vine: Breaking Through to Abundance*, which seemed to promise an inner change towards prosperity. But Rick Warren accused, "The only people getting prosperous from the prosperity gospel are the preachers."[44]

The Return of the Pharisees

Clearly modern Christians had major differences over what values they held most godly. As in the divisions over what kinds of men or women were most admirable, people had different gut-level feelings about what was sacred. Their different ideals ultimately meant different images of God. And looking over the big sweep of Judeo-Christian history, Marcus Borg felt there were two main religious visions, which had always competed for the soul of monotheism, through all the history recorded in the Bible and down to the present time. As Borg saw it, these two kinds of monotheistic religion were:

A) a "monarchical" religion, stressing God as an ultimate ruler whose orders must be obeyed, which led to a "performance model" for winning God's mercy through proper obedience, and

B) a "spirit" religion, focusing on the quality of care between souls, and a "relational model" for better living.[45]

In Jesus' time, the "monarchical" legalists for obedience to all holy laws were the Pharisees. And these people were Jesus' primary debating partners. The Pharisees felt that faith in the Bible required holding all traditions mentioned in its pages as equally inerrant and binding. But

Jesus engaged in heated debates over what was right and wrong in the Bible. Where Jesus stressed the prophets who saw God as a loving parent, the Pharisees preferred other visions where God was an almighty emperor, demanding obedience or death. These legalists objected to Jesus because he judged everything by the quality of relations involved, and he was willing to break any rule standing in the way of compassion.

To argue with the Pharisees was as difficult as arguing with Islamist fanatics. For them, everything recorded in the holy book was from God. Any deviation from the customs it described had to be punished, either in the next life, or by God's self-appointed agents on earth. To the Pharisees, a religion that emphasized better relations between human beings simply missed the main point of religion. Surely obeying God was infinitely more important than serving any mortal creature. So for these legalists, the pursuit of ever more perfect compliance with hundreds of ancient rules became the most important aim in life.

These ancient "culture wars" continued in modern North America with surprisingly little change, except that North America's debates included the New Testament material.[46] For modern Pharisees, Jesus had sacrificed himself to pay for all violations of the Bible's holy laws. But salvation still depended on following all those rules, and for many pharisaic preachers this seemed to require a "tyranny of legalistic perfection." These people didn't directly insist that legalism and dogma were more important than compassion. They just believed that getting people to obey the right rules *was* compassion.

Naturally, the first requirement for a legalistic religion was naming which authority to obey. And where medieval Christians felt sure the church hierarchy spoke for God, modern ones commonly made the Bible their court of highest appeal. Though the Eastern Orthodox churches warned of the dangers in "bibliolatry," many modern Pharisees took devotion to their book as far as Iran's Ayatollah Murtaza Mutahhari took his: "We [Muslims] have no doubt that all narrations in the Quran, in their form and content, are manifest realities and there is no need to support Quranic anecdotes by books of history; rather, history should be supported by the Quran."[47] As theologian Benjamin B. Warfield affirmed in the 1890s, the Bible is "not as man's report to us of what God says, but the very word of God itself, spoken by God himself through human lips and pens."[48] Without such belief in a fail-safe authority, many legalists felt that humanity would be lost in a sea of uncertainty.

As much of history shows, there's always been a vast popular demand for superhuman authority. Huge numbers of people have wanted an infallible guide to follow. It seemed far better than guessing and making perhaps disastrous mistakes. Many modern Christians like Phillip Johnson have defended this desire as a basic spiritual aspiration. For Johnson, the "mere concept of God in the human mind is no help at all, because a God created by human philosophy is just another idol . . . What we need is for God himself to speak, to give us a secure foundation on which we can build . . ."[49] For James Davison Hunter, real religion was commitment "to an external, definable, transcendent authority," which "tells us what is good, what is true, how we should live, and who we are."[50]

Instead of telling people to use their minds and hearts, legalists urged that every human tendency should be overcome though obedience to a higher will. And some sections of the Bible certainly took this principle to an extreme, as when the Levite priests announced orders from God: " 'Get your swords and go back and forth from one end of the camp to the other and kill even your brothers, friends, and neighbors.' So they did, and about three thousand men died that day. Then Moses told the Levites, 'Today you have ordained yourselves for the service of the Lord, for you obeyed him even though it meant killing your own sons and brothers; now he will give you a great blessing.' "(Exodus 32:27–29)

Jesus must have known such things were in the Book. And he clearly respected his heritage. But for him, respect involved denouncing what was cruel, and reinforcing what was just in his nation's traditions. After all his ridicule of Pharisees and official priests, it would be a stunning rejection of his own arguments if he then proclaimed "My tradition right or wrong." But that was just what many new Pharisees of modern times said about the Bible. Though the book itself was full of pro and con arguments over duty, freedom, marriage, slavery, patriotism, war, and taxes, the new Pharisees treated the whole book as a string of non-contradictory commands from God. And if the book was inerrant, then the priest who preached it also seemed to speak for God. So in his Radio Bible Class, Richard W. De Hann said of the scriptural pastor, "Yes, he is a fallible human being, but God has entrusted His infallible Word to that man. He therefore has a great message to proclaim, and you are under obligation to heed the exhortations and obey the directives which come from the Scriptures through the pastor to you."[51] This seemed to require a less critical sort of customer in an increasingly critical age. Many modern people questioned their pastors' interpretations of Bible teachings on child-care, marital strife, worldly wealth, or dispensationalism. But some of the more Pharisaical pastors tried to protect their authority from real debate. As Joe T. Odle advised the Southern Baptist clergy, "No one will deny that Biblical criticism, when carefully and wisely used, has a proper place, but many would question whether that place is in the quarterlies used by the rank and file of Southern Baptists."[52]

If these leaders and their book of rules were infallible within the church, then another question naturally arose. Why shouldn't they lead the whole community beyond the church as well? Why not impose their holy law across the land? When people of other cultures were diluting America's heritage, and America's power seemed in steady decline, was it not time to stand up for God's way? Previous generations of devout Christians had often avoided involvement in worldly affairs. But by the

1960s, many religious legalists started to go on the political offensive. In both the USA and Russia, some church leaders insisted that only a revived Christian state could avert a future of moral depravity. As a committee of Russian clerics wrote in the 1990s,

> The debasing of Russian history, the humiliating of Russian culture and self-awareness are carried on today as before, and cosmopolitanism and ethno-nihilism are openly propagated. Again and again we observe, in addition to the catastrophic material situation of the Russian people, moral degeneration, absolute legal nihilism, and the further disintegration of spirituality . . . Where is the way out of this situation? We must find the way out by means of restoring Russian national consciousness and Orthodoxy.[53]

For serious new Pharisees, the problems of modern society were primarily due to declining personal faith and morals. As evangelical cartoonist Jack Chick warned in the early 1970s, American values would soon be so enfeebled that communist thugs would overrun the country with impunity. Chick drew these new barbarians breaking into suburban homes, starting fires, dragging off women and children by the hair, murdering anybody who stood in their way. Another of Chick's cartoons showed parks full of kids sucking reefers, with perverts in raincoats emerging from X-rated theatres to chase little girls. Chick's cartoon exclaimed, "Only a revival could slow down this juggernaut!"[54] Clearly only fundamentalist Christians could halt the decline of the West; liberal Christians had nothing to say but "God is love, man."

Dr. D. James Kennedy, a leader of the Center for Reclaiming America, called for a new political activism: "Our job is to reclaim America for Christ, whatever the cost. As the vice regents of God we are to exercise godly dominion and influence over our neighborhoods, our schools, our government, our literature and arts, our sports arenas, our entertainment media, our scientific endeavors — in short, over every aspect and institution of human society."[55] We might think these reformers meant to defend freedom and apply sound management practice. But some of these legalists, like R.J. Rushdoony, viewed modern "secular humanist" America roughly the way John of Patmos viewed Rome. Though America was a democracy rather than a military dictatorship, Rushdoony viewed his country with a hostility approaching that of radical Islamists: "The humanist West is our modern throne of iniquity, framing mischief by enacting laws. We must return to God's law. We must work towards a true Christendom. Thy Kingdom come, O Lord!"[56]

For David Chilton, the task before Jesus' church was obvious: "The Christian goal for the world is the universal development of biblical theocratic republics, in which every area of life is redeemed and placed under the Lordship of Jesus Christ and the rule of God's law."[57] Of course many Christians and Muslims argued there must be no compulsion in religion. But Gary Bauer felt the struggle to establish Christian laws was unavoidable: "So the question," he argued, "is not whether you legislate morality. The question is whose morality you're going to legislate. Somebody's values are going to win. We just have to have the confidence to get in the public square and say that our values will be best for the country."[58] By such logic, somebody had to lose in both religion and politics. Howard Phillips put it even more bluntly: "The overarching question we face today is: 'Who is America's sovereign?' and 'What is his law?' . . . The holy Bible makes clear that Jesus Christ is our sovereign. He is King of Kings, lord of lords, the ruler of all nations. America's founding fathers understood and acted on this biblical truth . . . Clearly, if the words of the fathers are honored, Congress has no authority to restrict the establishment of Biblical religion in the State of Alabama . . ."[59]

If religion was a matter of obeying the correct master, then the world seemed split in two — between loyal subjects of the lawful king, and rebels who served another master. And why, in that case, should there be "tolerance" for relativity and pluralism, when other religions were treason against God's rule? As Tom DeLay insisted, "Only Christianity offers a comprehensive worldview that covers all areas of life and thought, every aspect of creation. Only Christianity offers a way to live in response to the realities that we find in this world." As if directly refuting similar Islamist claims to offer complete guidance in life, DeLay repeated, "Only Christianity."[60]

What sort of society did the new Pharisees envision? Some Christian Nationalists boldly called for a full restoration of Old Testament law as practiced by the Puritans of Massachusetts Bay Colony, including the death penalty for witchcraft, blasphemy, adultery, and homosexuality. Some even demanded a new crusade to establish Christianity throughout the world. As George Grant proclaimed in the late 1980s:

> *Christians have an obligation, a mandate, a commission, a holy responsibility to reclaim the land for Jesus Christ — to have dominion in civil structures, just as in every other aspect of life and godliness.*
> *But it is dominion we are after; Not just a voice.*
> *It is dominion we are after. Not just influence.*
> *It is dominion we are after. Not just equal time.*
> *It is dominion we are after.*
> *World conquest. That's what Christ has commissioned us to accomplish. We must win the world with the power of the Gospel. And we must never settle for anything less . . ."[61]*

Many of these new Pharisees displayed the wounded outrage of people whose birthright had been stolen. Rather than feeling fortunate that their churches were free from government control, they felt oppressed that their church could not control the government. Rather than feeling equally free with others to express their beliefs and values, they felt insulted by anyone who believed something else. Like some angry Muslims, they seemed to assume that other people had no right to offend them. Perhaps making the country officially Christian would end that problem. Maybe Christian Pharisees would find common cause with King Abdullah of Saudi Arabia, who recently proposed a U.N. resolution to defend "respect for religions, their places of worship, and their symbols . . . therefore preventing the derision of what people consider sacred."[62] In other words, a proposal to ban blasphemy as defined by the rulers of each country.

Like political movements everywhere, the new Pharisees championed political platforms for reform. And as in efforts to establish "Islamic law," there was difficulty agreeing just what the scriptures implied for public administration. Certainly the law should protect the traditional family, but different groups of Christians had different family traditions. There should be law and order, but improving the justice system was a huge, complicated challenge. Concerning "Christian laws," it would be very difficult for the leaders of numerous churches to agree what they were. So long as the new Pharisees didn't really hold power, it was easier for them to say what they opposed. So, in the 1970s the Protestant Pro-Family Forum listed the following "secular-humanist" beliefs to be rejected by proper Christians: "Belief in removal of distinctive roles of male and female . . . belief in the equal distribution of America's wealth to reduce poverty and bring about equality, belief in control of energy and its limitation, and belief in the removal of American patriotism and the free enterprise system, disarmament, and the creation of one-world socialistic government."[63]

For a time, it seemed that the modern Pharisees had a hammer-lock on the title of "real Christians." When they spoke of "values voters," they didn't mean the values of traditional evangelicals as seen in the movement against slavery, or the 1908 "social creed" of the Federal Council of

Churches, with its concerns to end child labor, require minimum wages, protect the Sabbath as a day for families, etc. They didn't mean the "social gospel" values of those who built the YMCA, the Salvation Army, the New Deal, or the Civil Rights movement. The new Pharisee values voters were less concerned with social fairness than controlling personal sin, especially if it related to sex.

Should rules on sex from ancient West Asia be imposed in the bedrooms of modern North America? Senator Rick Santorum argued they must:

> [I]f the Supreme Court says that you have the right to consensual sex within your home, then you have the right to bigamy, you have the right to polygamy, you have the right to incest, you have the right to adultery. You have the right to anything. Does that undermine the fabric of society? I would argue Yes, it does. It all comes from, I would argue, this right to privacy that doesn't exist in my opinion in the United States Constitution . . . You say, well, it's my individual freedom. Yes, but it destroys the basic unit of our society because it condones behavior that is antithetical to strong healthy families.[64]

As far as we know, Jesus never said anything about virginity, save to forgive a woman accused of forbidden love. But to fight premarital sex, the modern Pharisees felt it imperative to oppose education on sex in schools. As a result, a recent survey showed that American teenagers had rates of HIV infection 4 or 5 times higher, and a gonorrhea rate 70 times higher than better informed teenagers in the Netherlands or France.[65] Pope Paul VI even condemned masturbation (in 1975) as a mortal sin which forfeited the love of God, "even though it is not possible to prove unequivocally that Holy Scripture expressly repudiates this sin as such."[66]

Though the whole Bible gave no clear judgment about contraception, this became another primary issue for biblical legalists.[67] The medieval

Catholic Church had defined "conception" as the time the soul enters and "quickens" a fetus. As St. Jerome wrote back around 400, "The seed gradually takes shape in the uterus, and it does not count as killing until individual elements have acquired their external appearance and their limbs."[68] Both the canon law expert Gratian (1100s) and the Council of Trent (1545–63) upheld this understanding. But many modern leaders of Catholic and Protestant churches insisted on denying all rights of birth control to women.[69] And to win a political ally in this fight, the Catholic Church in America made a political deal. It dropped agitating for its traditional values of compassion for the working poor, the unemployed, the homeless, and the sick, in exchange for a Republican Party platform opposed to contraception, sterilization, or abortion.[70] Then, as Republican administrations tried to export this agenda through pressure on world health organizations, they found international allies against birth control, mainly from legalist Islamic states.[71] The values and tactics of legalists in both these religions showed a certain similarity. Where U.S. courts defended womens' rights to have an abortion, extremist Christians "zealous for the law," such as the Army of God and the Lambs of Christ, published lists of abortion providers on their websites for targeting by fellow fanatics.[72]

The traditions which the new Pharisees deemed most fundamental often flatly contradicted what Jesus taught. Marcus Borg said, "It is a sad irony that these groups, many of which are seeking earnestly to be faithful to the Scripture, end up emphasizing those parts of the Scripture that Jesus himself challenged and opposed."[73] As Riane Eisler saw their common pattern across the world:

If you look at the political agenda of fundamentalists — Muslim, Hindu, Jewish, or Christian — what really interests them is reimposing the system of rigid top-down control basic to the domination configuration. This configuration consists of strong-man rule in both the family and the state, the ranking of the male half of humanity over the female half, and fear and institutionalized violence to maintain rankings — be they man over woman, man over man, race over race, or religion over religion.[74]

Eisler questioned whether such religion should even be associated with Jesus:

If you look closely at the teachings and policies advocated by leaders of the Christian Right in the United States, you will see that they are often the polar opposite of the teachings of Jesus. Whereas Jesus challenged the rigid rule of the religious hierarchies of his time, these men (and occasional women) are bent on controlling all aspects of our lives — from our family relations to our political relations. Whereas Jesus taught caring, compassion, empathy, and non-violence — in a word, the fundamentals of partnership — the leaders of the Christian Right preach the fundamentals of the dominator model.[75]

Back in 1947, the Rev. Harold Ockenga had famously asked, "Can Fundamentalism Win America?" And he claimed it could not. He said fundamentalism had been "Weighed in the balances and found wanting," due to its spirit of "Fragmentation, segregation, separation, criticism, censoriousness, suspicion, solecism..."[76] Ockenga looked to a more generous kind of evangelism, animated by care and respect rather than legalistic judgment. Obviously Ockenga was decades premature in declaring that fundamentalist legalism would not prevail. But gradually most people in North America grew distrustful of all religious fanatics, be they Muslim, Christian, or even Jewish. By 2005, Arthur Schlesinger Jr. could seem wise rather than sacrilegious to warn "There is no greater human presumption than to read the mind of the Almighty, and no more dangerous individual than the one who has convinced himself that he is executing the Almighty's will."[77]

For many evangelical Christians, fundamentalist doctrines like dispensationalism, literal inerrancy, nationalism, subordination of women, or demands for separation from other sinners, were add-on teachings that had no basis in what Jesus taught.[78] The most widely popular evangelists like Billy Graham or Charles Templeton appealed to the general public, across ethnic, racial, or denominational lines, and didn't stress divisive judgmental doctrines. Of course Will Herberg could still complain that these preachers "speak the language of individualistic piety, which in lesser men frequently degenerates into a smug and nagging moralism."[79] But there were also Christians like Dorothy Day, Martin Luther King, Oscar Ramero, Desmond Tutu, Dom Helder Camara, Mother Teresa, Jaime Sin, Marianne Williamson, or Jim Wallis, who clearly stood for compassion in matters bigger than individual affairs.

At a Human Life International conference in 1994, Randall Terry spoke of the difficulties in making America a truly Christian republic. And he was quite despairing over the prospects of success. With commendable honesty he told the conference:

We're losing the fight, friends. I am a general in this war and I would be ill-serving if I did not tell you the truth. We're not just losing. We're getting our tails whipped, and it's not just happening in America . . . Why are we losing? . . . We are losing because of a lack of strong, righteous, courageous, visionary Christian leadership. The USA and the nations represented here tonight . . . we're locked into a cultural war.[80]

According to the National Opinion Research Center at the University of Chicago, the period of 1972 to 1994 had seen a decline in support for the values Terry felt were essential to Christianity. Opposition to freedom for homosexuals declined from 85% to 70% of the population. Those who felt it was wrong for mothers to have a career beyond parenting fell from 66% to 34%. The number wanting at least some legal restrictions on a woman's right to abortion slipped from 62% to 59%. The portion of people who would ban pornography to adults declined from 44% to 39%.[81] During his preaching career, Jesus hadn't mentioned any of these issues, except to stress the value of granting to others what we wish for ourselves. On that score, maybe the world was moving slowly toward Jesus' actual values, and dispensing with traditional corrections of what he said.

Postscript

In writing this book, I've aimed to speak as a citizen of the Western world, not as a defender of some religious sect. My attempt here has been something like an ordinary citizen of the USA or Canada, who tries to point out differences between his country's constitution and the record of his government. I wouldn't have to be some kind of super-patriot or a high court justice to write something like that. It would basically be a matter of common sense opinion. In the same way I've tried to talk about the religious side of our heritage, without any claim to be holier or wiser than most others in this society.

I should mention that a few years ago I married a Muslim woman. So now half or more of "my people" are Muslims, and I've had a chance to see some of their struggles with various supposedly Islamic traditions. My relatives aren't into any dogmatism. But they do feel strongly about rejecting the notion that fanatical people are the "real" Muslims, or "better" Muslims than ordinary people with common decency. My relatives are averse to arguing about religion, like many Christians are. But in doing a bit of reading about Islam, I immediately see issues that seem similar to what I've been talking about in Christianity. For example, Muhammad started out as an employee of his first wife, and in terms of the trading company, she was his boss. Yet after he died, some of his followers claimed he had said, "Those who entrust their affairs to a woman will never know prosperity."

In the decades after Muhammad died, a great trade arose in sayings attributed to him. And many of these sayings or interpretations of sayings contradicted what was written in the Quran, as when some clerics argued that women were mentally unfit to inherit property. Concerning such things, the Egyptian scholar Muhammad Abu Zahra wrote a history book with a chapter called "The Increase in Lying Concerning the Prophet and the Schisms and Divisions in the Ranks of the Fuqaha." During those early centuries, Muhammad ibn Ismail al-Bukhari (d. 870) tried to investigate some 600,000 sayings attributed to Muhammad. He concluded that only about 8,200 of them were authentic.

I suspect this is a universal problem of religions, though some Muslims or Christians would deny that any such problem exists in their own tradition. Obviously, I think it's good when people try to think critically about these things. And fortunately, there are many Muslims like Fatima Mernissi, Abdolkarim Soroush, and others who are doing that in Islamic culture. But I only have the background to talk about the tradition I grew up with.

Of course a lot of Muslims and Christians assume that only highly professional experts or designated leaders can properly evaluate what's authentic or fraudulent in their tradition. And this seems like a respectful attitude towards religion. But it also resembles the attitude that only leading politicians can tell what's right for their country. And in that case, it would be "loyal" and "faithful" for ordinary citizens to shut up and trust what they're told. Like perhaps most people these days, I figure a better kind of mutual accountability happens when everybody thinks for themselves about what's right. And it seems to me the world will be better as ordinary Muslims, Christians, etc. do that more.

Notes

Notes to chapter 1 : Correcting Jesus in Sunday School

[1] Ruether, Rosemary Radford, *Christianity and the Making of the Modern Family*, 104.
[2] Gaustad, Edwin, and Schmidt, Leigh, *The Religious History of America*, 235.
[3] *Recognitions of Clement*, 3.42, cited by Akers, Kieth, *The Lost Religion of Jesus*, 92.
[4] Bader-Saye, Scott, "Living the gospels: morality and politics," in *The Cambridge Companion to the Gospels*, 274–275.
[5] Gaustad, Edwin, and Schmidt, Leigh, *The Religious History of America*, 187.
[6] Jacobs, A.J., *The Year of Living Biblically*, 266.
[7] Jacobs, A.J., *The Year of Living Biblically*, 270.
[8] Manning, Joanna, *Take Back the Truth*, 99–100.

Notes to chapter 2 : Correcting Jesus' Jewish Religion

[1] Josephus Flavius, *Jewish War*, vii. 3. 35.
[2] Seneca, cited by Augustine, *The City of God*, Book VI, Chapter II.
[3] Jacobs, A.J., *The Year of Living Biblically*, 119.
[4] Wilson, Barrie, *How Jesus Became Christian*, 114.
[5] Frend, W.H.C., *The Rise of Christianity*, 98–99, 38–39.
[6] Wilson, Barrie, *How Jesus Became Christian*, 119.
[7] Wilson, Barrie, *How Jesus Became Christian*, 115.
[8] Epistle to Diognetus, 4, cited by Wilson, Barrie, *How Jesus Became Christian*, 191–92.
[9] Frend, W.H.C., *Martyrdom and Persecution in the Early Church*, 136–137.
[10] Durant, Will, *Caesar and Christ*, 543–544.
[11] Frend, W.H.C., *Martyrdom and Persecution in the Early Church*, 102.
[12] Josephus, Jewish War, 7.417–419, cited in Horsey, Richard A., and Hanson, John S., *Bandits, Prophets and Messiahs*, 215.
[13] Josephus, Jewish War 7.421, cited by Stegemann, Ekkard W. and Wolfgang, *The Jesus Movement: A Social History of its First Century*, 327–328.
[14] Wills, Garry, *What the Gospels Meant*, 109.
[15] Ashton, John, *The Religion of Paul the Apostle*, 89.
[16] Wilson, Barrie, *How Jesus Became Christian*, 199.
[17] Ignatius, Letters, cited in Frend, W.H.C., *The Rise of Christianity*, 124.
[18] Schoeps, Hans-Joachim, *Jewish Christianity*, 34, referring to Eusebius, *History of the Church*, 3.32.3–6
[19] Cheetham, Nicolas, *Keepers of the Keys: The Pope in History*, 10.
[20] Dudley, Donald, *The Romans*, 250.
[21] Irenaeus, *Libris Quinque Adversus Haereses*, 5.24.2, cited in Pagels, Elaine, *Adam, Eve, and the Serpent*, 116.
[22] Schoeps, Hans-Joachim, *Jewish Christianity*, 92.
[23] Warner, Marina, *Alone of All Her Sex: The Myth and Cult of the Virgin Mary*, 3.
[24] Campbell, Joseph, *Occidental Mythology*, 350
[25] Ehrman, Bart E., *Misquoting Jesus*, 96.
[26] Crossan, John Dominic, *God & Empire*, 28,
[27] Ruprecht, Louis A. Jr., *This Tragic Gospel*, 69–70, 94–95.
[28] Wills, Garry, *What the Gospels Meant*, 156, citing Augustine, "Interpreting John's Gospel," 36:1.
[29] Crossan, John Dominic, *The Birth of Christianity*, 336–337.
[30] Rossner, John, *In Search of the Primordial Tradition and the Cosmic Christ*, 116.
[31] Wilson, Barrie, *How Jesus Became Christian*, 100.
[32] Epiphanius of Salamis, *The Panarion of*, 30.20.5, cited by Akers, Kieth, *The Lost Religion of Jesus*, 235.
[33] Eusebius, *Eccesiastical History*, Book III, chapter 27, cited by Ehrman, Bart D., *The Orthodox Corruption of Scripture*, 51.
[34] Falwell, Jerry, *Finding Inner Peace and Strength*, 47.
[35] Eliade, Mircea, and Couliano Ioan P., *The Eliade Guide to World Religion*, 81.

[36] Spong, John Shelby, *Jesus for the Non-Religious*, xii.
[37] Christie-Murray, David, *A History of Heresy*, 48–49.
[38] Young, Frances, "The gospels and the development of doctrine," in *The Cambridge Companion to the Gospels*, 210.
[39] Ruprecht, Louis A. Jr., *This Tragic Gospel*, 152.
[40] Raschenbush, Paul, "Christian Gate-Keepers Declare Obama Not Christian," Progressive Revival blog, Nov. 17, 2008, beliefnet.com.
[41] Aslan, Reza, *No god but God*, 182.
[42] Wilson, Barrie, *How Jesus Became Christian*, 259.
[43] Ehrman, Bart D., *Misquoting Jesus*, 112–113.
[44] Ehrman, Bart D., *The Orthodox Corruption of Scripture*, 85.
[45] Borg, Marcus J., *Jesus, Uncovering the Life, Teachings and Relevance of a Religious Revolutionary*, 15–16.
[46] Graham, Billy, cited in the Herald Tribune, p. D14, March 26, 1998.
[47] Bokenkotter, Thomas, *A Concise History of the Catholic Church*, 55–56.
[48] Markschies, Christoph, *Between Two Worlds: Structures of Early Christianity*, 38.
[49] Wilson, Barrie, *How Jesus Became Christian*, 231–232.
[50] Cornwall, John, *Hitler's Pope*, 25–26.
[51] Kertzer, David I., *The Popes Against the Jews*, 185.
[52] Kertzer, David I., *The Popes Against the Jews*, 207.
[53] Kertzer, David I., *The Popes Against the Jews*, 17.
[54] Luther, cited by Ruprecht, Louis A. Jr., *This Tragic Gospel*, 169.
[55] Durant, Will and Ariel, *Rousseau and Revolution*, 632–633.
[56] Kertzer, David I., *The Popes Against the Jews*, 130.
[57] Kertzer, David I., *The Popes Against the Jews*, 65.
[58] McPherson, James M., *Ordeal by Fire: The Civil War and Reconstruction*, 377.
[59] Bernal, Martin, *Black Athena*, vol. 1, 343.
[60] Arnold, Matthew, quoted by Bernal, Martin, *Black Athena*, 348.
[61] Bernal, Martin, *Black Athena*, vol. 1, 349.
[62] Kertzer, David I., *The Popes Against the Jews*, 102.
[63] Kertzer, David I., *The Popes Against the Jews*, 143.
[64] Kertzer, David I., *The Popes Against the Jews*, 149–150.
[65] Kertzer, David I., *The Popes Against the Jews*, 252, 261.
[66] Kertzer, David I., *The Popes Against the Jews*, 271.
[67] Kertzer, David I., *The Popes Against the Jews*, 272–273.
[68] Kertzer, David I., *The Popes Against the Jews*, 257.
[69] Harris, Sam, *Letter to a Christian Nation*, 40.
[70] Goldberg, Michelle, *Kingdom Coming: The Rise of Christian Nationalism*, 73.
[71] Kertzer, David I., *The Popes Against the Jews*, 283.
[72] Cornwall, John, *Hitler's Pope*, 279.
[73] Cornwall, John, *Hitler's Pope*, 191.
[74] "Religion and Society Report," May 2000, Howard Institute, cited by Manning, Joanna, *Take Back the Truth*, 116.
[75] Spong, John Shelby, *Jesus for the Non-Religious*, 233–234.
[76] Bivins, Jason C., *Religion of Fear*, 189–191, citing *Tribulation Force*, 373–374.
[77] Cornwall, John, *Hitler's Pope*, 378.

Notes to chapter 3 : Correcting Forgiveness

[1] Hedges, Chris, *American Fascists*, 68–69.
[2] Epictetus of Hierapolis, cited by Durant, Will, *Caesar and Christ*, 492–493.
[3] Spong, John Shelby, *Jesus for the Non-Religious*, 235.
[4] Whitlock, Dorothy, *The Beginnings of English Society*, 42.
[5] Taibbi, Matt, *The Great Derangement*, 70.
[6] Kramer, Samuel Noah, *History Begins at Sumer*, University of Pennsylvania Press, Philadelphia, c. 1981, 1990, 110
[7] Spong, John Shelby, *Jesus for the Non-Religious*, 78.

CORRECTING JESUS

8 Ranke-Heinemann, Uta, *Putting Away Childish Things*, 101.

9 Vermes, G., citing 1 QS, Manual of Disciple, *The Dead Sea Scrolls in English*, Penguin, London, 1987, 62.

10 Wills, Garry, *What the Gospels Meant*, 82.

11 Jacobs, A.J., *The Year of Living Biblically*, 262.

12 Butt, Gerald, *The Arabs: Myth and Reality*, 216.

13 Akers, Keith, *The Lost Religion of Jesus*, 44.

14 Chilton, Bruce, citing the Targum Zechariah, 14:21, in *Rabbi Jesus: An Intimate Biography*, 198.

15 Spiegel, Shalom, cited by Rabbi Joseph Telushkin, *Biblical Literacy*, 313.

16 Nolan, Albert, *Jesus Before Christianity*, 159.

17 Durant, Will, *Caesar and Christ*, 588.

18 Spong, John Shelby, *Jesus for the Non-Religious*, 162–165.

19 Chilton, Bruce, citing Parah 4: 3, in *Rabbi Jesus: An Intimate Biography*, 252.

20 Chilton, Bruce, *Rabbi Jesus: An Intimate Biography*, 252–254.

21 Avot de Rabbi Nathan, 6, cited by Armstrong, Karen, in *Jerusalem: One City, Three Faiths*, 156

22 Gospel of Philip, 62:35–63:5, *The Nag Hammadi Library in English*, 147.

23 I Clement: 55, cited by Grant, Robert M., *Augustus to Constantine*, 104.

24 Acts of the Christian Martyrs, re: Bishop Polycarp, cited by Pagels, Elaine, *The Gnostoc Gospels*, 92.

25 Tertullian, Apology, 50, cited by Pagels, Elaine, *The Gnostoc Gospels*, 92.

26 Lambert, Malcolm, *Medieval Heresy*, 221.

27 Schoeps, Hans-Joachim, *Jewish Christianity: Factional Disputes in the Early Church*, 82.

28 Rubenson, Samuel, *The Letters of St. Antony: Monasticism and the Making of a Saint*, 77–78.

29 Augustine, *De Tinitate* 4,14,19, cited in Bonner, Gerald, "The Doctrine of Sacrifice: Augustine and the Latin Patristic Tradition," in *Sacrifice and Redemption: Durham Essays in Theology*, Sykes, S.W., editor, 105.

30 Cox, Harvey, *Fire From Heaven*, 71.

31 Gaustad, Edwin, and Schmidt, Leigh, *The Religious History of America*, 158–159.

32 Wills, Garry, *Papal Sin: Structures of Deceit*, 307.

33 Borg, Marcus J., *Meeting Jesus Again for the First Time*, 129.

34 Ranke-Heinemann, Uta, *Putting Away Childish Things*, 271–272.

35 Falwell, Jerry, with Dobson, Ed and Hindson, Ed, editors, *The Fundamentalist Phenomenon: The Resurgence of Conservative Christianity*, 10–11.

36 Spoto, Donald, *The Hidden Jesus*, 146.

37 Nolan, Albert, *Jesus Before Christianity*, 47.

38 Clement of Rome, 1 Clement 3: 3, cited in Pagels, Elaine, *The Gnostic Gospels*, 34.

39 Tertullian, cited in Eisler, Riane, *The Chalice & the Blade*, 127.

40 Wills, Garry, *What the Gospels Meant*, 179.

41 Gaustad, Edwin, and Schmidt, Leigh, *The Religious History of America*, 66

42 Jacobs, A.J., *The Year of Living Biblically*, 258.

43 Rohr, Richard, *Things Hidden*, 149.

44 Tertullian, *Against Marcion*, I.27, cited in *A New Eusebius*, edited by J. Stevenson, revised by W.H.C. Frend, 94–95.

45 Grant, Robert, *Augustus to Constantine*, 182.

46 Tertullian, *On Modesty*, cited in *A New Eusebius*, edited by J. Stevenson, revised by W.H.C. Frend, 176.

47 Russell, Jeffrey Burton, *A History of Heaven*, 74.

48 Wills, Garry, *What the Gospels Meant*, 147.

49 Campbell, Joseph, *Creative Mythology*, 50.

50 Celsus, *On the True Doctrine*, IV.

51 Tertullian, De Spectaculus, 30, cited by Frend, W.H.C., *Martyrdom and Persecution in the Early Church*, 274.

52 Frend, W.H.C., *The Rise of Christianity*, 147–148.

53 Bivins, Jason C., *Religion of Fear*, 85.

54 Bivins, Jason C., *Religion of Fear*, 155–156, 162.

55 Russell, Jeffrey Burton, *A History of Heaven*, 123.

56 Wills, Garry, *Papal Sin: Structures of Deceit*, 209.

57 Warner, Marina, *Alone of All Her Sex*, 327–328.

58 Durant, Will, *The Reformation*, 304.

59 Ruether, Rosemary Radford, *Christianity and the Making of the Modern Family*, 72.

Notes

[60] Durant, Will and Ariel, Rousseau and Revolution, 320–321.

[61] Hedges, Chris, *American Fascists*, 12–13.

[62] Harris, Sam, Letter to a Christian Nation, 44–45.

[63] Frend, W.H.C., *The Early Church*, 31.

[64] Crossan, John Dominic, *God & Empire*, 199, citing quotations from Boyer, Paul, *When Time Shall Be No More*.

[65] Crossan, John Dominic, *God & Empire*, 235, citing LaHaye, Tim and Jenkins, *Glorious Appearing: The End Days*, p. ix.

[66] LaHaye, Tim and Jenkins, *Glorious Appearing: The End Days*, Tyndale, Wheaton, IL, 2004, 225–226.

[67] Bivins, Jason C., *Religion of Fear*, 169, citing LaHaye, Tim and Jenkins, *Glorious Appearing: The End Days*.

[68] Bivins, Jason C., *Religion of Fear*, 182–183.

[69] Kloppenborg, John S., *The Formation of Q*, 299, as discussed by Crossan, John Dominic, *The Birth of Christianity*, 283.

[70] Bivins, Jason C., *Religion of Fear*, 208.

[71] Gaustad, Edwin, and Schmidt, Leigh, *The Religious History of America*, 306.

[72] Crossan, John Dominic, *God & Empire*, 88.

[73] Taibbi, Matt, *The Great Derangement*, 136.

Notes to chapter 4 : Correcting Respect for Women

[1] Ranke-Heinemann, Uta, *Eunuchs for the Kingdom of Heaven*, 120–121.

[2] Ye'or, Bat, *The Decline of Eastern Christianity Under Islam*, 67.

[3] King, Karen L., *The Gospel of Mary of Magdala*, Polebridge Press, Santa Rosa, CA, 2003, 149.

[4] Ben-Chorin, Shalom, cited in Ranke-Heinemann, Uta, *Eunuchs for the Kingdom of Heaven*, 44–45.

[5] King, Karen L., *The Gospel of Mary of Magdala*, Polebridge Press, Santa Rosa, CA, 2003, 15, 17..

[6] Clement of Alexandria, Stromateis 3.6.53. 3–4, in Kraemer, Ross Shepard, *Her Share of the Blessings: Women's Religions Among Pagans, Jews and Christians in the Greco-Roman World*, 188.

[7] Longenecker, Richard N., "Taking Up the Cross Daily: Discipleship in Luke-Acts," in *Patterns of Discipleship in the New Testament*, edited by Longenecker, Richard N., 72.

[8] Wills, Garry, *Papal Sin: Structures of Deceit*, 115–116.

[9] Ehrman, Bart E., *Misquoting Jesus*, 185–186.

[10] Jerome, Letters, xxii, 14, cited by Durant, Will, *The Age of Faith*, 53.

[11] Johnson, Elizabeth E., "Ephesians," in *The Women's Bible Commentary*, Newsome, Carol A., and Ringe, Sharon H., editors, 340.

[12] Livy, 34.2.14–34.3.3.

[13] Akers, Keith, *The Lost Religion of Jesus*, 56.

[14] Bassler, Jouette M., "I Corinthians" in *The Women's Bible Commentary*, Newsome, Carol A., and Ringe, Sharon H., editors, 324.

[15] Armstrong, Karen, *The Gospel According to Woman*, 19.

[16] Kraemer, Ross Shepard, *Her Share of the Blessings: Women's Religions Among Pagans, Jews and Christians in the Greco-Roman World*, 52.

[17] Minucius Felix, *Octavius*, cited by Smith John Holland, *The Death of Classical Paganism*, London and Dublin, Geoffrey Chapman Publishers. 5

[18] Verhey, Allen, *The Great Reversal*, 116.

[19] Johnson, Elizabeth E., "Colossians," in *The Women's Bible Commentary*, Newsome, Carol A., and Ringe, Sharon H., editors, 347.

[20] Brown, Peter, "Late Antiquity," in *A History of Private Life, I: From Pagan Rome to Byzantium*, 263.

[21] Clement of Alexandria, *Pedagogus*, III, 79, 4, cited by Ranke-Heinemann, *Eunuchs for the Kingdom of Heaven*, 127–128.

[22] Clement of Alexandria, *Pedagogus*, II, 10, 102, 1, cited by Ranke-Heinemann, *Eunuchs for the Kingdom of Heaven*, 49–50.

[23] Grant, Robert M., *Augustus to Constantine*, 271.

[24] Frend, W.H.C., *The Rise of Christianity*, 562.

[25] Ranke-Heinemann, Uta, *Eunuchs for the Kingdom of Heaven*, 24.

[26] Murphy, Cullen, *The Word According to Eve*, 173.

[27] Epiphianus, cited by Kraemer, Ross Shepard, *Her Share of the Blessings*, 166.

CORRECTING JESUS

[28] Kraemer, Ross Shepard, *Her Share of the Blessings*, 132.
[29] Council of Nicea canon XIX, cited on www.womanpriest.org/tradio/can_nic1.htm#cohabit
[30] Pelagius, in *Pelagius's Commentary on St. Paul's Epistle to the Romans*, translated by Theodore De Bruyn, Clarendon Press, Oxford, 1993, 150–151.
[31] Chrysostom, John, "First Homily on 'Salute Priscilla and Aquila,'" cited by Kraemer, Ross Shepard, *Her Share of the Blessings*, 188.
[32] Chrysostom, "On the Priesthood," cited in Kraemer, Ross Shepard, *Her Share of the Blessings*, 132.
[33] Ranke-Heinemann, Uta, *Eunuchs for the Kingdom of Heaven*, 134.
[34] Crossan, John Dominic, *God & Empire*, 177–179
[35] Murphy, Cullen, *The Word According to Eve*, 181–182.
[36] Wills, Garry, *Papal Sin: Structures of Deceit*, 107, quoting Thomas Aquinas, *Summa Theologica*, Suppl. Q. 39r.
[37] Gaustad, Edwin, and Schmidt, Leigh, *The Religious History of America*, 389.
[38] Gaustad, Edwin, and Schmidt, Leigh, *The Religious History of America*, 390.
[39] Manning, Joanna, *Is the Pope Catholic?*, 8, 96.
[40] Manning, Joanna, *Take Back the Truth*, 95–96,
[41] Tertullian, "On the Veiling of Virgins," cited in Armstrong, Karen, *The Gospel According to Woman*, 166.
[42] Cornwall, John, *Hitler's Pope*, 346.
[43] Harris, Sam, *Letter to a Christian Nation*, 28.
[44] Markschies, Christoph, *Between Two Worlds: Structures of Early Christianity*, SCM Press, London, 1999, 105.
[45] Ranke-Heinemann, Uta, *Eunuchs for the Kingdom of Heaven*, 130.
[46] Frend, William H.C., "Christianity in the Roman Empire," in *The Christian World: A Social and Cultural History*, ed. Barraclough, Geoffrey, 50.
[47] De Rosa, Peter, *Vicars of Christ*, 424.
[48] Markschies, Christoph, *Between Two Worlds: Structures of Early Christianity*, 57.
[49] De Rosa, Peter, *Vicars of Christ*, 476.
[50] Apostolic Constitutions, I, 9, cited in Ranke-Heinemann, Uta, *Eunuchs for the Kingdom of Heaven*, 130.
[51] Manning, Joanna, *Take Back the Truth*, 19, 116.
[52] Harris, Sam, *Letter to a Christian Nation*, 37
[53] Rouche, Michele, "the Early Middle Ages in the West," in *A History of Private Life, I, From Pagan Rome to Byzantium*, 533.
[54] Ranke-Heinemann, Uta, *Eunuchs for the Kingdom of Heaven*, 36–37.
[55] Rouche, Michele, "The Early Middle Ages in the West," in *A History of Private Life I, From Pagan Rome to Byzantium*, editor, Veyne, Paul, 475–476.
[56] Campbell, Joseph, *Creative Mythology*, 53.
[57] Durant, Will, *The Age of Faith*, 20.
[58] McNamara, Jo Ann, and Wemple, Suzanne, "The Power of Women Through the Family in Medieval Times, 500–1100," in *Women and Power in the Middle Ages*, eds., Erler, Mary, and Kowalski, Maryanne, 89.
[59] McNamara, Jo Ann, and Wemple, Suzanne, "The Power of Women Through the Family in Medieval Times, 500–1100," in *Women and Power in the Middle Ages*, eds., Erler, Mary, and Kowalski, Maryanne, 89.
[60] Durant, Will and Ariel, *The Age of Voltaire*, 290.
[61] De Mause, Lloyd, *The History of Childhood*, 29, citing Emily R. Coleman, "Medieval Marriage Characteristics: A Neglected Factor in the History of Medieval Serfdom."
[62] Jerome, *Against Jovinian*, 7, cited by Ruether, Rosemary Radford, *Christianity and the Making of the Modern Family*, 44–45.
[63] Ambrose, cited in Ranke-Heinemann, Uta, *Eunuchs for the Kingdom of Heaven*, 103.
[64] Augustine, Soliloquies, cited, de Rosa, Peter, *Vicars of Christ*, 444.
[65] Ruether, Rosemary Radford, *Christianity and the Making of the Modern Family*, 44.
[66] Ranke-Heinemann, Uta, *Eunuchs for the Kingdom of Heaven*, 6.
[67] Ruether, Rosemary Radford, *Christianity and the Making of the Modern Family*, 43–44, with of citing Jerome, *On the Perpetual Virginity of Mary Against Helvidius*.
[68] Jerome, cited in Ranke-Heinemann, Uta, *Eunuchs for the Kingdom of Heaven*, 103.
[69] Augustine, (De genesi ad litteram, 9, 5–9), cited by Ranke-Heinemann, Uta, *Eunuchs for the Kingdom of Heaven*, 88.
[70] De Rosa, Peter, *Vicars of Christ*, 564.
[71] Markus, Robert, *The End of Ancient Christianity*, 17.

Notes

[72] Constantelos, Demitrios J., *Understanding the Greek Orthodox Church*. 73.

[73] Grant, Robert M., *Augustus to Constantine*, 277.

[74] Leo I, Letter 167, 3, cited in Ranke-Heinemann, Uta, *Eunuchs for the Kingdom of Heaven*, 103.

[75] Gregory I, *Dialogues*, IV, 11, cited in Ranke-Heinemann, Uta, *Eunuchs for the Kingdom of Heaven*, 104–105.

[76] Ranke-Heinemann, Uta, *Eunuchs for the Kingdom of Heaven*, 102–03.

[77] De Rosa, Peter, *Vicars of Christ*, 565.

[78] Ranke-Heinemann, Uta, *Eunuchs for the Kingdom of Heaven*, 102–03.

[79] Durant, Will, *The Age of Faith*, 528, Christie-Murray, Donald, *A History of Heresy*, 98.

[80] Ranke-Heinemann, Uta, *Eunuchs for the Kingdom of Heaven*, 107.

[81] Durant, Will and Ariel, *The Age of Faith*, 528.

[82] Bernard of Clairvaux, *Sermones in Cantica*, lxv., cited in Southern, R.W., *Western Society and the Church in the Middle Ages*, 314–15.

[83] De Rosa, Peter, *Vicars of Christ*, 574.

[84] Morris, Colin, "Medieval Christendom," in *The Christian World: A Social and Cultural History*, 138.

[85] De Rosa, Peter, *Vicars of Christ*, 566.

[86] De Rosa, Peter, *Vicars of Christ*, 570.

[87] De Rosa, Peter, *Vicars of Christ*, 589.

[88] Bokenkotter, Thomas, *A Concise History of the Catholic Church*, 141.

[89] De Rosa, Peter, *Vicars of Christ*, 569.

[90] Ranke-Heinemann, Uta, *Eunuchs for the Kingdom of Heaven*, 108.

[91] Durant, Will and Ariel, *The Age of Faith*, 546.

[92] Ranke-Heinemann, Uta, *Eunuchs for the Kingdom of Heaven*, 100.

[93] De Rosa, Peter, *Vicars of Christ*, 61.

[94] Ranke-Heinemann, Uta, *Eunuchs for the Kingdom of Heaven*, 108–09.

[95] Ranke-Heinemann, Uta, *Eunuchs for the Kingdom of Heaven*, 107.

[96] Canon 66, Council of Nicea, 325 CE.

[97] Ruether, Rosemary Radford, *Christianity and the Making of the Modern Family*, 57.

[98] Ranke-Heinemann, Uta, *Eunuchs for the Kingdom of Heaven*, 109, 111.

[99] De Rosa, Peter, *Vicars of Christ*, 577.

[100] Ranke-Heinemann, Uta, *Eunuchs for the Kingdom of Heaven*, 110–11.

[101] Ruether, Rosemary Radford, *Christianity and the Making of the Modern Family*, 58.

[102] De Rosa, Peter, *Vicars of Christ*, 479–81.

[103] Warner, Maria, *Alone of All Her Sex*, 153.

[104] Durant, Will, *The Age of Faith*, 1044.

[105] Campbell, Joseph, *The Flight of the Wild Gander*, 218.

[106] Durant, Will, *The Age of Faith*, 576.

[107] De Rosa, Peter, *Vicars of Christ*, 571.

[108] Durant, Will, *The Reformation*, 22, 501.

[109] Durant, Will, *The Reformation*, 13.

[110] Luther, "To the Christian Nobility of the German Nation," cited in Ranke-Heinemann, Uta, *Eunuchs for the Kingdom of Heaven*, 28.

[111] Ranke-Heinemann, Uta, *Eunuchs for the Kingdom of Heaven*, 113–114.

[112] Manning, Joanna, *Take Back the Truth*, 131.

[113] Ranke-Heinemann, Uta, *Eunuchs for the Kingdom of Heaven*, 248.

[114] Ranke-Heinemann, Uta, *Eunuchs for the Kingdom of Heaven*, 113–114.

[115] Ruether, Rosemary Radford, *Christianity and the Making of the Modern Family*, 74.

[116] Schulenburg, Jane Tibbetts, "Female Sanctity: Public and Private Roles, ca. 500–1100, in Erler, Mary, and Kowalski, Maryanne, *Women and Power in the Middle Ages*, 117.

[117] Durant, Will, *The Age of Faith*, 986.

[118] Armstrong, Karen, *The Gospel According to Woman*, 117.

[119] Durant, Will, *The Age of Faith*, 985.

[120] Patai, Raphael, *The Hebrew Goddess*, 225.

[121] *Malleus Maleficarum*, Jacob Sprenger & Heinrich Kramer, cited in Armstrong, Karen, *The Gospel According to Woman*, 112.

[122] Bethancourt, W. J., "The Killings of Witches: A Chronicle of the Burning Times," posted to the internet, and

Sinton, D. Christie, "Christian crimeline," posted to the internet.

[123] Briggs, Robin, *Witches and Neighbors*, 361.

[124] Briggs, Robin, *Witches and Neighbors*, 145.

[125] Southern, R.W., *Western Society and the Church in the Middle Ages*, 310–11.

[126] Southern, R.W., *Western Society and the Church in the Middle Ages*, 313–14.

[127] Armstrong, Karen, *The Gospel According to Woman*, 166.

[128] Barraclough, Geoffrey, ed., *The Christian World*, 124.

[129] Armstrong, Karen, *The Gospel According to Woman*, 157–59

[130] St. Teresa of Avila, cited by Armstrong, Karen, *The Gospel According to Woman*, 91.

[131] Durant, Will, *The Reformation*, 904.

[132] St. Teresa of Avila, cited by Armstrong, Karen, *The Gospel According to Woman*, 261–63.

[133] Marvick, Elizabeth Wirth, "Nature Versus Nurture: Patterns and Trends in Seventeenth-Century French Child Rearing"" in *The History of Childhood*, 285.

[134] Durant, Will and Ariel, *Rousseau and Revolution*, 900.

[135] Durant, Will and Ariel, *The Age of Napoleon*, 27.

[136] Ruether, Rosemary Radford, *Christianity and the Making of the Modern Family*, 72.

[137] Durant, Will, *The Reformation*, 767.

[138] Chadwick, Owen, "Great Britain and Europe (since 1800)," in *The Oxford History of Christianity*, ed. McManners, John, 392.

[139] Blackbourne, David, *Fontana History of Germany, 1780–1918: The Long Nineteenth Century*, 349.

[140] Ruether, Rosemary Radford, *Christianity and the Making of the Modern Family*, 106, 112.

[141] Gaustad, Edwin, and Schmidt, Leigh, *The Religious History of America*, 250.

Notes to chapter 5 : Correcting Freedom

[1] Taibbi, Matt, *The Great Derangement*, 70.

[2] Mencius, Introduction, 42, cited by Durant, *Will, Our Oriental Heritage*, 42.

[3] Boorstin, Daniel J., *The Seekers*, 282.

[4] Senator Rick Santorum, quoted by Waldman, Steve, "Santorum: Obama's Faith is 'Phoney'," "Progressive Revival" blog on beliefnet.com, posted August 1, 2008.

[5] Didache, 11, 3–12, as cited in *A New Eusebius*, edited by J. Stevenson, revised by W.H.C. Frend, 11.

[6] Mack, Burton L., *The Lost Gospel: The Book of Q and Christian Origins*, 137.

[7] Rules of Pachomius, 9, cited by Rousseau, Philip, *Pachomius: The Making of a Community in Fourth-Century Egypt*, 116–17

[8] Philo of Alexandria, *Contemplative Life*, 70, cited in Crossan, John Dominic, *The Birth of Christianity*, 576.

[9] Dewey, Joanna, "1 Timothy," in *The Women's Bible Commentary*, Newsome, Carol A., and Ringe, Sharon H., editors, 357–358.

[10] Harris, Sam, *Letter to a Christian Nation*, 17.

[11] Gaustad, Edwin, and Schmidt, Leigh, *The Religious History of America*, 110.

[12] Celsus, *On the True Doctrine: A Discourse Against the Christians*, translated with general introduction, R. Joseph Hoffmann, VIII.

[13] Grant, Robert M., *Augustus to Constantine*, 71.

[14] Pagels, Elaine, *The Gnostic Gospels*, 15.

[15] Pagels, Elaine, *The Gnostic Gospels*, 122–123.

[16] Hippolytus, *Refutation of All Heresies*, cited by Pagels, Elaine, *The Gnostic Gospels*, xiv.

[17] Ireneaus, *Against the Heresies*, 2.13.3–10, cited by Pagels, Elaine, *The Gnostic Gospels*, 15.

[18] Ireneaus, *Against the Heresies*, 1.13.6, cited by Pagels, Elaine, *The Gnostic Gospels*, 21.

[19] Grant, Robert M., *Augustus to Constantine*, 72.

[20] Ireneaus, *Against the Heresies*, 1.13.4 and 3.15.2, cited by Pagels, Elaine, *The Gnostic Gospels*, 41–42, 39.

[21] Pagels, Elaine, *The Gnostic Gospels*, 39–40, 26.

[22] Ignatius, cited by Frend, W.H.C., *The Early Church*, 50.

[23] Ireneaus, *Against the Heresies*, 3.11.9, cited by Pagels, Elaine, *The Gnostic Gospels*, 17.

[24] Tertullian, *De Praescre*, 7, cited by Pagels, Elaine, *The Gnostic Gospels*, 114.

[25] *Apocalypse of Peter*, cited by Perkins, Pheme, *Peter: Apostle for the Whole Church*, 164, *Testimony of Truth*, 73.18.22, cited by Pagels, Elaine, *The Gnostic Gospels*, 111.

Notes

[26] Ignatius, *Magnesians* 6.1, *Trallians* 3.1, *Ephesians* 5.3, cited in Pagels, Elaine, *The Gnostic Gospels*, 35., also Brown, Schuyler, *The Origins of Christianity: A Historical Introduction to the New Testament*, 148–149.

[27] Ignatius, *Smyrnaeans*, VIII, cited in *A New Eusebius*, edited by J. Stevenson, revised by W.H.C. Frend, 15.

[28] Ireneaus, *Against the Heresies*, 4.26.2, cited by Pagels, Elaine, *The Gnostic Gospels*, 44–45.

[29] Frend, W.H.C., *The Early Church*, 103.

[30] Gaustad, Edwin, and Schmidt, Leigh, *The Religious History of America*, 350–352.

[31] Conway, J.S., *The Nazi Persecution of the Churches, 1933-45*, 157.

[32] Frend, H.W.C., *The Rise of Christianity*, 407–408.

[33] Bokenkotter, Thomas, *A Concise History of the Catholic Church*, 63.

[34] Rouche, Michele, "The Early Middle Ages in the West," in *A History of Private Life, I From Pagan Rome to Byzantium*, 544–545.

[35] Bokenkotter, Thomas, *A Concise History of the Catholic Church*, 63.

[36] Frend, W.H.C., *The Rise of Early Christianity*, 462, *Martyrdom and Persecution in the Early Church*, 374.

[37] Cornwall, John, *Hitler's Pope*, 322.

[38] Bonner, Gerald, "Schism and Church Unity," in *Church and Faith in the Patristic Tradition*, 223.

[39] Stewart-Gambino, Hannah, "Redefining the Changes and Politics in Chile," in *Conflict and Competition: The Latin American Church in a Changing Environment*, editors Cleary, Edward L., and Stewart-Gambino, Hannah, 36.

[40] Frend, W.H.C., *The Rise of Early Christianity*, 534–35.

[41] Canons of the Council of Arles, 314, cited in Stevenson J., editor, *A New Eusebius*, 296.

[42] Grant, Robert M., *Augustus to Constantine*, 237–38.

[43] Constantine, Letter to Domitius Celsus, in Optatus of Milevis, App. Vii, cited by Frend, W.H.C., *The Early Church*, 131–132.

[44] *Sermo de Passione Donati*, 3, cited in Stevenson J., editor, *A New Eusebius*, 309.

[45] Frend, W.H.C., *The Early Church*, 220.

[46] Alexander of Alexandria, cited in *A New Eusebius*, ed. J. Stevenson, revised by W.H.C. Frend, 328.

[47] Grant, Michael, *Constantine the Great: The Man and His Times*, 159.

[48] Barnes, Timothy D., *Athanasius and Constantius*, 174.

[49] Theodosian Code, cited in Lewis, Naphtali and Reinhold, Meyer, editors, *Roman Civilization, Sourcebook II: The Empire*, 607.

[50] Edict of Constantine, cited by Misha'al ibn Abdullah, *What Did Jesus Really Say?*, 148.

[51] Socrates, *Ecclesiastical History*, I.9, cited by Frend, W.H.C., *The Rise of Christianity*, 500.

[52] Jerome, Epistles, CXLVI.I.I, 1–5, cited in *A New Eusebius*, ed. J. Stevenson, revised by W.H.C. Frend, 356.

[53] Frend, W.H.C., *The Early Church*, 170.

[54] Rousseau, Philip, *Pachomius: The Making of a Community in Fourth-Century Egypt*, 117, 109.

[55] Smith, John Holland, *The Death of Classical Paganism*, 160–162.

[56] Bonner, Gerald, "Schism and Church Unity," in *Church and Faith in the Patristic Tradition*, 224.

[57] Bonner, Gerald, "Schism and Church Unity," in *Church and Faith in the Patristic Tradition*, 224.

[58] Augustine, "Free Choice," cited by Scott, T. Kermit, *Augustine: His Thought in Context*, 137.

[59] Augustine, *City of God*, chapter 14, as described by Bonner, Gerald, "Augustine and Pelagianism," in *Augustinian Studies*, no. 24, 40.

[60] Taibbi, Matt, *The Great Derangement*, 108.

[61] Augustine, "To Simplician," 2, 12, cited by Scott, T. Kermit, *Augustine: His Thought in Context*, 181.

[62] Augustine, Letter 93, 16, cited in Markschies, Christoph, *Between Two Worlds: Structures of Early Christianity*, 48–49.

[63] Augustine, quoted by Cahill, Thomas, *How the Irish Saved Civilization*, 64–65.

[64] Augustine, *The City of God*, book 22, chapter 30. cited by Campbell, Joseph, *Occidental Mythology*, 393.

[65] Augustine, *The City of God*, 14:12.

[66] Rohr, Richard, *Things Hidden*, 50.

[67] Pagels, Elaine, *Adam, Eve, and the Serpent*, 113–114.

[68] Pagels, Elaine, *Adam, Eve, and the Serpent*, 125.

[69] Frend, W.H.C., *The Rise of Christianity*, 674.

[70] De Bruyn, Theodore, Introduction to *Pelagius's Commentary on St. Paul's Epistle to the Romans*, 41.

[71] Antony, Letter VII, 7b–d, cited by Rubenstson, Samuel, *The Letters of Saint Antony*, 229.

[72] Pagels, Elaine, *Adam, Eve and the Serpent*, 129.

[73] Augustine, *The City of God*, Book II, chapter 1.

[74] Christie-Murray, Donald, *A History of Heresy*, 91–92.

[75] Randers-Pehrson, Justine Davis, *Barbarians and Romans*, 248.

[76] Runciman, Steven, "The Greek Church and the People of Eastern Europe," *The Christian World*, 110.

[77] Atiya, Aziz S., *A History of Eastern Christianity*, 307.

[78] Constantelos, Demetrios, *The Greek Orthodox Church*, 45–46.

[79] De Rosa, Peter, *Vicars of Christ*, 71–73.

[80] Durant, Will, *The Reformation*, 375, *The Renaissance*, 449.

[81] Fox, Matthew, *Sins of the Spirit, Blessings of the Flesh*, 16.

[82] Durant, Will, *Our Oriental Heritage*, 874.

[83] Grant, Michael, *Constantine the Great: The Man and His Times*, 149.

[84] Barraclough, Geoffrey, *The Christian World: A Social and Cultural History*, 32.

[85] Malina, Bruce, and Rohrbaugh, Richard L., *Social Science Commentary on the Synoptic Gospels*, 328–329.

[86] Runciman, Steven, "The Greek Church and the People of Eastern Europe," in *The Christian World: A Social and Cultural History*, 32.

[87] Cohn, Samuel K., Jr., *Lust for Liberty*, 15.

[88] Cohn, Samuel K., Jr., *Lust for Liberty*, 226, 85.

[89] Cohn, Samuel K., Jr., *Lust for Liberty*, 241.

[90] Durant, Will, *The Reformation*, 190.

[91] Durant, Will and Ariel, *The Age of Louis XIV*, 17.

[92] Gernet, Jacques, *China and the Christian Impact*, 223.

[93] Durant, Will, *The Reformation*, 787, 813.

[94] Durant, Will and Ariel, *The Age of Louis XIV*, 555.

[95] Durant, Will and Ariel, *Rousseau and Revolution*, 737.

[96] Durant, Will and Ariel, *The Age of Louis XIV*, 579.

[97] Runcimen, Steven, *The Orthodox Churches and the Secular State*, 42.

[98] Durant, Will, *The Reformation*, 628–630.

[99] Durant, Will and Ariel, *The Age of Louis XIV*, 256.

[100] Gaustad Edwin, Schmidt, Leigh, *The Religious History of America*, 108.

[101] Noll, Mark A., *A History of Christianity in the United States and Canada*, 89.

[102] Noll, Mark A., *A History of Christianity in the United States and Canada*, 58–59.

[103] Gaustad Edwin, Schmidt, Leigh, *The Religious History of America*, 70.

[104] Mayhew, Jonathan, cited by Rifkin, Jeremy, and Howard, Ted, *The Emerging Order: God in the Age of Scarcity*, 136–137.

[105] Boétie, Étienne de la, Discous sur la servitude voluntaire, cited by Durant, Will, *The Renaissance*, 882.

[106] Pelikan, Jaroslav, *The Illustrated Jesus Through the Centuries*, 49

[107] Gaustad Edwin, Schmidt, Leigh, *The Religious History of America*, 121, 48, 138.

[108] Cornwall, John, *Hitler's Pope*, 43–44.

[109] Manning, Joanna, *Take Back the Truth*, 144–145.

Notes to chapter 6 : And How About Equality?

[1] Durant, Will and Ariel, *The Age of Napoleon*, 185.

[2] Lord Cromer, cited by Karabell, Zachery, *Peace Be Upon You*, 240.

[3] Greenberg, Amy S., *Manifest Manhood and the Antebellum American Empire*, 260.

[4] John Adams, cited by Gore, Al, *The Assault on Reason*, 84.

[5] Gaustad, Edwin, and Schmidt, Leigh, *The Religious History of America*, 191.

[6] Gaustad, Edwin, and Schmidt, Leigh, *The Religious History of America*, 184.

[7] McPherson, James M., *Ordeal by Fire: The Civil War and Reconstruction*, 33.

[8] McPherson, James M., *Ordeal by Fire: The Civil War and Reconstruction*, 46–47.

[9] Durant, Will, *The Reformation*, 621.

[10] De Rosa, Peter, *Vicars of Christ*, 146.

[11] Kertzer, David I., *The Popes Against the Jews*, 126–127.

[12] Catholic Church canon of July 18, 1870, cited by Averill, Lloyd J., *Religious Right, Religious Wrong*, 72.

[13] Cornwall, John, *Hitler's Pope*, 14–15.

Notes

[14] Christie-Murray, Donald, *A History of Heresy*, 209.

[15] Durant, Will and Ariel, *Rousseau and Revolution*, 801.

[16] Kertzer, David I., *The Popes Against the Jews*, 126–127.

[17] Hawken, Paul, *Blessed Unrest*, 5.

[18] Chadwick, Owen, "Christianity and Industrial Society," *The Christian World: A Social and Cultural History*, 254.

[19] Cornwall, John, *Hitler's Pope*, 114.

[20] Cornwall, John, *Hitler's Pope*, 115.

[21] Cornwall, John, *Hitler's Pope*, 147, 197.

[22] Cornwall, John, *Hitler's Pope*, 183.

[23] Taylor, A.J.P., "The Course of German History," cited in Derfler, Leslie, editor, *An Age of Conflict: Readings in Twentieth-Century European History*, 118.

[24] Strauss, Gerald, *Luther's House of Learning*, 136.

[25] Cornwall, John, *Hitler's Pope*, 202–203.

[26] Cornwall, John, *Hitler's Pope*, 261–263.

[27] Cornwall, John, *Hitler's Pope*, 327–328.

[28] Mark A. Beliles and Stephen K. McDowell, *America's Providential History*, c. 1989, p. 265, cited by Hedges, Chris, *American Fascists*, 180.

[29] James, Gordon, in *Inerrancy and the Southern Baptist Convention*, cited by Bawer, Bruce, *Stealing Jesus: How Fundamentalism Betrays Christianity*, 156.

[30] Bawer, Bruce, *Stealing Jesus: How Fundamentalism Betrays Christianity*, 80.

[31] Roof, Wade Clark, and McKinney, William, in *American Religion: Its Changing Shape and Future*, cited by Reeves, Thomas C., *The Empty Church: The Suicide of Liberal Christianity*, 193.

[32] Durant, Will, *The Reformation*, 370–371.

[33] Noll, Mark A., *A History of Christianity in the United States and Canada*, 208.

[34] Klinghoffer, David, in *Dumbing Down: Essays on the Strip Mining of American Culture*, cited by Bawer, Bruce, *Stealing Jesus: How Fundamentalism Betrays Christianity*, 283.

[35] Conciliar Document no. 4, chapter IV, Second Vatican Council, 1962–65, page 53.

[36] Freston, Paul, *Evangelicals and Politics in Asia, Africa, and Latin America*, 318.

[37] Manning, Joanna, *Is the Pope Catholic?*, 64–65.

[38] Gaustad, Edwin, and Schmidt, Leigh, *The Religious History of America*, 345–347.

[39] Rosenberg, Tina, *The Haunted Land: Facing Europe's Ghosts After Communism*, 161–62.

[40] Rosenburg, Tina, *The Haunted Land: Facing Europe's Ghosts After Communism*, 160.

[41] Pope John Paul II, *Veritas Splendor*, Libreria Editrice Vaticana, Vatican City, 1993, 7.

[42] Hackel, Sergei, "The Orthodox Churches of Eastern Europe" (after 1800), in *The Oxford History of Christianity*, ed. McManners, John, 552.

[43] Pope John Paul II, *Veritas Splendor*, paragraph 1, cited by Manning Joanna, *Take Back the Truth*, 61.

[44] Falwell, Jerry, cited by Averill, Lloyd J., *Religious Right, Religious Wrong*, 113.

[45] Ellis, Jane, *The Russian Orthodox Church: Triumphalism and Defensiveness*, 41.

[46] Spong, John Shelby, *Jesus for the Non-Religious*, 135.

[47] Fox, Matthew, *Sins of the Spirit, Blessings of the Flesh*, 177.

[48] Bradshaw, John, *Creating Love*, 26, 58, 89.

[49] Carl F.H. Henry, in an opening address to the Evangelical Theological Society in 1949, cited by Hart, D.G., *Deconstructing Evangelicalism*, 131–132.

[50] Hedges, Chris, *American Fascists*, 124.

[51] Manning, Joanna, *Take Back the Truth*, 115.

[52] Manning, Joanna, *Take Back the Truth*, 113.

[53] Falwell, Jerry, *Finding Inner Peace and Strength*, 67, 93.

Notes to chapter 7 : Correcting Non-Violence

[1] Greenberg, Amy S., *Manifest Manhood and the Antebellum American Empire*, 159.

[2] Gandhi, cited by Rabbi Joseph Telushkin, *Biblical Literacy*, 286

[3] Wink, Walter, *The Powers That Be*, 104–105.

[4] Eisler, Riane, and Loye, David, *The Partnership Way*, 116, 182.

[5] Idliby, Ranya, Oliver, Suzanne Warner, Priscilla, *The Faith Club*, 145.

[6] Tatian, *Oration Against the Greeks*, 11, cited in Grant, Robert M., *Augustus to Constantine*, 115.

[7] Minucius Felix, *Octavius*, xxv.5, cited by Frend, W.H.C., *The Rise of Christianity*, 292.

[8] *Recognitions of Clement*, 3.42, cited by Akers, Kieth, *The Lost Religion of Jesus*, 92.

[9] Celsus, *On the True Doctrine*, X, translated by Hoffmann, R. Joseph, 124–125.

[10] Toynbee, Arnold J., *A Study of History, Abridgement of Volumes VII to X*, edited by Somervell, D.C., 65.

[11] Hippolytus, *Apostolic Tradition*, cited by Spoto, Donald, *The Hidden Jesus*, 148.

[12] Grant, Robert M., *Augustus to Constantine*, 90–91.

[13] Smith, John Holland, *The Death of Classical Paganism*, 157.

[14] Crossan, John Dominic, *The Birth of Christianity*, 262.

[15] Toynbee, Arnold J., *A Study of History, Abridgement of Volumes VII to X*, edited by Somervell, D.C., 67.

[16] Smith, John Holland, *The Death of Classical Paganism*, 81.

[17] Smith, John Holland, *The Death of Classical Paganism*, 22.

[18] Campbell, Joseph, *Occidental Mythology*, 387.

[19] Patlagean, Evelyne, "Byzantium in the Tenth and Eleventh Centuries," in *A History of Private Life: From Pagan Rome to Byzantium*, 633.

[20] Nicholson, Helen J., "Serious Violence: Church justification for violence in the Middle Ages," posted to the internet

[21] Whitlock, Dorothy, *The Beginning of English Society*, 42–43.

[22] Nicholson, Helen J., "Serious Violence: Church justification for violence in the Middle Ages," posted to the internet

[23] Urban II, cited by Housley, Norman, "The Mercenary Companies, The Papacy, and the Crusades, 1356–1378," in *Crusading and Warfare in Medieval and Renaissance Europe*, 270.

[24] Durant, Will, *The Age of Faith*, 593.

[25] Orderic Vitalis, loosely quoting Count Helias of Maine, cited by Housley, Norman, "Jerusalem and the Development of the Crusade Idea, 1099–1128," in *Crusading and Warfare in Medieval and Renaissance Europe*, 37.

[26] Lambert, Malcolm, *Medieval Heresy*, 27.

[27] Cohn, Samuel K., Jr., *Lust for Liberty*, 5–6, 106.

[28] Durant, Will, *The Age of Faith*, 778.

[29] Durant, Will, *The Age of Faith*, 595–596.

[30] Durant, Will, *The Age of Faith*, 777.

[31] Innocent III, cited by Housley, Norman, "Crusades Against Christians: Their Origins and Development, 1000–1216," in *Crusading and Warfare in Medieval and Renaissance Europe*, 37.

[32] Christie_Murray, Donald, *A History of Heresy*, 104–105.

[33] Durant, Will, *The Age of Faith*, 779.

[34] Durant, Will, *The Age of Faith*, 780.

[35] Durant, Will, *The Age of Faith*, 388.

[36] Durant, Will, *The Age of Faith*, 778.

[37] Durant, Will, *The Reformation*, 8.

[38] Nirenburg, David, *Communities of Violence: Persecution of Minorities in the Middle Ages*, 132.

[39] Durant, Will, *The Renaissance*, 252.

[40] Durant, Will, *The Reformation*, 351

[41] Durant, Will, *The Reformation*, 614.

[42] Durant, Will, *The Reformation*, 166.

[43] Gerant, Jacques, *China and the Christian Impact*, 110.

[44] Gaustad, Edwin, and Schmidt, Leigh, *The Religious History of America*, 21.

[45] Durant, Will, *Our Oriental Heritage*, 843.

[46] Gaustad, Edwin, and Schmidt, Leigh, *The Religious History of America*, 96.

[47] Greenberg, Amy, *Manifest Manhood and the Antebellum American Empire*, 221.

[48] Greenberg, Amy, *Manifest Manhood and the Antebellum American Empire*, 180.

[49] Greenberg, Amy, *Manifest Manhood and the Antebellum American Empire*, 248.

[50] Greenberg, Amy, *Manifest Manhood and the Antebellum American Empire*, 99.

[51] Greenberg, Amy, *Manifest Manhood and the Antebellum American Empire*, 154.

[52] Greenberg, Amy, *Manifest Manhood and the Antebellum American Empire*, 172.

[53] Aslan, Reza, *No god but God*, 224–225.

Notes

[54] Karabell, Zachary, *Peace Be Upon You*, 217.

[55] Greenberg, Amy, *Manifest Manhood and the Antebellum American Empire*, 255.

[56] Manning, Joanna, *Take Back the Truth*, 137.

[57] Lieven, Dominic, "Western Scholarship on the Fall of the Soviet Regime," in *An Age of Conflict: Readings in Twentieth-Century European History*, 372

[58] Taylor, A.J.P., "The Course of German History," in *An Age of Conflict: Readings in Twentieth-Century European History*, 121–123

[59] Gaustad, Edwin, and Schmidt, Leigh, *The Religious History of America*, 256.

[60] Gaustad, Edwin, and Schmidt, Leigh, *The Religious History of America*, 267.

[61] Ponting, Clive, *A Green History of the World*, 148-149.

[62] Badr-Saye, Scott, "Living the Gospels: Morality and Politics," in *The Cambridge Companion to the Gospels*, 276.

[63] Cornwall, John, *Hitler's Pope*, 68.

[64] Loye, David, *Darwin's Lost Theory*, Benjamin Franklin Press, Carmel, CA, 2007.

[65] Margulis, Lynn, and Sagan, Dorian, *Microcosmos: Four Billion Years of Evolution from our Microbal Ancestors*, 248.

[66] Hodgson, Godfrey, *America in Our Time*, 130.

[67] Goldberg, Michelle, *Kingdom Coming*, 12.

[68] Wink, Walter, *The Powers That Be*, 162.

[69] Camara, Dom Helder, *Questions for Living*, 92.

[70] Isichei, Elizabeth, *A History of Christianity in Africa*, 312.

[71] Wink, Walter, *The Powers That Be*, 121.

[72] Hedges, Chris, *American Fascists*, 29–30.

[73] Manning, Joanna, *Take Back the Truth*, 94.

[74] Aslan, Reza, *No god but God*, xxiii–xxiv.

[75] Goldberg, Michelle, *Kingdom Coming*, 163–164.

[76] Kohut, Andrew, and Stokes, Bruce, *America Against the World*, 116.

[77] Klein, Naomi, *The Shock Doctrine*, 366–367.

[78] Kohut, Andrew, and Stokes, Bruce, *America Against the World*, 117, 99.

[79] Klein, Naomi, *The Shock Doctrine*, 443, 446.

[80] Moore, Robin, *Dreams and Shadows*, 414.

[81] Borg, Marcus J. *Jesus: Uncovering the Life, Teachings, and Relevance of a Religious Revolutionary*, 506.

[82] Safi, Omid, "Palin Hears Voices," Progressive Revival blog, beliefnet.com, Sept. 8, 2008.

[83] Hedges, Chris, *American Fascists*, 30.

[84] Crossan, John Dominic, *God & Empire*, 224.

Notes to chapter 8 : Correcting Compassion

[1] Manning, Joanna, *Take Back the Truth*, 94–95.

[2] McPherson, James, *Ordeal by Fire: The Civil War and Reconstruction*, 19.

[3] Day, Dorothy, cited by McCarthy, David Matzko, "The gospels embodied: the lives of the saints and martyrs," in *The Cambridge Companion to the Gospels*, 236–237.

[4] Borg, Marcus A., *Jesus: Uncovering the Life, Teachings, and Relevance of a Religious Revolutionary*, 307–308.

[5] Schaeffer, Frank, *Crazy for God*, 30.

[6] Manning, Joanna, *Take Back the Truth*, 67.

[7] Pew Research Center, cited by Kohut, Andrew, and Stokes, Bruce, *America Against the World*, 18–19.

[8] Armstrong, Karen, *The Battle for God*, 361.

[9] Klein, Naomi, *The Shock Doctrine*, 545.

[10] Klein, Naomi, *The Shock Doctrine*, 123.

[11] Manning, Joanna, *Take Back the Truth*, 154–155.

[12] Briggs, Robin, *Witches and Neighbors*, 205.

[13] McPherson, James M., *Ordeal by Fire: The Civil War and Reconstruction*, 14.

[14] Durant, Will and Ariel, *Rousseau and Civilization*, 677.

[15] Durant, Will and Ariel, *Rousseau and Civilization*, 680, 732, 708.

[16] Durant, Will, *The Reformation*, 764.

[17] Warner, Marina, *Alone of All Her Sex*, 190.

[18] Hedges, Chris, *American Fascists*, 82.

[19] Eisler, Riane, *The Chalice & the Blade*, 146–47.

[20] Kellner, L., cited by Miller, Alice, *For Your Own Good*, 40.

[21] Illick, Joseph E., "Child Rearing in Seventeenth Century England and America," in *The History of Childhood*, edited by Lloyd deMause, 312, 315–316, 337.

[22] Dunn, Patrick P., "That Enemy is the Baby: Childhood in Imperial Russia" in *The History of Childhood*, edited by Lloyd deMause, 393.

[23] Durant, Will and Ariel, *The Age of Voltaire*, 289.

[24] Durant, Will and Ariel, *The Age of Louis XIV*, 591.

[25] Briggs, Asa, *A Social History of England*, 118–119,158–159.

[26] Durant, Will and Ariel, *The Age of Napoleon*, 365.

[27] Greenberg, Amy S., *Manifest Manhood and the Antebellum American Empire*, 11–12.

[28] Durant, Will and Ariel, *The Age of Napoleon*, 348.

[29] Greenberg, Amy S., *Manifest Manhood and the Antebellum American Empire*, 152.

[30] Gaustad, Edwin, and Schmidt, Leigh, *The Religious History of America*, 189.

[31] Gaustad, Edwin, and Schmidt, Leigh, *The Religious History of America*, 238.

[32] Hart, D.H., *Deconstructing Evangelicalism*, 70–71.

[33] Raushenbach, Paul, "Rick Warren and the Social Gospel," Progressive Revival blog, Dec. 15, 2008, beliefnet.com

[34] Gaustad, Edwin, and Schmidt, Leigh, *The Religious History of America*, 339.

[35] Gaustad, Edwin, and Schmidt, Leigh, *The Religious History of America*, 345.

[36] Hedges, Chris, *American Fascists*, 179.

[37] Hedges, Chris, *American Fascists*, 123.

[38] Hedges, Chris, *American Fascists*, 180.

[39] Taibbi, Matt, *The Great Derangement*, 177–178.

[40] Klein, Naomi, *The Shock Doctrine*, 194–195, 65.

[41] Klein, Naomi, *The Shock Doctrine*, 536–537.

[42] Wilcox, Clyde, and Larson, Wilcox, *Onward Christian Soldiers?*, 187.

[43] Klein, Naomi, *The Shock Doctrine*, 267.

[44] Rauschenbush, "Main Street Casualties of the Prosperity Gospel," Progressive Revival blog, beliefnet.com, October 4, 2008.

[45] Borg, Marcus J., *The God We Never Knew*, 61.

[46] Borg, Marcus, J., *Jesus: Uncovering the Life, Teachings, and Relevance of a Religious Revolutionary*, 8.

[47] Mutahhari, Murtaza, *Noble Character of the Holy Prophet*, 76.

[48] Warfield, Benjamin B., cited by Boone, Kathleen C., *The Bible Tells Them So*, 31, 65.

[49] Goldberg, Michelle, *Kingdom Coming: The Rise of Christian Nationalism*, 86, citing Johnson, Phillip in *The Wedge of Truth*.

[50] Hart, D.G., *Deconstructing Evangelicalism*, 172–173, citing Hunter, James Davison, *Culture Wars: The Struggle to Define America*, 44.

[51] De Hann, Richard W., cited by Boone, Kathleen C., *The Bible Tells Them So*, 87.

[52] Olde, Joe T., cited by Boone, Kathleen C., *The Bible Tells Them So*, 84.

[53] Ellis, Jane, *The Russian Orthodox Church: Triumphalism and Defensiveness*, 106–107.

[54] Bivins, Jason C., *Religion of Fear*, 73, citing Jack Chick's cartoon "Communist Time-Table for the U.S — 1973."

[55] Hedges, Chris, *American Fascists*, 58.

[56] Rushdoony, R.J., cited by Goldberg, Michelle, *Kingdom Coming: The Rise of Christian Nationalism*, 158.

[57] Manning, Joanna, *Take Back the Truth*, 93–94.

[58] Bauer, Gary, *New York Times*, A12, August 17, 1999.

[59] Phillips, Howard, quoted by Goldberg, Michelle, *The Rise of Christian Nationalism*, 167.

[60] Goldberg, Michelle, *Kingdom Coming: The Rise of Christian Nationalism*, 40.

[61] Grant, George, *The Changing of the Guard: Biblical Principles for Political Action*, Dominion Press, Fort Worth, 1987, 50–51, cited in Goldberg, Michelle, *Kingdom Coming: The Rise of Christian Nationalism*, 158.

[62] Raushenbach, Paul, "The Saudis dubious interfaith agenda at the U.N.," Progressive Revival blog, Nov. 14, 2008, beliefnet.com.

[63] Manning, Joanna, *Take Back the Truth*, 92.

[64] Goldberg, Michelle, *Kingdom Coming: The Rise of Christian Nationalism*, 156–157.

[65] Harris, Sam, *Letter to a Christian Nation*, 27–28.

Notes

[66] Ranke-Heinemann, Uta, *Eunuchs for the Kingdom of God*, 319.

[67] Wills, Garry, *Papal Sin: Structures of Deceit*, 221.

[68] Ranke-Heinemann, Uta, *Eunuchs for the Kingdom of God*, 75, citing St Jerome, Epistle 121.4.

[69] Manning, Joanna, *Take Back the Truth*, 72.

[70] Manning, Joanna, *Take Back the Truth*, 91.

[71] Hedges, Chris, *American Fascists*, 24.

[72] Manning, Joanna, *Take Back the Truth*, 102.

[73] Borg, Marcus J., *Meeting Jesus Again for the First Time*, 59.

[74] Eisler, Riane, *The Power of Partnership*, 108.

[75] Eisler, Riane, *The Power of Partnership*, 107.

[76] Hart, D.G., *Deconstructing Evangelicalism*, 24–25.

[77] Kohut, Andrew, and Stokes, Bruce, *America Against the World*, 96.

[78] Hart, D.G., *Deconstructing Evangelicalism*, 26.

[79] Hart, D.G., *Deconstructing Evangelicalism*, 64, citing Herberg, Will, *Protestant, Catholic, Jew*, 134.

[80] Manning, Joanna, *Take Back the Truth*, 117.

[81] Wilcox, Clyde, and Larson, Carin, *Onward Christian Soldiers?*, 178.

Bibliography

Akers, Keith, *The Lost Religion of Jesus:Simple Living and Nonviolence in Early Christianity*, Lantern Books, New York, 2000.

Armstrong, Karen, *Jerusalem: One City, Three Faiths*, Alfred A. Knopf, New York, 1996.

Armstrong, Karen, *The Battle for God*, Alfred A. Knopf, New York, 2000.

Armstrong, Karen, *The Gospel According to Woman: Christianity's Creation of the Sex War in the West,* Anchor Books, Doubleday, New York, London, 1987 (c.1986).

Ashton, John, *The Religion of Paul the Apostle*, Yale University Press, New Haven and London, 2000.

Aslan, Reza, *No god but God*, Random House, New York, 2006, (c.2005).

Atiya, Aziz S., *A History of Eastern Christianity*, Butler and Tanner, Frome aud London, 1968.

Averill, Lloyd J., *Religious Right, Religious Wrong: A Critique of the Fundamentalist Phenomenon*, The Pilgrim Press, New York, 1989.

Barnes, Timothy D., *Athanasius and Constantius: Theology and Politics in the Constantinian Empire*, Harvard University Press, Cambridge and London, 1993.

Barraclough, Geoffrey, ed., *The Christian World: A Social and Cultural History*, Harry N. Abrams, Inc., Publishers, New York, 1981.

Barton, Stephen C., editor, *The Cambridge Companion to the Gospels*, Cambridge University Press, Cambridge, 2006.

Bawer, Bruce, *Stealing Jesus: How Fundamentalism Betrays Christianity*, Crown Publishers, Inc., New York, 1997.

Bernal, Martin, *Black Athena: The Afroasiatic Roots of Classical Civilization, Volume 1: Fabrication of Ancient Greece, 1785 – 1985,* Free Association Books, London, 1987.

Bivins, Jason C., *Religion of Fear: The Politics of Horror in Conservative Evangelicalism*, Oxford University Press, New York, 2008.

Blackbourn, David, *Fontana History of Germany, 1780–1918: The Long Nineteenth Century*, Fontana Press, London, 1997.

Bokenkotter, Thomas, *A Concise History of the Catholic Church*, Doubleday & Company, Inc., Garden City, NY, 1977.

Bonner, Gerald, *Church and Faith in the Patristic Tradition: Augustine, Pelagianism and Early Christian Northumbria*, Ashgate Publishing Ltd., Aldershot, UK, 1996.

Boone, Kathleen C., *The Bible Tells Them So: The Discourse of Protestant Fundamentalism*, Sate University of New York Press, Albany, 1989.

Boorstin, Daniel J., *The Seekers: The Story of Man's Continuing Quest to Understand His World*, Vintage Books, New York, 1998.

Borg, Marcus J., *Jesus: Uncovering the Life, Teachings, and Relevance of a Religious*

Revolutionary, HarperOne, New York, 2006.

Borg, Marcus J., *Meeting Jesus Again for the First Time: The Historical Jesus & the Heart of Contemporary Faith*, HarperSanFrancisco, 1995, (c. 1994).

Borg, Marcus J., *The God We Never Knew: Beyond Dogmatic Religion to a More Authentic Contemporary Faith*, HarperSanFrancisco, 1998, (c. 1997).

Bradshaw, John, *Creating Love: The Next Great Stage of Growth*, Bantam Books, New York, Toronto, 1992.

Briggs, Asa, *A Social History of England*, Third edition, 3rd edition, Penguin, London, 1999 (c. 1983).

Briggs, Robin, *Witches and Neighbors: The Social and Cultural Context of European Witchcraft,* Penguin, New York, 1998.

Brown, Schuyler, *The Origins of Christianity: A Historical Introduction to the New Testament*, Oxford University Press, Oxford, New York, 1984.

Butt, Gerald, *The Arabs: Myth and Reality*, I.B. Tauris, Publishers, London, New York, 1997.

Cahill, Thomas, *How the Irish Saved Civilization*, Doubleday, New York, 1995.

Camara, Dom Helder, *Questions for Living*, translated from French by Barr, Robert R., Orbis Books, Maryknoll, New York, 1984.

Campbell, Joseph, *Creative Mythology*, Penguin Books, Harmondsworth, New York, Victoria, Markham, Auckland, 1986 (c. 1968).

Campbell, Joseph, *Occidental Mythology*, Penguin Books, Harmondsworth, New York, Victoria, Markham, Auckland, 1986 (c. 1964).

Campbell, Joseph, *The Flight of the Wild Gander*, Harper Collins, New York, 1990 (c.1951).

Cheetham, Nicolas, *Keepers of the Keys: The Pope in History*, MacDonald & Co., London and Sydney, 1982.

Chilton, Bruce, *Rabbi Jesus: An Intimate Biography*, Doubleday, New York, London, 2000.

Christie-Murray, David, *A History of Heresy*, Oxford University Press, Oxford, New York, 1976.

Cleary, Edward L., and Stewart-Gambino, Hannah, editors, *Conflict and Competition: The Latin American Church in a Changing Environment*, Lynne Rienner Publishers, Boulder and London, 1992.

Cohn, Samuel K., Jr., *Lust for Liberty: The Politics of Social Revolt in Medieval Europe, 1200 – 1425*, Harvard University Press, Cambridge, 2006.

Constantelos, Demetrios, *The Greek Orthodox Church*, The Seabury Press, New York, 1967.

Constantelos, Demetrios, *Understanding the Greek Orthodox Church*, The Seabury Press, New York, 1982.

309

Conway, J.S., *The Nazi Persecution of the Churches, 1933-45*, The Ryerson Press, Toronto, 1968.

Cornwell, John, *Hitler's Pope: The Secret History of Pious XII*, Viking, London, 1999.

Cox, Harvey, *Fire From Heaven The Rise of Pentacostal Spirituality and the Reshaping of Religion in the Twenty-first Century*, Addison-Wesley Publishing Company, 1995.

Crossan, John Dominic, *God & Empire: Jesus Against Rome, Then and Now*, Harper, San Francisco, 2007.

Crossan, John Dominic, *The Birth of Christianity: Discovering What Happened in the Years Immediately After the Execution of Jesus*, HarperSanFrancisco, 1998.

De Bruyn, Theodore, Translator and Editor, *Pelagius's Commentary on St. Paul's Epistle to the Romans*, Clarendon Press, Oxford, 1993.

De Mause, Lloyd, *The History of Childhood* , The Psychology Press, Atcom Inc., New York, 1974.

De Rosa, Peter, *Vicars of Christ*, Corgi, London, 1989 (c.1988).

Derfler, Leslie, editor, *An Age of Conflict: Readings in Twentieth-Century European History*, Second edition, Harcourt Brace College Publishers, Toronto, 1997, (c. 1990).

Dudley, Donald, *The Romans,* Hutchinson, London, 1970.

Durant, Will and Ariel, *Rousseau and Revolution: A History of Civilization in France, England and Germany from 1756, and the Remainder of Europe from 1715 to 1789*, Simon and Schuster, New York, 1967.

Durant, Will and Ariel, *The Age of Faith: A History of Medieval Civilization —Christian, Islamic, and Judaic—From Constantine to Dante: 325 – 1300*, Simon & Schuster, New York, 1950.

Durant, Will and Ariel, *The Age of Louis XIV: A History of European Civilization in the Period of Pascal, Moliere, Milton, Peter the Great, Newton and Spinoza: 1648 – 1715*, Simon & Schuster, New York, 1963.

Durant, Will and Ariel, *The Age of Napoleon: A History of European Civilization from 1789 to 1815*, Simon and Schuster, New York, 1975.

Durant, Will and Ariel, *The Age of Voltaire: A History of Civilization in Western Europe from 1715 to 1756*, Simon and Schuster, New York, 1965.

Durant, Will, *Caesar and Christ: A History of Roman Civilization and of Christianity from Their Beginnings to A.D. 325.* Simon and Schuster, New York, 1944.

Durant, Will, *Our Oriental Heritage: The Story of Civilization Part 1*, Simon and Schuster, New York, 1954.

Durant, Will, *The Reformation: A History of Civilization from Wyclife to Calvin: 1300 –1564*, Simon and Schuster, New York, 1957.

Durant, Will, *The Renaissance: A History of Civilization in Italy from 1304 –1576*, Simon and Schuster, New York, 1953.

Ehrman, Bart D., *Misquoting Jesus: The Story Behind Who Changed the Bible and Why*, HarperOne, New York, 2007.

Bibliography

Ehrman, Bart D., *The Orthodox Corruption of Scripture: The Effect of Early Christological Controversies on the Text of the New Testament*, Oxford University Press, New York, 1993.

Eisler, Riane, and Loye, David, *The Partnership Way: New Tools for Learning and Living*, Harper San Francisco, 1990.

Eisler, Riane, *The Chalice & the Blade: Our History, Our Future*, Harper & Row, San Francisco, 1987.

Eisler, Riane, *The Power of Partnership: Seven Relationships that Will Change Your Life*, New World Library, Novato, California, 2002.

Eliade, Mircea, and Couliano, Ioan P. with Wiesner, Hillary S., *The Eliade Guide to World Religions*, HarperSanFrancisco, 1991.

Ellis, Jane, *The Russian Orthodox Church: Triumphalism and Defensiveness*, MacMillan Press, Hampshire and London, 1996.

Erler, Mary, and Kowaleski, Maryanne, editors, *Women and Power in the Middle Ages*, University of Georgia Press, Athens, GA, 1988.

Falwell, Jerry, *Finding Inner Peace and Strength*, Doubleday, Garden City, New York, 1982.

Falwell, Jerry, with Dobson, Ed and Hindson, Ed, editors, *The Fundamentalist Phenomenon: The Resurgence of Conservative Christianity*, A Doubleday-Galilee Original, Doubleday & Company Inc., Garden City, New York, 1981.

Fox, Matthew, *Sins of the Spirit, Blessings of the Flesh: Lessons for Transforming Evil in Soul and Society*, Three Rivers Press, New York, 1999.

Frend, W.H.C., *Martyrdom and Persecution in the Early Church: A Study of a Conflict from the Maccabees to Donatus*, New York University Press, 1967.

Frend, W.H.C., *The Early Church*, Fortress Press, Philadelphia, 1982 (c. 1965).

Frend, W.H.C., *The Rise of Christianity*, Fortress, Press, Philadelphia, 1984.

Freston, Paul, *Evangelicals and Politics in Asia, Africa, and Latin America*, Cambridge University Press, Cambridge, 2001.

Gaustad, Edwin, and Schmidt, Leigh, *The Religious History of America: The Heart of the American Story from Colonial Times to Today*, HarperOne, New York, revised edition, 2002.

Gernet, Jacques, *China and the Christian Impact*, Cambridge University Press, Cambridge and New York, 1885 (c. 1982).

Goldberg, Michelle, *Kingdom Coming: The Rise of Christian Nationalism*, W.W. Norton & Company, New York, 2006.

Gore, Al, *The Assault on Reason*, The Penguin Press, New York, 2007.

Grant, Michael, *Constantine the Great: The Man and His Times*, Charles Scribner's Sons, New York, Oxford, 1994 (c. 1993).

Grant, Robert M., *Augustus to Constantine: The Trust of the Christian Movement into the Roman World*, Harper & Row, Publishers, New York, Evanston, London, 1970.

CORRECTING JESUS

Greenberg, Amy S., *Manifest Manhood and the Antebellum American Empire*, Cambridge University Press, Cambridge, 2005.

Griffith, Brian, *Different Visions of Love: Partnership and Dominator Values in Christian History*, Outskirts Press, Parker, CO, 2008.

Griffith, Brian, *The Gardens of Their Dreams: Desertification and Culture in World History*, Zed Books, London and Fernwood Publishing, Halifax, 2001.

Harris, Sam, *Letter to a Christian Nation*, Alfred A Knopf, New York, 2006.

Hart, D.G., *Deconstructing Evangelicalism: Conservative Protestantism in the Age of Billy Graham*, Baker Academic, Grand Rapids, MI, 2004.

Hawken, Paul, *Blessed Unrest: How the Largest Movement in the World Came into Being and Why No One Saw It Coming*, Viking, New York, 2007.

Hedges, Chris, *American Fascists: The Christian Right and the War on America*, Free Press, New York, 2006.

Hodgson, Godfrey, *America in Our Time: From WWII to Nixon — What Happened and Why*, Princeton University Press, Princeton and Oxford, 1976.

Hoffmann, R. Joseph, translator, Celsus, *On the True Doctrine: A Discourse Against the Christians*, Oxford University Press, Oxford, 1987.

Horsley, Richard A., and Hanson, John S., *Bandits, Prophets and Messiahs: Popular Movements in the Time of Jesus*, Winston Press, Minneapolis, Chicago, 1985.

Housley, Norman, *Crusading and Warfare in Medieval and Renaissance Europe*, Ashgate/Valiorum, Aldershot, 2001.

Idliby, Ranya, Oliver, Suzanne Warner, Priscilla, *The Faith Club: A Muslim, A Christian, and a Jew — Three Women Search for Understanding*, Free Press, New York, 2006.

Isichei, Elizabeth, *A History of Christianity in Africa: From Antiquity to the Present*, William B. Eerdmans Publishing Company, Grand Rapids and Lawrenceville, 1995.

Jacobs, A.J., *The Year of Living Biblically: One Man's Humble Quest to Follow the Bible as Literally as Possible*, Simon & Schuster, New York, 2007.

Karabell, Zachary, *Peace Be Upon You: Fourteen Centuries of Muslim, Christian and Jewish Conflict and Cooperation*, Vintage Books, New York, 2007.

Kertzer, David I., *The Popes Against the Jews: The Vatican's Role in the Rise of Modern Anti-Semitism*, Vintage Books, New York, 2002.

King, Karen L., *The Gospel of Mary of Magdala*, Polebridge Press, Santa Rosa, CA, 2003.

Klein, Naomi, *The Shock Doctrine The Rise of Disaster Capitalism*, Alfred A. Knopf Canada, Toronto, 2007.

Kohut, Andrew, and Stokes, Bruce, *America Against the World: How We are Different and Why We are Disliked,* Times Books, New York, 2006.

Kraemer, Ross Shepard, *Her Share of the Blessings: Women's Religions Among Pagans, Jews and Christians in the Greco-Roman World*, Oxford University Press, Oxford and New York, 1992.

312

Bibliography

Kramer, Samuel Noah, *History Begins at Sumer*, University of Pennsylvania Press, Philadelphia,1990 (c. 1981).

LaHaye, Tim and Jenkins, Jerry B. *Glorious Appearing: The End Days*, Tyndale, Wheaton, IL, 2004.

Lambert, Malcolm, *Medieval Heresy: Popular Movements from the Gregorian Reform to the Reformation*, Second Edition, Blackwell Publishers, Oxford, 1992 (1977).

Lewis, Naphtali and Reinhold, Meyer, editors, *Roman Civilization, Sourcebook II: The Empire*, Harper & Row Publishers, New York, San Francisco, Hagerstown, London, 1966 (c. 1955).

Longenecker, Richard N., editor, *Patterns of Discipleship in the New Testament*, William B. Eerdmans Publishing Co., Grand Rapids, MI, 1996.

Loye, David, *Darwin's Lost Theory*, Benjamin Franklin Press, Carmel, CA, 2007.

Mack, Burton L., *The Lost Gospel: The Book of Q and Christian Origins*, HarperSanFrancisco, 1993.

Malina, Bruce, and Rohrbaugh, Richard L., *Social Science Commentary on the Synoptic Gospels*, Fortress Press, Minneapolis, 1992.

Manning, Joanna, *Is the Pope Catholic?: A Woman Confronts Her Church*, Malcolm Lester Books, Toronto, 1999.

Manning, Joanna, *Take Back the Truth: Confronting Papal Power and the Religious Right,* The Crossroad Publishing Company, New York, 2002.

Margulis, Lynn, and Sagan, Dorion, *Microcosmos: Four Billion Years of Evolution from our Microbal Ancestors*, Summit Books, New York, 1986.

Markschies, Christoph, *Between Two Worlds: Structures of Early Christianity*, SCM Press, London, 1999.

Markus, Robert, *The End of Ancient Christianity*, Cambridge University Press, Cambridge, 1990.

McManners, John, ed., *The Oxford History of Christianity*, Oxford University Press, Oxford and New York, 1993.

McPherson, James M., *Ordeal by Fire: The Civil War and Reconstruction*, Alfred A. Knopf, New York, 1982.

Misha'al ibn Abdullah, *What Did Jesus Really Say?*, Islamic Assembly of North America, 1996.

Murphy, Cullen, *The Word According to Eve: Women and the Bible in Ancient Times and Our Own*, Houghton Mifflin Company, Boston, New York, 1998.

Mutahhari, Murtaza, *Noble Character of the Holy Prophet*, Alhoda Publications, London, 2003.

Newsom, Carol A., and Ringe, Sharon H., editors, *The Women's Bible Commentary*, SPCK, London and Westminster, and John Knox Press, Louisville, KY, 1992.

Nirenberg, David, *Communities of Violence: Persecution of Minorities in the Middle*

SPCK, London and Westminster, and John Knox Press, Louisville, KY, 1992.

Nirenberg, David, *Communities of Violence: Persecution of Minorities in the Middle Ages*, Princeton University Press, Princeton, 1996.

Nolan, Albert, *Jesus Before Christianity*, Orbis Books, Maryknoll, New York, 1992 (c.1976).

Noll, Mark A., *A History of Christianity in the United States and Canada*, William B. Eerdmans Publishing Co., Grand Rapids, MI, 1992.

Pagels, Elaine, *Adam, Eve, and the Serpent: Sex and Politics in Early Christianity*, Vintage Books, New York, 1989.

Pagels, Elaine, *The Gnostic Gospels*, Vintage Books, New York, 1989 (c.1988).

Patai, Raphael, *The Hebrew Goddess*, Wayne State University Press, Detroit, third enlarged edition, 1990 (c. 1967).

Pelikan, Jaroslav, *The Illustrated Jesus Through the Centuries*, Yale University Press, New Haven, 1997.

Ponting, Clive, *A Green History of the World*, Sinclair-Stevenson, Ltd., 1991.

Randers-Pehrson, Justine Davis, *Barbarians and Romans: The Birth Struggle of Europe, A.D. 400–700*, University of Oklahoma Press, Norman, OK, 1983.

Ranke-Heinemann, Uta, *Eunuchs for the Kingdom of God: Women, Sexuality, and the Catholic Church*, English translation by Peter Heinegg, Doubleday, New York, London, Toronto, Sydney, Auckland, 1990.

Ranke-Heinemann, Uta, *Putting Away Childish Things: The Virgin Birth, the Empty Tomb, and Other Fairy Tales You Don't Need to Believe to Have a Living Faith*, translation by Peter Heinegg, HarperSanFrancisco, 1994.

Reeves, Thomas C., *The Empty Church: The Suicide of Liberal Christianity*, The Free Press, New York, London, 1996.

Rifkin, Jeremy, and Howard, Ted, *The Emerging Order: God in the Age of Scarcity*, G.P. Putnam's Sons, New York, 1979.

Robinson, James M., *The Nag Hammadi Library in English*, Harper & Row, New York, 1988.

Rohr, Richard, *Things Hidden: Scripture as Spirituality*, St. Anthony Messenger Press, Cincinnati, 2007.

Rosenberg, Tina, *The Haunted Land: Facing Europe's Ghosts After Communism*, Random House, New York, 1995, 161–62.

Rossner, John, *In Search of the Primordial Tradition and the Cosmic Christ*, Llewellyn Publications, Woodbury, MN, 1989.

Rousseau, Philip, *Pachomius: The Making of a Community in Fourth-Century Egypt*, University of California Press, Berkeley, Los Angeles, London, 1985.

Rubenson, Samuel, *The Letters of St. Antony: Monasticism and the Making of a Saint*, Fortress Press, Minneapolis, 1995 (c. 1990).

Bibliography

Runciman, Steven, *The Orthodox Churches and the Secular State*, Oxford University Press, New York and Oxford, 1972.

Ruprecht, Louis A. Jr., *This Tragic Gospel: How John Corrupted the Heart of Christianity*, Jossey-Bass, San Francisco, 2008.

Russell, Jeffrey Burton, *A History of Heaven: The Singing Silence*, Princeton University Press, Princeton, 1997.

Schaeffer, Frank, *Crazy for God: How I Grew Up as One of the Elect, Helped Found the Religious Right, and Lived to Take All (or Almost All) of It Back*, Carroll & Graf Publishers, New York, 2007.

Schoeps, Hans-Joachim, *Jewish Christianity: Factional Disputes in the Early Church*, Translated by Douglas R.A. Hare, Fortress Press, Philadelphia, 1969.

Scott, T. Kermit, *Augustine: His Thought in Context*, Paulist Press, New York, Mahwah, NJ, 1995.

Smith, John Holland, *The Death of Classical Paganism*, Geoffrey Chapman Publishers, London and Dublin, 1976.

Southern, R.W., *Western Society and the Church in the Middle Ages*, Pelican Books, Harmondsworth, New York, 1986 (c. 1970).

Spong, John Shelby, *Jesus for the Non-Religious: Recovering the Divine at the Heart of the Human*, HarperSanFrancisco, 2007.

Spoto, Donald, *The Hidden Jesus: A New Life*, St. Martin's Press, New York, 1998.

Stegemann, Ekkehard W. and Wolfgang, *The Jesus Movement: A Social History of its First Century*, Fortress Press, Minneapolis, 1999 (c.1995).

Stevenson, J., editor, *A New Eusebius: Documents Illustrating the History of the Church to AD 337*, revised by W.H.C. Frend, University of Cambridge Press, Cambridge, 1987.

Strauss, Gerald, *Luther's House of Learning: Indoctrination of the Young in the German Reformation*, John Hopkins University Press, Baltimore, 1981.

Sykes, S.W., editor, *Sacrifice and Redemption: Durham Essays in Theology*, Cambridge University Press, Cambridge, 1990.

Taibbi, Matt, *The Great Derangement: A Terrifying True Story of War, Politics, and Religion at the Twilight of the American Empire*, Spiegel & Grau, New York, 2008.

Telushkin, Joseph, *Biblical Literacy*, William Morrow and Company, Inc., New York, 1997.

Toynbee, Arnold J., *A Study of History, Abridgement of Volumes VII to X*, edited by Somervell, D.C., Oxford University Press, New York and Oxford, 1987 (c. 1957).

Verhey, Allen, *The Great Reversal: Ethics and the New Testament*, William B. Eerdmans Publishing Co., Grand Rapids, MI, 1984.

Vermes, G., citing 1 QS, Manual of Disciple, *The Dead Sea Scrolls in English*, Penguin, London, 1987.

315

Veyne, Paul, editor, *A History of Private Life Volume I, From Pagan Rome to Byzantium*, The Belknap Press of Harvard University Press, Cambridge, MS, London, 1987.

Warner, Marina, *Alone of All Her Sex: The Myth and Cult of the Virgin Mary*, Vintage, London, 2000. (c. 1976).

Whitelock, Dorothy, *The Beginning of English Society*, Penguin, Harmondsworth, 1976 (c.1952).

Wilcox, Clyde, and Larson, Carin, *Onward Christian Soldiers: The Religious Right In American Politics*, 3rd edition, Westview Press, Boulder, CO, 2006.

Wills, Garry, *Papal Sin: Structures of Deceit*, Doubleday, New York and London, 2000.

Wills, Garry, *What the Gospels Meant*, Viking, New York, 2008.

Wilson, Barrie, *How Jesus Became Christian*, Random House Canada, Toronto, 2008.

Wink, Walter, *The Powers That Be: Theology for a New Millennium*, Galilee Doubleday, New York and London, 1998.

Wright, Robin, *Dreams and Shadows: The Future of the Middle East*, Penguin Press, New York, 2008.

Ye'or, Bat, *The Decline of Eastern Christianity Under Islam: From Jihad to Dhimmitude*, Fairleigh Dickinson Press, Madison, NJ, 1996.

Index

BRIAN GRIFFITH is an independent historian who's interested in the whole world's "culture wars," scavenging history books for 25 years to learn more about them. His two previous books are *The Gardens of Their Dreams: Desertification and Culture in World History*, and *Different Visions of Love: Partnership and Dominator Values in Christian History*, with a foreword by Riane Eisler. He's married and lives near Toronto, Ontario.